KT-569-809

GOD AND THE PROBLEM OF EVIL

LEEDS TRINITY LIBRARY

316604 8

BLACKWELL READINGS IN PHILOSOPHY

Series Editor: Steven M. Cahn

Blackwell Readings in Philosophy are concise, chronologically arranged collections of primary readings from classical and contemporary sources. They represent core positions and important developments with respect to key philosophical concepts. Edited and introduced by leading philosophers, these volumes provide valuable resources for teachers and students of philosophy, and for all those interested in gaining a solid understanding of central topics in philosophy.

1. *God and the Problem of Evil*
   Edited by William L. Rowe

2. *Epistemology: Internalism and Externalism*
   Edited by Hilary Kornblith

3. *Free Will*
   Edited by Robert Kane

4. *Democracy*
   Edited by David Estlund

5. *Meaning*
   Edited by Mark Richard

6. *Philosophical Skepticism*
   Edited by Charles Landesman and Roblin Meeks

7. *Consequentialism*
   Edited by Stephen Darwall

8. *Contractarianism/Contractualism*
   Edited by Stephen Darwall

9. *Deontology*
   Edited by Stephen Darwall

10. *Virtue Ethics*
    Edited by Stephen Darwall

11. *Personal Identity*
    Edited by Raymond Martin and John Barresi

12. *Perception*
    Edited by Robert Schwartz

13. *Theories of Truth*
    Edited by Frederick F. Schmitt

14. *Social Justice*
    Edited by Matthew Clayton and Andrew Williams

GOD AND THE PROBLEM OF EVIL

Edited by William L. Rowe

Blackwell
Publishing

214 ROW

3166048

© 2001 by Blackwell Publishing Ltd 2001
Editorial matter and organization © 2001 by William L. Rowe

BLACKWELL PUBLISHING   LEEDS TRINITY UNIVERSITY AB.
350 Main Street, Malden, MA 02148-5020, USA
108 Cowley Road, Oxford OX4 1JF, UK
550 Swanston Street, Carlton, Victoria 3053, Australia

All rights reserved. No part of this publication may be reproduced, stored in a retrieval system,
or transmitted, in any form or by any means, electronic, mechanical, photocopying, recording or
otherwise, except as permitted by the UK Copyright, Designs and Patents Act 1988, without the
prior permission of the publisher.

First published 2001
Reprinted 2005

Library of Congress Cataloging-in-Publication Data

God and the problem of evil / edited by William L. Rowe.
    p. cm.—(Blackwell readings in philosophy; 1)
    Includes bibliographical references and index.
    ISBN 0-631-22220-0 (alk. paper)—ISBN 0-631-22221-9
    1. Good and evil. 2. Theodicy. I. Rowe, William L. II. Title. III. Series.

BJ1401 .G63 2001
214—dc21
                                                        00-051918

A catalogue record for this title is available from the British Library.

Set in 11 on 13 pt Baskerville
by Kolam Information Services Pvt. Ltd, Pondicherry, India

The publisher's policy is to use permanent paper from mills that operate a sustainable forestry
policy, and which has been manufactured from pulp processed using acid-free and elementary
chlorine-free practices. Furthermore, the publisher ensures that the text paper and cover board
used have met acceptable environmental accreditation standards.

For further information on
Blackwell Publishing, visit our website:
www.blackwellpublishing.com

CONTENTS

CONTRIBUTORS

Marilyn McCord Adams is Professor of Historical Theology at Yale Divinity School and Professor of Philosophy at Yale University.

Robert Merrihew Adams is Professor of Philosophy and Religious Studies at Yale University.

Michael Bergmann is Assistant Professor of Philosophy at Purdue University.

Paul Draper is Professor of Philosophy at Florida International University.

John Hick is a former H. G. Wood Professor of Theology at the University of Birmingham and Danforth Professor of the Philosophy of Religion at the Claremont Graduate School in California.

Daniel Howard-Snyder is Associate Professor of Philosophy at Seattle Pacific University.

David Hume was a distinguished Scottish philosopher and historian. His *Dialogues Concerning Natural Religion* has been influential in shaping philosophical thought about religion.

Gottfried Wilhelm Leibniz was an influential German rationalist philosopher who argued in his *Theodicy* that since a perfect being exists, this world is the best of all possible worlds.

J. L. Mackie was Reader in Philosophy and Fellow of University College, Oxford.

Nelson Pike is Professor Emeritus at the University of California, Irvine.

Alvin Plantinga is John A. O'Brien Professor of Philosophy at the University of Notre Dame.

William L. Rowe is Professor of Philosophy at Purdue University.

J. L. Schellenberg is Associate Professor of Philosophy and Chair of the Philosophy Department, Mount Saint Vincent University.

Richard Swinburne is the Nolloth Professor of Philosophy of the Christian Religion at Oriel College, Oxford University.

Peter van Inwagen is John Cardinal O'Hara Professor of Philosophy at the University of Notre Dame.

PREFACE

The problem of evil is the problem of understanding why there is so much evil in the world if the world is created by, and under the providential care of, a being who is infinitely powerful, all-knowing, and perfectly good. For if God is all-knowing and infinitely powerful, he certainly could have prevented many, if not all of the terrible evils that afflict our world. And, being infinitely good he would surely want to prevent such evils. But then why is there so much horrendous evil in our world? This question has plagued philosophers and theologians for centuries. Indeed, some religious thinkers have argued that it is impossible both that such a divine being exists and that the world contains evil. They have concluded that God is *limited* in power and, therefore, not able to prevent the occurrence of terrible evil in the world. Other religious thinkers have supposed not only that God is *limited* in power but that there exists a powerful evil being, *independent* of God's power, who is responsible for the terrible evil in the world. But, as attractive as these views may be in terms of reconciling the existence of some sort of divine being with the presence of considerable evil in the world, the predominant view of God in western civilization has been, and continues to be, that he is an *infinitely* powerful, all-knowing, perfectly good being on whom all other things depend for their existence. We will call this "the *theistic* idea of God." It is this idea of God that has dominated religious thinking in the West even in the face of the fact that so much horrendous evil afflicts human and animal life.

But what is evil? How are we to characterize it? A complete characterization of evil is a philosophical task in itself. But for our purposes it will suffice to think of evil as *undeserved suffering*, both human and animal. Here are two of examples of such evil: A five-year-old girl's being brutally beaten, raped, and strangled; a fawn's being horribly burned in a forest fire, lying for five days on the forest floor before death relieves its suffering. The first instance is called a "moral" evil since the little girl's suffering presumably resulted from a wicked, intentional act of a conscious agent. The second is called a "natural" evil since the fawn's suffering presumably resulted from the activity of the forces of nature – lightning striking a dead tree and starting the fire in which the fawn was trapped and horribly burned. It is the proliferation in our world of evils (undeserved suffering), often on a scale – e.g., the Holocaust – beyond our imagination, that constitutes the problem of evil in a world we suppose to be created by, and under the providential care of, a being who is unlimited in goodness, knowledge, and power.

As discussed by philosophers, the problem of evil concerns the question of whether it is *rational* to believe in the existence of an all-powerful, all-knowing, perfectly good creator given our knowledge of the horrendous evils that afflict our world. As we shall see, some philosophers think it cannot possibly be rational to believe such a being exists given our knowledge of the evils in our world. For they hold that the existence of such a being *logically excludes* the existence of any evil at all in the world he creates. Those who hold such a view see the existence of evil in the world as constituting a *logical problem* for belief in the theistic God. Other philosophers allow that it is, or may be, logically possible for the world to contain the evils it does and yet be the creation of the theistic God. But they go on to claim that the evils in the world make it *unlikely* that the theistic God exists. For even though they see no logical inconsistency in this world, with all of its evil, being the creation of the theistic God, they think it *unlikely* that such a being would need to permit all the terrible evils that occur in our world. Those who hold such a view see the existence of evil in the world as constituting an *evidential problem* for belief in the theistic God. Still other philosophers think that unless we have some not implausible account of the goods for the sake of which God may permit all these evils, we should conclude that theism is unlikely. Accordingly, some have proposed *theodicies*, suggestions as to what the goods are that may constitute God's reason for permitting these evils. Finally, there are philosophers who think we simply lack sufficient reason to think that the evils in our world logically preclude, or even provide significant evidence against, the existence of the theistic God. For, they reason, given our limited knowledge in comparison with the mind of God we are simply unable to make any judgment at all about whether there is a justifying reason for God to permit the evils we see about us. In this book the reader will become acquainted with the writings of philosophers representing each of these four views of the problem of evil.

The aim of this book is to provide the reader with some of the more important philosophical essays in print on the problem of evil. Although most of the included essays were published late in the twentieth or early in the twenty-first century, the book begins with two essays authored by major eighteenth-century philosophers, Leibniz and Hume, whose writings have had a profound effect on subsequent discussions of the problem. Part I (Historically Important Essays and Contemporary Responses) contains these two essays along with responses and clarifications by two contemporary philosophers. Part II (The Logical Problem of Evil) provides the reader with the two most widely read twentieth-century essays on the logical problem of evil. In Part III (The Evidential Problem of Evil) the reader will find a debate on the question of whether the evils in our world make it likely that the theistic God does not exist, along with an essay seeking to make an advance in our understanding of the evidential argument from evil. In addition, Part III includes two important essays on whether theism or naturalism provides the best explanation of the role of pleasure and pain in human life. Part IV (Theodicies) contains three major twentieth-century contributions to the task of providing an account of why God may be justified in permitting the kinds and amount of evil that are found in our world.

ACKNOWLEDGMENTS

The authors and publishers gratefully acknowledge the following for permission to reproduce copyright material:

Adams, Marilyn McCord, "The Problem of Hell: A Problem of Evil for Christians" from *Reasoned Faith* (ed. Eleonore Stump) (Cornell University Press, Ithaca, 1993);

Adams, Robert Merrihew, "Must God Create the Best?" from *The Philosophical Review* 81 (1972). Copyright 1972 Cornell University. Reprinted by permission of the publisher;

Draper, Paul, "Pain and Pleasure: An Evidential Problem for Theists," *Noûs*, vol. 23 (1989);

Hick, John, "Soul-Making Theodicy" from *Encountering Evil* (ed. Steven T. Davis) © 1981 Steven T. Davis. Used by permission of Westminster/John Knox Press;

Howard-Snyder, Daniel, Michael Bergmann, and W. L. Rowe, "An Exchange on the Problem of Evil," forthcoming in a Reader to be published by Blackwell Publishers: *Contemporary Debates in Philosophy of Religion* (ed., Michael Peterson);

Hume, David, *Dialogues Concerning Natural Religion* (ed. Henry D. Aiken) (Hafner Publishing, 1948);

Leibniz, G. W., *Theodicy* (Routledge and Kegan Paul, London, 1951);

Mackie, J. L., "Evil and Omnipotence," *Mind*, vol. 64 (1955). Reprinted by permission of Oxford University Press, Oxford;

Pike, Nelson, "Hume on Evil" from *The Philosophical Review* 72 (1963). Copyright 1963 Cornell University. Reprinted by permission of the publisher;

Plantinga, Alvin, "The Free Will Defense" from *The Nature of Necessity* (Clarendon Press, Oxford, 1971);

Schellenberg, J. L., "Stalemate and Strategy: Rethinking the Evidential Argument from Evil," *American Philosophical Quarterly* 37 (4). Reprinted by courtesy of North American Philosophical Association Publications Inc., Pittsburgh;

Swinburne, Richard, "Some Major Strands of Theodicy" from *The Evidential Argument from Evil* (ed. Daniel Howard-Snyder) (Indiana University Press, Bloomington, 1996);

van Inwagen, Peter, "The Problem of Evil, the Problem of Air, and the Problem of Silence," *Philosophical Perspectives* 5, *Philosophy of Religion*, 1991.

The publishers apologize for any errors or omissions in the above list and would be grateful to be notified of any corrections that should be incorporated in the next edition or reprint of this book.

Part I

Historically Important Essays and Contemporary Responses

Although the existence of evil is discussed in the literature of the East, it has played a larger role in Western religious thought owing to the western emphasis on sin rather than ignorance as constituting the human predicament, and personal salvation rather than enlightenment constituting the solution to the human predicament. Moreover, in Eastern thought evil has sometimes been regarded as unreal; whereas in the West evil is almost always regarded as a real component of our world. In the West, early religious thinkers (for example, Augustine, Maimonides, and Aquinas) viewed evil as resulting from the abuse of human free will. More extensive treatments of the problem of evil appeared in the seventeenth and eighteenth centuries, particularly in the works of Leibniz and Hume. Both Leibniz and Hume saw that evil in the world doesn't consist just of abuses of human free will, resulting in punishments imposed by God, but often arises from the sort of environment the world (God's creation) provides. And Leibniz undertook the task of proving, despite appearances to the contrary, that among possible worlds – all the ways things might be – God would of course create the very best world, making this world the best of all possible worlds, a view Voltaire ridiculed in his work *Candide*. Nevertheless, Leibniz developed a rigorous argument for his conclusion that this world must be the best of all possible worlds. What then of the evils in this world? Drawing on the aesthetic analogy that dates as far back as Augustine, Leibniz argued that rather than detracting from the overall goodness of the world, the evils that occur are actually *essential* to the superior goodness of the whole of which they are a part. Suppose that we could rank colors in their degree of beauty. Purple, we may suppose, is objectively near the top in the scale of beauty, whereas chartreuse, let us say, is close to the bottom. Consider, then, an exceedingly beautiful painting. It may well be that bits of chartreuse here and there in the painting are such that substituting purple, or some other color near the top of the scale of beauty, would detract from the overall beauty of the painting. So too, Leibniz argued, the great evils in our world may contribute to the overall goodness of the world. Certainly, the Holocaust is a terrible evil. Leibniz would say nothing to the contrary. But just as the chartreuse may actually contribute to the overall beauty of the whole picture even though in itself chartreuse is an ugly color, so too, Leibniz would say, the evilness of the Holocaust may actually contribute to the overall goodness of the world. Of course, if we reflect only on the goods and evils in the world, we have no reason at all to think that the Holocaust actually contributes to the overall goodness of the world. But Leibniz was convinced of the existence of a wholly perfect being. And from this he deduced that this world must be the best of all possible worlds. For otherwise this perfect being would lack a sufficient reason to create it.

In his essay "Must God Create the Best?" Robert Adams challenges the idea that God must create the best world, assuming there is a best among possible worlds. Adams supposes that the world God creates contains creatures each of whom is as happy as it could be in any possible world in which it exists. Moreover, suppose no creature in this world is so miserable that it would be better had it not existed. Suppose also that there is some other possible world with different creatures that exceeds this world in its degree of happiness, a world that God could have created. If so, God has created a world with a lesser degree of happiness than he could have. But has God wronged anyone in creating this world? Adams argues that God cannot have wronged the creatures in the other possible world, for merely possible beings don't have rights. Nor can he have wronged the creatures in the world he has created, for their lives could not be made more happy. Adams notes that God would have done something wrong in creating this world were the following principle true.

> It is wrong to bring into existence, knowingly, a being less excellent than one could have brought into existence.

But this principle, Adams argues, is subject to counter-examples. Parents do no wrong, for example, when they refrain from taking drugs that would result in an abnormal gene structure in their children, even though taking the drugs would result in children who are superhuman both in intelligence and in prospects for happiness. In this way Adams challenges Leibniz's assumption that a perfectly good being must create the best world it can.

It is likely that Hume thought that the existence of an all-powerful, all-knowing, perfectly good being is *logically inconsistent* with the existence of all the evil (undeserved suffering) in our world. But in his penetrating essay on Hume, Nelson Pike notes that in order to *establish* inconsistency we would have to know that God could not have a morally sufficient reason to permit the evils in our world. For if God could have a morally sufficient reason for permitting the evils in our world, there simply would be no inconsistency in the idea both that God exists and that the world contains all the evil it does. But Hume also develops a different attack against traditional theistic belief. Imagine that we were to visit our planet for the first time, having been assured in advance that it is the product of an all-powerful, all-knowing, perfectly good being. Would we expect to find a world "so full of vice and misery and disorder, as it appears in this life"? Surely not, says Hume. Of course, if we *knew* in advance that God exists we would simply have to accept our surprise and believe that God has unknown reasons for permitting all the evils in the world. But what if we don't *know* that God exists? Indeed, suppose we are considering whether we should believe that there is a God and that we are examining the world to see whether it provides us with good evidence for or against the existence of God as its maker. If this is how we approach the matter of whether to believe in the theistic God, Hume's point is difficult to turn aside. Looking at our world with all its evil, it would not be reasonable to infer that its maker, if it has a maker, is a completely *malicious* being. For there is a great deal of good in our world – pleasure, happiness, love, beauty, etc. – that a thoroughly malicious being would have good reason to prevent. But, by the same token, looking at the good in our world, it would not be reasonable to infer that its maker, if it has a maker, is a thoroughly beneficent being. For there is a great deal of bad in our world – pain, unhappiness, hate, ugliness, etc. – that a thoroughly beneficent being would have good reason to prevent. If we infer a maker at all, Hume suggests, we should infer a being who is *indifferent* to the sentient beings he creates. Pike sees this point as Hume's major contribution to the problem of evil. He suggests, however, that most theists do not treat the existence of God as an empirical hypothesis by which to explain the world. Rather they take it as an item of faith.

1

GOTTFRIED WILHELM LEIBNIZ
Theodicy, sections 218–236

218. I come now to the principal objection M. Bayle, after M. Arnauld, brings up against me. It is complicated: they maintain that God would be under compulsion, that he would act of necessity, if he were bound to create the best; or at least that he would have been lacking in power if he could not have found a better expedient for excluding sins and other evils. That is in effect denying that this universe is the best, and that God is bound to insist upon the best. I have met this objection adequately in more than one passage: I have proved that God cannot fail to produce the best; and from that assumption it follows that the evils we experience could not have been reasonably excluded from the universe, since they are there. Let us see, however, what these two excellent men bring up, or rather let us see what M. Bayle's objection is, for he professes to have profited by the arguments of M. Arnauld.

219. 'Would it be possible', he says, *Reply to the Questions of a Provincial*, vol. III, ch. 158, p. 890, 'that a nature whose goodness, holiness, wisdom, knowledge and power are infinite, who loves virtue supremely, and hates vice supremely, as our clear and distinct idea of him shows us, and as well-nigh every page of Scripture assures us, could have found in virtue no means fitting and suited for his ends? Would it be possible that vice alone had offered him this means? One would have thought on the contrary that nothing beseemed this nature more than to establish virtue in his work to the exclusion of all vice.' M. Bayle here exaggerates things. I agree that some vice was connected with the

Original publication: Pp. 264–73, 377–88, G. W. Leibniz, *Theodicy: Essays on the Goodness of God, the Freedom of Man and the Origin of Evil* (London: Routledge and Kegan Paul, 1951).

best plan of the universe, but I do not agree with him that God could not find in virtue any means suited for his ends. This objection would have been valid if there were no virtue, if vice took its place everywhere. He will say it suffices that vice prevails and that virtue is trifling in comparison. But I am far from agreeing with him there, and I think that in reality, properly speaking, there is incomparably more moral good than moral evil in rational creatures; and of these we have knowledge of but few.

220.   This evil is not even so great in men as it is declared to be. It is only people of a malicious disposition or those who have become somewhat misanthropic through misfortunes, like Lucian's Timon, who find wickedness everywhere, and who poison the best actions by the interpretations they give to them. I speak of those who do it in all seriousness, to draw thence evil conclusions, by which their conduct is tainted; for there are some who only do it to show off their own acumen. People have found that fault in Tacitus, and that again is the criticism M. Descartes (in one of his letters) makes of Mr. Hobbes's book *De Cive*, of which only a few copies had at that time been printed for distribution among friends, but to which some notes by the author were added in the second edition which we have. For although M. Descartes acknowledges that this book is by a man of talent, he observes therein some very dangerous principles and maxims, in the assumption there made that all men are wicked, or the provision of them with motives for being so. The late Herr Jacob Thomasius said in his admirable *Tables of Practical Philosophy* that the $\pi\rho\hat{\omega}\tau o\nu\ \psi\epsilon\hat{\upsilon}\delta o\varsigma$, the primary cause of errors in this book by Mr. Hobbes, was that he took *statum legalem pro naturali*, that is to say that the corrupt state served him as a gauge and rule, whereas it is the state most befitting human nature which Aristotle had had in view. For according to Aristotle, that is termed *natural* which conforms most closely to the perfection of the nature of the thing; but Mr. Hobbes applies the term *natural state* to that which has least art, perhaps not taking into account that human nature in its perfection carries art with it. But the question of name, that is to say, of what may be called natural, would not be of great importance were it not that Aristotle and Hobbes fastened upon it the notion of natural right, each one following his own signification. I have said here already that I found in the book on the Falsity of human Virtues the same defect as M. Descartes found in Mr. Hobbes's *De Cive*.

221.   But even if we assume that vice exceeds virtue in the human kind, as it is assumed the number of the damned exceeds that of the

elect, it by no means follows that vice and misery exceed virtue and happiness in the universe: one should rather believe the opposite, because the City of God must be the most perfect of all possible states, since it was formed and is perpetually governed by the greatest and best of all Monarchs. This answer confirms the observation I made earlier, when speaking of the conformity of faith with reason, namely, that one of the greatest sources of fallacy in the objections is the confusion of the apparent with the real. And here by the apparent I mean not simply such as would result from an exact discussion of facts, but that which has been derived from the small extent of our experiences. It would be senseless to try to bring up appearances so imperfect, and having such slight foundation, in opposition to the proofs of reason and the revelations of faith.

222.   Finally, I have already observed that love of virtue and hatred of vice, which tend in an undefined way to bring virtue into existence and to prevent the existence of vice, are only antecedent acts of will, such as is the will to bring about the happiness of all men and to save them from misery. These acts of antecedent will make up only a portion of all the antecedent will of God taken together, whose result forms the consequent will, or the decree to create the best. Through this decree it is that love for virtue and for the happiness of rational creatures, which is undefined in itself and goes as far as is possible, receives some slight limitations, on account of the heed that must be paid to good in general. Thus one must understand that God loves virtue supremely and hates vice supremely, and that nevertheless some vice is to be permitted.

223.   M. Arnauld and M. Bayle appear to maintain that this method of explaining things and of establishing a best among all the plans for the universe, one such as may not be surpassed by any other, sets a limit to God's power. 'Have you considered', says M. Arnauld to Father Malebranche (in his *Reflexions on the New System of Nature and Grace*, vol. II, p. 385), 'that in making such assumptions you take it upon yourself to subvert the first article of the creed, whereby we make profession of believing in God the Father Almighty?' He had said already (p. 362): 'Can one maintain, without trying to blind oneself, that a course of action which could not fail to have this grievous result, namely, that the majority of men perish, bears the stamp of God's goodness more than a different course of action, which would have caused, if God had followed it, the salvation of all men?' And, as M. Jacquelot does not differ from the principles I have just laid

down, M. Bayle raises like objections in his case (*Reply to the Questions of a Provincial*, vol. III, ch. 151, p. 900): 'If one adopts such explanations', he says, 'one sees oneself constrained to renounce the most obvious notions on the nature of the supremely perfect Being. These teach us that all things not implying contradiction are possible for him, that consequently it is possible for him to save people whom he does not save: for what contradiction would result supposing the number of the elect were greater than it is? They teach us besides that, since he is supremely happy, he has no will which he cannot carry out. How, then, shall we understand that he wills to save all men and that he cannot do so? We sought some light to help us out of the perplexities we feel in comparing the idea of God with the state of the human kind, and lo! we are given elucidations that cast us into darkness more dense.'

224. All these obstacles vanish before the exposition I have just given. I agree with M. Bayle's principle, and it is also mine, that everything implying no contradiction is possible. But as for me, holding as I do that God did the best that was possible, or that he could not have done better than he has done, deeming also that to pass any other judgement upon his work in its entirety would be to wrong his goodness or his wisdom, I must say that to make something which surpasses in goodness the best itself, that indeed would imply contradiction. That would be as if someone maintained that God could draw from one point to another a line shorter than the straight line, and accused those who deny this of subverting the article of faith whereby we believe in God the Father Almighty.

225. The infinity of possibles, however great it may be, is no greater than that of the wisdom of God, who knows all possibles. One may even say that if this wisdom does not exceed the possibles extensively, since the objects of the understanding cannot go beyond the possible, which in a sense is alone intelligible, it exceeds them intensively, by reason of the infinitely infinite combinations it makes thereof, and its many deliberations concerning them. The wisdom of God, not content with embracing all the possibles, penetrates them, compares them, weighs them one against the other, to estimate their degrees of perfection or imperfection, the strong and the weak, the good and the evil. It goes even beyond the finite combinations, it makes of them an infinity of infinites, that is to say, an infinity of possible sequences of the universe, each of which contains an infinity of crea-tures. By this means the divine Wisdom distributes all the possibles it had already contemplated separately, into so many universal systems

which it further compares the one with the other. The result of all these comparisons and deliberations is the choice of the best from among all these possible systems, which wisdom makes in order to satisfy goodness completely; and such is precisely the plan of the universe as it is. Moreover, all these operations of the divine understanding, although they have among them an order and a priority of nature, always take place together, no priority of time existing among them.

226.   The careful consideration of these things will, I hope, induce a different idea of the greatness of the divine perfections, and especially of the wisdom and goodness of God, from any that can exist in the minds of those who make God act at random, without cause or reason. And I do not see how they could avoid falling into an opinion so strange, unless they acknowledged that there are reasons for God's choice, and that these reasons are derived from his goodness: whence it follows of necessity that what was chosen had the advantage of goodness over what was not chosen, and consequently that it is the best of all the possibles. The best cannot be surpassed in goodness, and it is no restriction of the power of God to say that he cannot do the impossible. Is it possible, said M. Bayle, that there is no better plan than that one which God carried out? One answers that it is very possible and indeed necessary, namely that there is none: otherwise God would have preferred it.

227.   It seems to me that I have proved sufficiently that among all the possible plans of the universe there is one better than all the rest, and that God has not failed to choose it. But M. Bayle claims to infer thence that God is therefore not free. This is how he speaks on that question (*ubi supra*, ch. 151, p. 899): 'I thought to argue with a man who assumed as I do that the goodness and the power of God are infinite, as well as his wisdom; and now I see that in reality this man assumes that God's goodness and power are enclosed within rather narrow bounds.' As to that, the objection has already been met: I set no bounds to God's power, since I recognize that it extends *ad maximum, ad omnia*, to all that implies no contradiction; and I set none to his goodness, since it attains to the best, *ad optimum*. But M. Bayle goes on: 'There is therefore no freedom in God; he is compelled by his wisdom to create, and then to create precisely such a work, and finally to create it precisely in such ways. These are three servitudes which form a more than Stoic *fatum*, and which render impossible all that is not within their sphere. It seems that, according to this system, God could have said, even before

shaping his decrees: I cannot save such and such a man, nor condemn such and such another, *quippe velor fatis*, my wisdom permits it not.'

228. I answer that it is goodness which prompts God to create with the purpose of communicating himself; and this same goodness combined with wisdom prompts him to create the best: a best that includes the whole sequence, the effect and the process. It prompts him thereto without compelling him, for it does not render impossible that which it does not cause him to choose. To call that *fatum* is taking it in a good sense, which is not contrary to freedom: *fatum* comes from *fari*, to speak, to pronounce; it signifies a judgement, a decree of God, the award of his wisdom. To say that one cannot do a thing, simply because one does not will it, is to misuse terms. The wise mind wills only the good: is it then a servitude when the will acts in accordance with wisdom? And can one be less a slave than to act by one's own choice in accordance with the most perfect reason? Aristotle used to say that that man is in a natural servitude (*natura servus*) who lacks guidance, who has need of being directed. Slavery comes from without, it leads to that which offends, and especially to that which offends with reason: the force of others and our own passions enslave us. God is never moved by anything outside himself, nor is he subject to inward passions, and he is never led to that which can cause him offence. It appears, therefore, that M. Bayle gives odious names to the best things in the world, and turns our ideas upside-down, applying the term slavery to the state of the greatest and most perfect freedom.

229. He had also said not long before (ch. 151, p. 891): 'If virtue, or any other good at all, had been as appropriate as vice for the Creator's ends, vice would not have been given preference; it must therefore have been the only means that the Creator could have used; it was therefore employed purely of necessity. As therefore he loves his glory, not with a freedom of indifference, but by necessity, he must by necessity love all the means without which he could not manifest his glory. Now if vice, as vice, was the only means of attaining to this end, it will follow that God of necessity loves vice as vice, a thought which can only inspire us with horror; and he has revealed quite the contrary to us.' He observes at the same time that certain doctors among the Supralapsarians (like Rutherford, for example) denied that God wills sin as sin, whilst they admitted that he wills sin permissively in so far as it is punishable and pardonable. But he urges in objection, that an action is only punishable and pardonable in so far as it is vicious.

230. M. Bayle makes a false assumption in these words that we have just read, and draws from them false conclusions. It is not true that God loves his glory by necessity, if thereby it is understood that he is led by necessity to acquire his glory through his creatures. For if that were so, he would acquire his glory always and everywhere. The decree to create is free: God is prompted to all good; the good, and even the best, inclines him to act; but it does not compel him, for his choice creates no impossibility in that which is distinct from the best; it causes no implication of contradiction in that which God refrains from doing. There is therefore in God a freedom that is exempt not only from constraint but also from necessity. I mean this in respect of metaphysical necessity; for it is a moral necessity that the wisest should be bound to choose the best. It is the same with the means which God chooses to attain his glory. And as for vice, it has been shown in preceding pages that it is not an object of God's decree as *means*, but as *conditio sine qua non*, and that for that reason alone it is permitted. One is even less justified in saying that vice is *the only means*; it would be at most one of the means, but one of the least among innumerable others.

231. 'Another frightful consequence,' M. Bayle goes on, 'the fatality of all things, ensues: God will not have been free to arrange events in a different way, since the means he chose to show forth his glory was the only means befitting his wisdom.' This so-called fatality or necessity is only moral, as I have just shown: it does not affect freedom; on the contrary, it assumes the best use thereof; it does not render impossible the objects set aside by God's choice. 'What, then, will become', he adds, 'of man's free will? Will there not have been necessity and fatality for Adam to sin? For if he had not sinned, he would have overthrown the sole plan that God had of necessity created.' That is again a misuse of terms. Adam sinning freely was seen of God among the ideas of the possibles, and God decreed to admit him into existence as he saw him. This decree does not change the nature of the objects: it does not render necessary that which was contingent in itself, or impossible that which was possible.

232. M. Bayle goes on (p. 892): 'The subtle Scotus asserts with much discernment that if God had no freedom of indifference no creature could have this kind of freedom.' I agree provided it is not meant as an indifference of equipoise, where there is no reason inclining more to one side than the other. M. Bayle acknowledges (farther on in chapter 168, p. 1111) that what is termed indifference does not exclude prevenient inclinations and pleasures. It suffices therefore

that there be no metaphysical necessity in the action which is termed free, that is to say, it suffices that a choice be made between several courses possible.

233.   He goes on again in the said chapter 157, p. 893: 'If God is not determined to create the world by a free motion of his goodness, but by the interests of his glory, which he loves by necessity, and which is the only thing he loves, for it is not different from his substance; and if the love that he has for himself has compelled him to show forth his glory through the most fitting means, and if the fall of man was this same means, it is evident that this fall happened entirely by necessity and that the obedience of Eve and Adam to God's commands was impossible.' Still the same error. The love that God bears to himself is essential to him, but the love for his glory, or the will to acquire his glory, is not so by any means: the love he has for himself did not impel him by necessity to actions without; they were free; and since there were possible plans whereby the first parents should not sin, their sin was therefore not necessary. Finally, I say in effect what M. Bayle acknowledges here, 'that God resolved to create the world by a free motion of his goodness'; and I add that this same motion prompted him to the best.

234.   The same answer holds good against this statement of M. Bayle's (ch. 165, p. 1071): 'The means most appropriate for attaining an end is of necessity one alone' (that is very well said, at least for the cases where God has chosen). 'Therefore if God was prompted irresistibly to employ this means, he employed it by necessity.' (He was certainly prompted thereto, he was determined, or rather he determined himself thereto: but that which is certain is not always necessary, or altogether irresistible; the thing might have gone otherwise, but that did not happen, and with good reason. God chose between different courses all possible: thus, metaphysically speaking, he could have chosen or done what was not the best; but he could not morally speaking have done so. Let us make use of a comparison from geometry. The best way from one point to another (leaving out of account obstacles and other considerations accidental to the medium) is one alone: it is that one which passes by the shortest line, which is the straight line. Yet there are innumerable ways from one point to another. There is therefore no necessity which binds me to go by the straight line; but as soon as I choose the best, I am determined to go that way, although this is only a moral necessity in the wise. That is why the following conclusions fail.) 'Therefore he could only do that which he did. Therefore

that which has not happened or will never happen is absolutely impossible.' (These conclusions fail, I say: for since there are many things which have never happened and never will happen, and which nevertheless are clearly conceivable, and imply no contradiction, how can one say they are altogether impossible? M. Bayle has refuted that himself in a passage opposing the Spinozists, which I have already quoted here, and he has frequently acknowledged that there is nothing impossible except that which implies contradiction: now he changes style and terminology.) 'Therefore Adam's perseverance in innocence was always impossible; therefore his fall was altogether inevitable, and even antecedently to God's decree, for it implied contradiction that God should be able to will a thing opposed to his wisdom: it is, after all, the same thing to say, that it is impossible for God, as to say, God could do it, if he so willed, but he cannot will it.' (It is misusing terms in a sense to say here: one can will, one will will; 'can' here concerns the actions that one does will. Nevertheless it implies no contradiction that God should will – directly or permissively – a thing not implying contradiction, and in this sense it is permitted to say that God can will it.)

235.   In a word, when one speaks of the *possibility* of a thing it is not a question of the causes that can bring about or prevent its actual existence: otherwise one would change the nature of the terms, and render useless the distinction between the possible and the actual. This Abélard did, and Wyclif appears to have done after him, in consequence of which they fell needlessly into unsuitable and disagreeable expressions. That is why, when one asks if a thing is possible or necessary, and brings in the consideration of what God wills or chooses, one alters the issue. For God chooses among the possibles, and for that very reason he chooses freely, and is not compelled; there would be neither choice nor freedom if there were but one course possible.

236.   One must also answer M. Bayle's syllogisms, so as to neglect none of the objections of a man so gifted: they occur in Chapter 151 of his *Reply to the Questions of a Provincial* (vol. III, pp. 900, 901).

FIRST SYLLOGISM

'God can will nothing that is opposed to the necessary love which he has for his wisdom.

'Now the salvation of all men is opposed to the necessary love which God has for his wisdom.

'Therefore God cannot will the salvation of all men.'

The major is self-evident, for one can do nothing whereof the opposite is necessary. But the minor cannot be accepted, for, albeit God loves his wisdom of necessity, the actions whereto his wisdom prompts him cannot but be free, and the objects whereto his wisdom does not prompt him do not cease to be possible. Moreover, his wisdom has prompted him to will the salvation of all men, but not by a consequent and decretory will. Yet this consequent will, being only a result of free antecedent acts of will, cannot fail to be free also.

SECOND SYLLOGISM

'The work most worthy of God's wisdom involves amongst other things the sin of all men and the eternal damnation of the majority of men.

'Now God wills of necessity the work most worthy of his wisdom.

'He wills therefore of necessity the work that involves amongst other things the sin of all men and the eternal damnation of the majority of men.'

The major holds good, but the minor I deny. The decrees of God are always free, even though God be always prompted thereto by reasons which lie in the intention towards good: for to be morally compelled by wisdom, to be bound by the consideration of good, is to be free; it is not compulsion in the metaphysical sense. And metaphysical necessity alone, as I have observed so many times, is opposed to freedom.

SUMMARY OF THE CONTROVERSY REDUCED TO FORMAL ARGUMENTS

Some persons of discernment have wished me to make this addition. I have the more readily deferred to their opinion, because of the opportunity thereby gained for meeting certain difficulties, and for making observations on certain matters which were not treated in sufficient detail in the work itself.

OBJECTION I

Whoever does not choose the best course is lacking either in power, or knowledge, or goodness.

God did not choose the best course in creating this world.

Therefore God was lacking in power, or knowledge, or goodness.

ANSWER

I deny the minor, that is to say, the second premiss of this syllogism, and the opponent proves it by this

PROSYLLOGISM

Whoever makes things in which there is evil, and which could have been made without any evil, or need not have been made at all, does not choose the best course.

God made a world wherein there is evil; a world, I say, which could have been made without any evil or which need not have been made at all.

Therefore God did not choose the best course.

ANSWER

I admit the minor of this prosyllogism: for one must confess that there is evil in this world which God has made, and that it would have been possible to make a world without evil or even not to create any world, since its creation depended upon the free will of God. But I deny the major, that is, the first of the two premisses of the prosyllogism, and I might content myself with asking for its proof. In order, however, to give a clearer exposition of the matter, I would justify this denial by pointing out that the best course is not always that one which tends towards avoiding evil, since it is possible that the evil may be accompanied by a greater good. For example, the general of an army will prefer a great victory with a slight wound to a state of affairs without wound and without victory. I have proved this in further detail in this work by pointing out, through instances taken from mathematics and elsewhere, that an imperfection in the part may be required for a greater perfection in the whole. I have followed therein the opinion of St. Augustine, who said a hundred times that God permitted evil in order to derive from it a good, that is to say, a greater good; and Thomas Aquinas says (in libr. 2, *Sent. Dist.* 32, qu. 1, art. 1) that the permission of evil tends towards the good of the universe. I have shown that among older writers the fall of Adam was termed *felix culpa*, a fortunate sin, because it had been expiated with immense benefit by the incarnation of the Son of God: for he gave to the universe something more noble than anything there would otherwise have been amongst created beings. For the better understanding of the matter I added, following the example of many good authors, that it was consistent with order and the general good for God to grant to certain of his creatures the opportunity to exercise their freedom, even when he foresaw that they would turn to evil: for God could easily correct the evil, and it was not fitting that in order to prevent sin he should always act in an extraordinary way. It will therefore sufficiently refute the objection to show that a world with evil may be better than a world without evil. But I have gone still further in the work, and have even shown that this universe must be indeed better than every other possible universe.

OBJECTION II

If there is more evil than good in intelligent creatures, there is more evil than good in all God's work.

Now there is more evil than good in intelligent creatures.

Therefore there is more evil than good in all God's work.

ANSWER

I deny the major and the minor of this conditional syllogism. As for the major, I do not admit it because this supposed inference from the part to the whole, from intelligent creatures to all creatures, assumes tacitly and without proof that creatures devoid of reason cannot be compared or taken into account with those that have reason. But why might not the surplus of good in the non-intelligent creatures that fill the world compensate for and even exceed incomparably the surplus of evil in rational creatures? It is true that the value of the latter is greater; but by way of compensation the others are incomparably greater in number; and it may be that the proportion of number and quantity surpasses that of value and quality.

The minor also I cannot admit, namely, that there is more evil than good in intelligent creatures. One need not even agree that there is more evil than good in the human kind. For it is possible, and even a very reasonable thing, that the glory and the perfection of the blessed may be incomparably greater than the misery and imperfection of the damned, and that here the excellence of the total good in the smaller number may exceed the total evil which is in the greater number. The blessed draw near to divinity through a divine Mediator, so far as can belong to these created beings, and make such progress in good as is impossible for the damned to make in evil, even though they should approach as nearly as may be the nature of demons. God is infinite, and the Devil is finite; good can and does go on *ad infinitum*, whereas evil has its bounds. It may be therefore, and it is probable, that there happens in the comparison between the blessed and the damned the opposite of what I said could happen in the comparison between the happy and the unhappy, namely that in the latter the proportion of degrees surpasses that of numbers, while in the comparison between intelligent and non-intelligent the proportion of numbers is greater than that of values. One is justified in assuming that a thing may be so as long as one does not prove that it is impossible, and indeed what is here put forward goes beyond assumption.

But secondly, even should one admit that there is more evil than good in the human kind, one still has every reason for not admitting that there is more evil than good in all intelligent creatures. For there is an inconceivable number of Spirits, and perhaps of other rational creatures besides: and an opponent cannot prove that in the whole City of God, composed as much of Spirits as of rational animals without number and of endless different kinds, the evil exceeds the good. Although one need not, in order to answer an objection, prove that a thing is, when its mere possibility suffices, I have nevertheless shown in this present work that it is a result of the supreme perfection of the Sovereign of the Universe that the kingdom of God should be the most perfect of all states or governments possible, and that in consequence what little evil there is should be required to provide the full measure of the vast good existing there.

OBJECTION III

If it is always impossible not to sin, it is always unjust to punish.
Now it is always impossible not to sin, or rather all sin is necessary.
Therefore it is always unjust to punish.
The minor of this is proved as follows.

FIRST PROSYLLOGISM

Everything predetermined is necessary.
Every event is predetermined.
Therefore every event (and consequently sin also) is necessary.
Again this second minor is proved thus.

SECOND PROSYLLOGISM

That which is future, that which is foreseen, that which is involved in causes is predetermined.
Every event is of this kind.
Therefore every event is predetermined.

ANSWER

I admit in a certain sense the conclusion of the second prosyllogism, which is the minor of the first; but I shall deny the major of the first prosyllogism, namely that everything predetermined is necessary; taking 'necessity', say the necessity to sin, or the impossibility of not sinning, or of not doing some action, in the sense relevant to the argument, that is, as a necessity essential and absolute, which destroys the morality of action and the justice of punishment. If anyone meant a different necessity or impossibility (that is, a necessity only moral or hypothetical, which will be explained presently) it is plain that we would deny him the major stated in the objection. We might content ourselves with this answer, and demand the proof of the proposition denied: but I am well pleased to justify my manner of procedure in the present work, in order to make the matter clear and to throw more light on this whole subject, by explaining the necessity that must be rejected and the determination that must be allowed. The truth is that the necessity contrary to morality, which must be avoided and which would render punishment unjust, is an insuperable necessity, which would render all opposition unavailing, even though one should wish with all one's heart to avoid the necessary action, and though one should make all possible efforts to that end. Now it is plain that this is not applicable to voluntary actions, since one would not do them if one did not so desire. Thus their prevision and predetermination is not absolute, but it presupposes will: if it is certain that one will do them, it is no less certain that one will will to do them. These voluntary actions and their results will not happen whatever one may do and whether one will them or not; but they will happen because one will do, and because one will will to do, that which leads to them. That is involved in prevision and predetermination, and forms the reason thereof. The necessity of such events is called conditional or hypothetical, or again necessity of consequence, because it presupposes the will and the other requisites. But the necessity which destroys morality, and renders punishment unjust and reward unavailing, is found in the things that will be whatever one may do and whatever one may will to do: in a word, it exists in that which is essential. This it is which is called an absolute necessity. Thus it avails nothing with regard to what is necessary absolutely to ordain interdicts or commandments, to propose penalties or prizes, to blame or to praise; it will come to pass no more and no less. In voluntary actions, on the contrary, and in what depends upon them, precepts, armed with power to punish and to reward, very often serve, and are included in the order of causes that make action exist. Thus it comes about that not only pains and effort but also prayers are effective, God having had even these prayers in mind before he ordered things, and having made due allowance for them. That is why the precept *Ora et labora* (Pray and work) remains intact. Thus not only those who (under the empty pretext of the necessity of events) maintain that one can spare oneself the pains demanded by affairs, but also those who argue against prayers, fall into that which the ancients even in their time called 'the Lazy Sophism'. So the predetermination of events by their causes is precisely what contributes to morality instead of destroying it, and the causes incline the will without necessitating it. For this reason the determination we are concerned with is not a necessitation. It is certain (to him who knows all) that the effect will follow this inclination; but this effect does not follow thence by a consequence which is necessary, that is, whose contrary implies contradiction; and it is also by such an inward inclination that the will is determined, without the presence of necessity. Suppose that one has the greatest possible passion (for example, a great thirst), you will admit that the soul can find some reason for resisting it, even if it were only that of displaying its power. Thus though one may never have complete indifference of equipoise, and there is always a predominance of inclination for the course adopted, that predominance does not render absolutely necessary the resolution taken.

OBJECTION IV

Whoever can prevent the sin of others and does not so, but rather contributes to it, although he be fully apprised of it, is accessary thereto.

God can prevent the sin of intelligent creatures; but he does not so, and he rather contributes to it by his co-operation and by the opportunities he causes, although he is fully cognizant of it.

Therefore, etc.

ANSWER

I deny the major of this syllogism. It may be that one can prevent the sin, but that one ought not to do so, because one could not do so without committing a sin oneself, or (when God is concerned) without acting unreasonably. I have given instances of that, and have applied them to God himself. It may be also that one contributes to the evil, and that one even opens the way to it sometimes, in doing things one is bound to do. And when one does one's duty, or (speaking of God) when, after full consideration, one does that which reason demands, one is not responsible for events, even when one foresees them. One does not will these evils; but one is willing to permit them for a greater good, which one cannot in reason help preferring to other considerations. This is a *consequent* will, resulting from acts of *antecedent* will, in which one wills the good. I know that some persons, in speaking of the antecedent and consequent will of God, have meant by the antecedent that which wills that all men be saved, and by the consequent that which wills, in consequence of persistent sin, that there be some damned, damnation being a result of sin. But these are only examples of a more general notion, and one may say with the same reason, that God wills by his antecedent will that men sin not, and that by his consequent or final and decretory will (which is always followed by its effect) he wills to permit that they sin, this permission being a result of superior reasons. One has indeed justification for saying, in general, that the antecedent will of God tends towards the production of good and the prevention of evil, each taken in itself, and as it were detached (*particulariter et secundum quid*: Thom., I, qu. 19, art. 6) according to the measure of the degree of each good or of each evil. Likewise one may say that the consequent, or final and total, divine will tends towards the production of as many goods as can be put together, whose combination thereby becomes determined, and involves also the permission of some evils and the exclusion of some goods, as the best possible plan of the universe demands. Arminius, in his *Antiperkinsus*, explained very well that the will of God can be called consequent not only in relation to the action of the creature considered beforehand in the divine understanding, but also in relation to other anterior acts of divine will. But it is enough to consider the passage cited from Thomas Aquinas, and that from Scotus (I, dist. 46, qu. 11), to see that they make this distinction as I have made it here. Nevertheless if anyone will not suffer this use of the terms, let him put 'previous' in place of 'antecedent' will, and 'final' or 'decretory' in place of 'consequent' will. For I do not wish to wrangle about words.

OBJECTION V

Whoever produces all that is real in a thing is its cause.
God produces all that is real in sin.
Therefore God is the cause of sin.

ANSWER

I might content myself with denying the major or the minor, because the term 'real' admits of interpretations capable of rendering these propositions false. But in order to give a better explanation I will make a distinction. 'Real' either signifies that which is positive only, or else it includes also privative beings: in the first case, I deny the major and I admit the minor; in the second case, I do the opposite. I might have confined myself to that; but I was willing to go further, in order to account for this distinction. I have therefore been well pleased to point out that every purely positive or absolute reality is a perfection, and that every imperfection comes from limitation, that is, from the privative: for to limit is to withhold extension, or the more beyond. Now God is the cause of all perfections, and consequently of all realities, when they are regarded as purely positive. But limitations or privations result from the original imperfection of creatures which restricts their receptivity. It is as with a laden boat, which the river carries along more slowly or less slowly in proportion to the weight that it bears: thus the speed comes from the river, but the retardation which restricts this speed comes from the load. Also I have shown in the present work how the creature, in causing sin, is a deficient cause; how errors and evil inclinations spring from privation; and how privation is efficacious accidentally. And I have justified the opinion of St. Augustine (lib. I, *Ad. Simpl.*, qu. 2) who explains (for example) how God hardens the soul, not in giving it something evil, but because the effect of the good he imprints is restricted by the resistance of the soul, and by the circumstances contributing to this resistance, so that he does not give it all the good that would overcome its evil. 'Nec (*inquit*) ab illo erogatur aliquid quo homo fit deterior, sed tantum quo fit melior non erogatur.' But if God had willed to do more here he must needs have produced either fresh natures in his creatures or fresh miracles to change their natures, and this the best plan did not allow. It is just as if the current of the river must needs be more rapid than its slope permits or the boats themselves be less laden, if they had to be impelled at a greater speed. So the limitation or original imperfection of creatures brings it about that even the best plan of the universe cannot admit more good, and cannot be exempted from certain evils, these, however, being only of such a kind as may tend towards a greater good. There are some disorders in the parts which wonderfully enhance the beauty of the whole, just as certain dissonances, appropriately used, render harmony more beautiful. But that depends upon the answer which I have already given to the first objection.

Whoever punishes those who have done as well as it was in their power to do is unjust.

God does so.

Therefore, etc.

I deny the minor of this argument. And I believe that God always gives sufficient aid and grace to those who have good will, that is to say, who do not reject this grace by a fresh sin. Thus I do not admit the damnation of children dying unbaptized or outside the Church, or the damnation of adult persons who have acted according to the light that God has given them. And I believe that, *if anyone has followed the light he had,* he will undoubtedly receive thereof in greater measure as he has need, even as the late Herr Hulsemann, who was celebrated as a profound theologian at Leipzig, has somewhere observed; and if such a man had failed to receive light during his life, he would receive it at least in the hour of death.

Whoever gives only to some, and not to all, the means of producing effectively in them good will and final saving faith has not enough goodness.

God does so.

Therefore, etc.

I deny the major. It is true that God could overcome the greatest resistance of the human heart, and indeed he sometimes does so, whether by an inward grace or by the outward circumstances that can greatly influence souls; but he does not always do so. Whence comes this distinction, someone will say, and wherefore does his goodness appear to be restricted? The truth is that it would not have been in order always to act in an extraordinary way and to derange the connexion of things, as I have observed already in answering the first objection. The reasons for this connexion, whereby the one is placed in more favourable circumstances than the other, are hidden in the depths of God's wisdom: they depend upon the universal harmony. The best plan of the universe, which God could not fail to choose, required this. One concludes thus from the event itself; since God made the universe, it was not possible to do better. Such management, far from being contrary to goodness, has rather been prompted by supreme goodness itself. This objection with its solution might have been inferred from what was said with regard to the first objection; but it seemed advisable to touch upon it separately.

OBJECTION VIII

Whoever cannot fail to choose the best is not free.
God cannot fail to choose the best.
Therefore God is not free.

ANSWER

I deny the major of this argument. Rather is it true freedom, and the most perfect, to be able to make the best use of one's free will, and always to exercise this power, without being turned aside either by outward force or by inward passions, whereof the one enslaves our bodies and the other our souls. There is nothing less servile and more befitting the highest degree of freedom than to be always led towards the good, and always by one's own inclination, without any constraint and without any displeasure. And to object that God therefore had need of external things is only a sophism. He creates them freely: but when he had set before him an end, that of exercising his goodness, his wisdom determined him to choose the means most appropriate for obtaining this end. To call that a *need* is to take the term in a sense not usual, which clears it of all imperfection, somewhat as one does when speaking of the wrath of God.

Seneca says somewhere, that God commanded only once, but that he obeys always, because he obeys the laws that he willed to ordain for himself: *semel jussit, semper paret*. But he had better have said, that God always commands and that he is always obeyed: for in willing he always follows the tendency of his own nature, and all other things always follow his will. And as this will is always the same one cannot say that he obeys that will only which he formerly had. Nevertheless, although his will is always indefectible and always tends towards the best, the evil or the lesser good which he rejects will still be possible in itself. Otherwise the necessity of good would be geometrical (so to speak) or metaphysical, and altogether absolute; the contingency of things would be destroyed, and there would be no choice. But necessity of this kind, which does not destroy the possibility of the contrary, has the name by analogy only: it becomes effective not through the mere essence of things, but through that which is outside them and above them, that is, through the will of God. This necessity is called moral, because for the wise what is necessary and what is owing are equivalent things; and when it is always followed by its effect, as it indeed is in the perfectly wise, that is, in God, one can say that it is a happy necessity. The more nearly creatures approach this, the closer do they come to perfect felicity. Moreover, necessity of this kind is not the necessity one endeavours to avoid, and which destroys morality, reward and commendation. For that which it brings to pass does not happen whatever one may do and whatever one may will, but because one desires it. A will to which it is natural to choose well deserves most to be commended; and it carries with it its own reward, which is supreme happiness. And as this constitution of the divine nature gives an entire satisfaction to him who possesses it, it is also the best and the most desirable from the point of view of the creatures who are all dependent upon God. If the will of God had not as its rule the principle of the best, it would tend towards evil, which would be worst of all; or else it would be indifferent somehow to good and to evil, and guided by chance. But a will that would always drift along at random would scarcely be any better for the government of the universe than the fortuitous concourse of corpuscles, without the existence of divinity. And even though God should abandon himself to chance only in some cases, and in a certain way (as he would if he did not always tend entirely towards the best, and if he were capable of preferring a lesser good to a greater good, that is, an evil to a good, since that which prevents a greater good is an evil) he would be no less imperfect than the object of his choice. Then he would not deserve absolute trust; he would act without reason in such a case, and the government of the universe would be like certain games equally divided between reason and luck. This all proves that this objection which is made against the choice of the best perverts the notions of free and necessary, and represents the best to us actually as evil: but that is either malicious or absurd.

2

ROBERT MERRIHEW ADAMS

Must God Create the Best?

I

Many philosophers and theologians have accepted the following proposition:

(P) If a perfectly good moral agent created any world at all, it would have to be the very best world that he could create.

The best world that an omnipotent God could create is the best of all logically possible worlds. Accordingly, it has been supposed that if the actual world was created by an omnipotent, perfectly good God, it must be the best of all logically possible worlds.

In this chapter I shall argue that ethical views typical of the Judeo-Christian religious tradition do not require the Judeo-Christian theist to accept (P). He must hold that the actual world is a good world. But he need not maintain that it is the best of all possible worlds, or the best world that God could have made.[1]

The position which I am claiming that he can consistently hold is that *even if* there is a best among possible worlds, God could create another instead of it, and still be perfectly good. I do not in fact see any good reason to believe that there is a best among possible worlds. Why can't it be that for every possible world there is another that is better? And if there is no maximum degree of perfection among possible worlds, it would be unreasonable to blame God, or think less highly of His goodness, because He created a world less excellent than

Original Publication: Robert Merrihew Adams, "Must God Create the Best?," *The Philosophical Review* 81 (3) (1972): 317–32.

He could have created.[2] But I do not claim to be able to prove that there is no best among possible worlds, and in this essay I shall assume for the sake of argument that there is one.

Whether we accept proposition (P) will depend on what we believe are the requirements for perfect goodness. If we apply an act-utilitarian standard of moral goodness, we will have to accept (P). For by act-utilitarian standards it is a moral obligation to bring about the best state of affairs that one can. It is interesting to note that the ethics of Leibniz, the best-known advocate of (P), is basically utilitarian.[3] In his *Theodicy* (Part I, Section 25) he maintains, in effect, that men, because of their ignorance of many of the consequences of their actions, ought to follow a rule-utilitarian code, but that God, being omniscient, must be a perfect act utilitarian in order to be perfectly good.

I believe that utilitarian views are not typical of the Judeo-Christian ethical tradition, although Leibniz is by no means the only Christian utilitarian. In this essay I shall assume that we are working with standards of moral goodness which are not utilitarian. But I shall not try either to show that utilitarianism is wrong or to justify the standards that I take to be more typical of Judeo-Christian religious ethics. To attempt either of these tasks would unmanageably enlarge the scope of the chapter. What I can hope to establish here is therefore limited to the claim that the rejection of (P) is consistent with Judeo-Christian religious ethics.

Assuming that we are not using utilitarian standards of moral goodness, I see only two types of reason that could be given for (P). (1) It might be claimed that a creator would necessarily wrong someone (violate someone's rights), or be less kind to someone than a perfectly good moral agent must be, if he knowingly created a less excellent world instead of the best that he could. Or (2) it might be claimed that even if no one would be wronged or treated unkindly by the creation of an inferior world, the creator's choice of an inferior world must manifest a defect of character. I will argue against the first of these claims in section II. Then I will suggest, in section III, that God's choice of a less excellent world could be accounted for in terms of His grace, which is considered a virtue rather than a defect of character in Judeo-Christian ethics. A counter-example, which is the basis for the most persuasive objections to my position that I have encountered, will be considered in sections IV and V.

II

Is there someone *to* whom a creator would have an obligation to create the best world he could? Is there someone whose rights would be violated, or who would be treated unkindly, if the creator created a less excellent world? Let us suppose that our creator is God, and that there does not exist any being, other than Himself, which He has not created. It follows that if God has wronged anyone, or been unkind to anyone, in creating whatever world He has created, this must be one of His own creatures. To which of His creatures, then, might God have an obligation to create the best of all possible worlds? (For that is the best world He could create.)

Might He have an obligation to the creatures in the best possible world, to create them? Have they been wronged, or even treated unkindly, if God has created a less excellent world, in which they do not exist, instead of creating them? I think not. The difference between actual beings and merely possible beings is of fundamental moral importance here. The moral community consists of actual beings. It is they who have actual rights, and it is to them that there are actual obligations. A merely possible being cannot be (actually) wronged or treated unkindly. A being who never exists is not wronged by not being created, and there is no obligation to any possible being to bring it into existence.

Perhaps it will be objected that we believe we have obligations to future generations, who are not yet actual and may never be actual. We do say such things, but I think what we mean is something like the following. There is not merely a logical possibility, but a probability greater than zero, that future generations will really exist; and *if* they will in fact exist, we will have wronged them if we act or fail to act in certain ways. On this analysis we cannot have an obligation to future generations to bring them into existence.

I argue, then, that God does not have an obligation to the creatures in the best of all possible worlds to create them. If God has chosen to create a world less excellent than the best possible, He has not thereby wronged any creatures whom He has chosen not to create. He has not even been unkind to them. If any creatures are wronged, or treated unkindly, by such a choice of the creator, they can only be creatures that exist in the world He has created.

I think it is fairly plausible to suppose that God could create a world which would have the following characteristics:

(1) None of the individual creatures in it would exist in the best of all possible worlds.

(2) None of the creatures in it has a life which is so miserable on the whole that it would be better for that creature if it had never existed.

(3) Every individual creature in the world is at least as happy on the whole as it would have been in any other possible world in which it could have existed.

It seems obvious that if God creates such a world He does not thereby wrong any of the creatures in it, and does not thereby treat any of them with less than perfect kindness. For none of them would have been benefited by His creating any other world instead.[4]

If there are doubts about the possibility of God's creating such a world, they will probably have to do with the third characteristic. It may be worth while to consider two questions, on the supposition (which I am not endorsing) that no possible world less excellent than the best would have characteristic (3), and that God has created a world which has characteristics (1) and (2) but not (3). In such a case must God have wronged one of His creatures? Must He have been less than perfectly kind to one of His creatures?

I do not think it can reasonably be argued that in such a case God must have wronged one of His creatures. Suppose a creature in such a case were to complain that God had violated its rights by creating it in a world in which it was less happy on the whole than it would have been in some other world in which God could have created it. The complaint might express a claim to special treatment: "God ought to have created *me* in more favorable circumstances (even though that would involve His creating some *other* creature in less favorable circumstances than He could have created it in)." Such a complaint would not be reasonable, and would not establish that there had been any violation of the complaining creature's rights.

Alternatively, the creature might make the more principled complaint, "God has wronged me by not following the principle of refraining from creating any world in which there is a creature that would have been happier in another world He could have made." This also is an unreasonable complaint. For if God followed the stated principle, He would not create any world that lacked characteristic (3). And we are assuming that no world less excellent than the best possible would have characteristic (3). It follows that if God acted on the stated principle. He would not create any world less excellent than the best possible. But the complaining creature would not exist in the best of all possible worlds; for we are assuming that this creature exists in a world which has characteristic (1). The complaining creature, therefore, would never have existed if God had followed the principle that is urged in the complaint. There could not possibly be any advantage to this creature from God's having followed that principle; and the creature has not been wronged by God's not following the principle. (It would not be better for the creature if it had never existed; for we are assuming that the world God created has characteristic [2].)

The question of whether in the assumed case God must have been unkind to one of His creatures is more complicated than the question of whether He must have wronged one of them. In fact it is too complicated to be discussed adequately here. I will just make three observations about it. The first is that it is no clearer that the best of all possible worlds would possess characteristic (3) than that some less excellent world would possess it. In fact it has often been supposed that the best possible world might not possess it. The problem we are now discussing can therefore arise also for those who believe that God has created the best of all possible worlds.

My second observation is that if kindness to a person is the same as a tendency to promote his happiness, God has been less than perfectly (completely, unqualifiedly) kind to any creature whom He could have made somewhat happier than He has made it. (I shall not discuss here whether kindness to a person is indeed the same as a tendency to promote his happiness; they are at least closely related.)

But in the third place I would observe that such qualified kindness (if that is what it is) toward some creatures is consistent with God's being perfectly good, and with His being very kind to all His creatures. It is consistent with His being very kind to all His creatures because He may have prepared for all of them a very satisfying existence even though some of them might have been slightly happier in some other possible world. It is consistent with His being perfectly good because even a perfectly good moral agent may be led, by other considerations of sufficient weight, to qualify his kindness or beneficence toward some person. It has sometimes been held that a perfectly good God might cause or permit a person to have less happiness than he might otherwise have had, in order to punish him, or to avoid interfering with the freedom of another person, or in order to create the best of all possible worlds. I would suggest that the desire to create and love all of a certain group of possible creatures (assuming that all of them would have satisfying lives on the whole) might be an adequate ground for a perfectly good God to create them, even if His creating *all* of them must have the result that some of them are less happy than they might otherwise have been. And they need not be the best of all possible creatures, or included in the best of all possible worlds, in order for this qualification of His kindness to be consistent with His perfect goodness. The desire to create *those* creatures is as legitimate a ground for Him to qualify His kindness toward some, as the desire to create the best of all possible worlds. This suggestion seems to me to be in keeping with the aspect of the Judeo-Christian moral ideal which will be discussed in section III.

These matters would doubtless have to be discussed more fully if we were considering whether the *actual* world can have been created by a perfectly good God. For our present purposes, however, enough may have been said – especially since, as I have noted, it seems a plausible assumption that God could make a world having characteristics (1), (2), and (3). In that case He could certainly make a less excellent world than the best of all possible worlds without wronging any of His creatures or failing in kindness to any of them. (I have, of course, *not* been arguing that there is *no* way in which God could wrong anyone or be less kind to anyone than a perfectly good moral agent must be.)

III

Plato is one of those who held that a perfectly good creator would make the very best world he could. He thought that if the creator chose to make a world less good than he could have made, that could be understood only in terms of some defect in the creator's character. Envy is the defect that Plato suggests.[5] It may be thought that the creation of a world inferior to the best that he could make would manifest a defect in the creator's character even if no one were thereby wronged or treated unkindly. For the perfectly good moral agent must not only be kind and refrain from violating the rights of others, but must also have other virtues. For instance, he must be noble, generous, high-minded, and free from envy. He must satisfy the moral ideal.

There are differences of opinion, however, about what is to be included in the moral ideal. One important element in the Judeo-Christian moral ideal is *grace*. For present purposes, grace may be defined as a disposition to love which is not dependent on the merit of the person loved. The gracious person loves without worrying about whether the person he loves is worthy of his love. Or perhaps it would be better to say that the gracious person sees what is valuable in the person he loves, and does not worry about whether it is more or less valuable than what could be found in someone else he might have loved. In the Judeo-Christian tradition it is typically believed that grace is a virtue which God does have and men ought to have.

A God who is gracious with respect to creating might well choose to create and love less excellent creatures than He could have chosen. This is not to suggest that grace in creation consists in a preference for imperfection as such. God could have chosen to create the best of all possible creatures, and still have been gracious in choosing them. God's graciousness in creation does not imply that the creatures He has chosen to create must be less excellent than the best possible. It implies, rather, that even if they are the best possible creatures, that is not the ground for His choosing them. And it implies that there is nothing in God's nature or character which would require Him to act on the principle of choosing the best possible creatures to be the object of His creative powers.

Grace, as I have described it, is not part of everyone's moral ideal. For instance, it was not part of Plato's moral ideal. The thought that it may be the expression of a virtue, rather than a defect of character, in a creator, *not* to act on the principle of creating the best creatures he possibly could, is quite foreign to Plato's ethical viewpoint. But I believe that thought is not at all foreign to a Judeo-Christian ethical viewpoint.

This interpretation of the Judeo-Christian tradition is confirmed by the religious and devotional attitudes toward God's creation which prevail in the tradition. The man who worships God does not normally praise Him for His moral rectitude and good judgment in creating *us*. He thanks God for his existence as for an undeserved personal favor. Religious writings frequently deprecate the intrinsic worth of human beings, considered apart from God's love for them, and express surprise that God should concern Himself with them at all.

When I look at thy heavens, the work of thy fingers, the moon and the stars which thou hast established;
What is man that thou art mindful of him, and the son of man that thou dost care for him?

Yet thou hast made him little less than God, and dost crown him with
glory and honor.
Thou hast given him dominion over the works of thy hands; thou hast
put all things under his feet. (Psalm 8: 3–6)

Such utterances seem quite incongruous with the idea that God
created us because if He had not He would have failed to bring
about the best possible state of affairs. They suggest that God has
created human beings and made them dominant on this planet
although He could have created intrinsically better states of affairs
instead.

I believe that in the Judeo-Christian tradition the typical religious
attitude (or at any rate the attitude typically encouraged) toward the
fact of our existence is something like the following. "I am glad that I
exist, and I thank God for the life He has given me. I am also glad that
other people exist, and I thank God for them. Doubtless there could be
more excellent creatures than we. But I believe that God, in His grace,
created us and loves us; and I accept that gladly and gratefully." (Such
an attitude need not be complacent; for the task of struggling against
certain evils may be seen as precisely a part of the life that the religious
person is to accept and be glad in.) When people who have or endorse
such an attitude say that God is perfectly good, we will not take them as
committing themselves to the view that God is the kind of being who
would not create any other world than the best possible. For they
regard grace as an important part of perfect goodness.

IV

On more than one occasion when I have argued for the positions I
have taken in sections II and III above, a counterexample of the
following sort has been proposed. It is the case of a person who,
knowing that he intends to conceive a child and that a certain drug
invariably causes severe mental retardation in children conceived by
those who have taken it, takes the drug and conceives a severely
retarded child. We all, I imagine, have a strong inclination to say that
such a person has done something wrong. It is objected to me that our
moral intuitions in this case (presumably including the moral intuitions
of religious Jews and Christians) are inconsistent with the views I have
advanced above. It is claimed that consistency requires me to abandon

those views unless I am prepared to make moral judgments that none of us are in fact willing to make.

I will try to meet these objections. I will begin by stating the case in some detail, in the most relevant form I can think of. Then I will discuss objections based on it. In this section I will discuss an objection against what I have said in section II, and a more general objection against the rejection of proposition (P) will be discussed in section V.

Let us call this Case (A). A certain couple become so interested in retarded children that they develop a strong desire to have a retarded child of their own – to love it, to help it realize its potentialities (such as they are) to the full, to see that it is as happy as it can be. (For some reason it is impossible for them to *adopt* such a child.) They act on their desire. They take a drug which is known to cause damaged genes and abnormal chromosome structure in reproductive cells, resulting in severe mental retardation of children conceived by those who have taken it. A severely retarded child is conceived and born. They lavish affection on the child. They have ample means, so that they are able to provide for special needs, and to insure that others will never be called on to pay for the child's support. They give themselves unstintedly, and do develop the child's capacities as much as possible. The child is, on the whole, happy, though incapable of many of the higher intellectual, aesthetic, and social joys. It suffers some pains and frustrations, of course, but does not feel miserable on the whole.

The first objection founded on this case is based, not just on the claim that the parents have done something wrong (which I certainly grant), but on the more specific claim that they have *wronged the child*. I maintained, in effect, in section II that a creature has not been wronged by its creator's creating it if both of the following conditions are satisfied.[6] (4) The creature is not, on the whole, so miserable that it would be better for him if he had never existed. (5) No being who came into existence in better or happier circumstances would have been the same individual as the creature in question. If we apply an analogous principle to the parent–child relationship in Case (A), it would seem to follow that the retarded child has not been wronged by its parents. Condition (4) is satisfied: the child is happy rather than miserable on the whole. And condition (5) also seems to be satisfied. For the retardation in Case (A), as described, is not due to prenatal injury but to the genetic constitution of the child. Any normal child the parents might have conceived (indeed any normal child at all) would have had a different genetic constitution, and would therefore have been a different person, from the retarded child they actually did conceive. But it is objected to me – we do regard the parents in Case (A) as having wronged the child, and therefore we cannot consistently accept the principle that I maintained in section II.

My reply is that if conditions (4) and (5) are really satisfied the child cannot have been wronged by its parents' taking the drug and conceiving it. If we think otherwise we are being led, perhaps by our emotions, into a confusion. If the child is not worse off than if it had never existed, and if *its* never existing would have been a sure consequence of its not having been brought into existence as retarded, I do not see how *its* interests can have been injured, or *its* rights violated, by the parents' bringing it into existence as retarded.

It is easy to understand how the parents might come to feel that they had wronged the child. They might come to feel guilty (and rightly so), and the child would provide a focus for the guilt. Moreover, it would be easy, psychologically, to assimilate Case (A) to cases of culpability for prenatal injury, in which it is more reasonable to think of the child as having been wronged.[7] And we often think very carelessly about counterfactual personal identity, asking ourselves questions of doubtful intelligibility, such as, "What if I had been born in the Middle Ages?" It is very easy to fail to consider the objection, "But that would not have been the same person."

It is also possible that an inclination to say that the child has been wronged may be based, at least in part, on a doubt that conditions (4) and (5) are really satisfied in Case (A). Perhaps one is not convinced that in real life the parents could ever have a reasonable confidence that the child would be happy rather than miserable. Maybe it will be doubted that a few changes in chromosome structure, and the difference between damaged and undamaged genes, are enough to establish that the retarded child is a different person from any normal child that the couple could have had. Of course, if conditions (4) and (5) are not satisfied, the case does not constitute a counterexample to my claims in section II. But I would not rest any of the weight of my argument on doubts about the satisfaction of the conditions in Case (A), because I think it is plausible to suppose that they would be satisfied in Case (A) or in some very similar case.

V

Even if the parents in Case (*A*) have not wronged the child, I assume that they have done something wrong. It may be asked *what* they have done wrong, or *why* their action is regarded as wrong. And these questions may give rise to an objection, not specifically to what I said in section II, but more generally to my rejection of proposition (*P*). For it may be suggested that what is wrong about the action of the parents in Case (*A*) is that they have violated the following principle:

(*Q*) It is wrong to bring into existence, knowingly, a being less excellent than one could have brought into existence.[8]

If we accept this principle we must surely agree that it would be wrong for a creator to make a world that was less excellent than the best he could make, and therefore that a perfectly good creator would not do such a thing. In otherwords, (*Q*) implies (*P*).

I do not think (*Q*) is a very plausible principle. It is not difficult to think of counterexamples to it.

Case (*B*): A man breeds goldfish, thereby bringing about their existence. We do not normally think it is wrong, or even prima facie wrong, for a man to do this, even though he could equally well have brought about the existence of more excellent beings, more intelligent and capable of higher satisfactions. (He could have bred dogs or pigs, for example.) The deliberate breeding of human beings of subnormal intelligence is morally offensive; the deliberate breeding of species far less intelligent than retarded human children is not morally offensive.

Case (*C*): Suppose it has been discovered that if intending parents take a certain drug before conceiving a child, they will have a child whose abnormal genetic constitution will give it vastly superhuman intelligence and superior prospects of happiness. Other things being equal, would it be wrong for intending parents to have normal children instead of taking the drug? There may be considerable disagreement of moral judgment about this. I do not think that parents who chose to have normal children rather than take the drug would be doing anything wrong, nor that they would necessarily be manifesting any weakness or defect of moral character. Parents' choosing to have a normal rather than a superhuman child would not, at any rate, elicit the strong and universal or almost universal disapproval that would be elicited by the action of the parents in Case (A). Even with respect to the offspring of human beings, the principle we all confidently endorse is not that it is wrong to bring about, knowingly and voluntarily, the procreation of offspring less excellent than could have been procreated, but that it is wrong to bring about, knowingly and voluntarily, the procreation of a human offspring which is deficient by comparison with normal human beings.

Such counterexamples as these suggest that our disapproval of the action of the parents in Case (A) is not based on principle (Q), but on a less general and more plausible principle such as the following:

(R)   It is wrong for human beings to cause, knowingly and voluntarily, the procreation of an offspring of human parents which is notably deficient, by comparison with normal human beings, in mental or physical capacity.

One who rejects (Q) while maintaining (R) might be held to face a problem of explanation. It may seem arbitrary to maintain such a specific moral principle as (R), unless one can explain it as based on a more general principle, such as (Q). I believe, however, that principle (R) might well be explained in something like the following way in a theological ethics in the Judeo-Christian tradition, consistently with the rejection of (Q) and (P).[9]

God, in His grace, has chosen to have human beings among His creatures. In creating us He has certain intentions about the qualities and goals of human life. He has these intentions for us, not just as individuals, but as members of a community which in principle includes the whole human race. And His intentions for human beings as such extend to the offspring (if any) of human beings. Some of these intentions are to be realized by human voluntary action, and it is our duty to act in accordance with them.

It seems increasingly possible for human voluntary action to influence the genetic constitution of human offspring. The religious believer in the Judeo-Christian tradition will want to be extremely cautious about this. For he is to be thankful that we exist as the beings we are, and will be concerned lest he bring about the procreation of human offspring who would be deficient in their capacity to enter fully into the purposes that God has for human beings as such. We are not God. We are His creatures, and we belong to Him. Any offspring we have will belong to Him in a much more fundamental way than they can belong to their human parents. We have not the right to try to have as our offspring just any kind of being whose existence might on the whole be pleasant and of some value (for instance, a being of very low intelligence but highly specialized for the enjoyment of aesthetic pleasures of smell and taste). If we do intervene to affect the genetic constitution of human offspring, it must be in ways which seem likely to make them *more* able to enter fully into what we believe to be the purposes of God for human beings as such. The deliberate procreation of children deficient in mental or physical capacity would be an intervention which could hardly be expected to result in offspring more able to enter fully into God's purposes for human life. It would therefore be sinful, and inconsistent with a proper respect for the human life which God has given us.

On this view of the matter, our obligation to refrain from bringing about the procreation of deficient human offspring is rooted in our obligation to God, as His creatures, to respect His purposes for human life. In adopting this theological rationale for the acceptance of principle (R), one in no way commits oneself to proposition (P). For one does not base (R) on any principle to the effect that one must always try to bring into existence the most excellent things that one can. And the claim that, because of His intentions for human life, we have an obligation to God not to try to have as our offspring beings of certain sorts does not imply that it would be wrong for God to create such beings in other ways. Much less does it imply that it would be wrong for God to create a world less excellent than the best possible.

In this essay I have argued that a creator would not necessarily wrong anyone, or be less kind to anyone than a perfectly good moral agent must be, if he created a world of creatures who would not exist in the best world he could make. I have also argued that from the standpoint of Judeo-Christian religious ethics, a creator's choice of a less excellent world need not be regarded as manifesting a defect of character. It could be understood in terms of his *grace*, which (in that ethics) is considered an important part of perfect goodness. In this way I think the rejection of proposition (P) can be seen to be congruous with the attitude of gratitude and respect for human life as God's gracious gift which is encouraged in the Judeo-Christian religious tradition. And that attitude (rather than any belief that one ought to bring into existence only the best beings one can) can be seen as a basis for the disapproval of the deliberate procreation of deficient human offspring.[10]

NOTES

1 What I am saying in this essay is obviously relevant to the problem of evil. But I make no claim to be offering a complete theodicy here.

2 Leibniz held (in his *Theodicy*, pt. I, sec. 8) that if there were no best among possible worlds, a perfectly good God would have created nothing at all. But Leibniz is mistaken if he supposes that in this way God could avoid choosing an alternative less excellent than others He could have chosen. For the existence of no created world at all would surely be a less excellent state of affairs than the existence of some of the worlds that God could have created.

3 See Gaston Grua, *Jurisprudence universelle et théodicée selon Leibniz* (Paris, 1953), pp. 210–18.

4 Perhaps I can have a right to something which would not benefit me (e.g., if it has been promised to me). But if there are such non-beneficial rights, I do not see any plausible reason for supposing that a right not to be created could be among them.

5 *Timaeus*, 29E–30A.

6 I am not holding that these are necessary conditions, but only that they are jointly sufficient conditions, for a creature's not being wronged by its creator's creating it. I have numbered these conditions in such a way as to avoid confusion with the numbered characteristics of worlds in sec. II.

7 It may be questioned whether even the prenatally injured child is the same person as any unimpaired child that might have been born. I am inclined to think it is the same person. At any rate there is *more* basis for regarding it as the same person as a possible normal child than there is for so regarding a child with abnormal genetic constitution.

8 Anyone who was applying this principle to human actions would doubtless insert an "other things being equal" clause. But let us ignore that, since such a clause would presumably provide no excuse for an agent who was deciding an issue so important as what world to create.

9 I am able to give here, of course, only a very incomplete sketch of a theological position on the issue of "biological engineering."

10 Among the many to whom I am indebted for help in working out the thoughts contained in this chapter, and for criticisms of earlier drafts of it, I must mention Marilyn McCord Adams, Richard Brandt, Eric Lerner, the members of my graduate class on theism and ethics in the fall term of 1970 at the University of Michigan, and the editors of the *Philosophical Review*.

3

DAVID HUME

Dialogues Concerning Natural Religion, Parts X and XI

PART X

It is my opinion, I own, replied Demea, that each man feels, in a manner, the truth of religion within his own breast, and, from a consciousness of his imbecility and misery rather than from any reasoning, is led to seek protection from that Being on whom he and all nature is dependent. So anxious or so tedious are even the best scenes of life that futurity is still the object of all our hopes and fears. We incessantly look forward and endeavour, by prayers, adoration, and sacrifice, to appease those unknown powers whom we find, by experience, so able to afflict and oppress us. Wretched creatures that we are! What resource for us amidst the innumerable ills of life did not religion suggest some methods of atonement, and appease those terrors with which we are incessantly agitated and tormented?

I am indeed persuaded, said Philo, that the best and indeed the only method of bringing everyone to a due sense of religion is by just representations of the misery and wickedness of men. And for that purpose a talent of eloquence and strong imagery is more requisite than that of reasoning and argument. For is it necessary to prove what everyone feels within himself? It is only necessary to make us feel it, if possible, more intimately and sensibly.

The people, indeed, replied Demea, are sufficiently convinced of this great and melancholy truth. The miseries of life, the unhappiness of man, the general corruptions of our nature, the unsatisfactory enjoyment of pleasures, riches, honours – these phrases have

Original publication: Pp. 61–70, 71–81, David Hume, *Dialogues Concerning Natural Religion*, parts X–XI, ed. Henry D. Aiken (New York: Hafner, 1948).

become almost proverbial in all languages. And who can doubt of what all men declare from their own immediate feeling and experience?

In this point, said Philo, the learned are perfectly agreed with the vulgar; and in all letters, *sacred* and *profane*, the topic of human misery has been insisted on with the most pathetic eloquence that sorrow and melancholy could inspire. The poets, who speak from sentiment, without a system, and whose testimony has therefore the more authority, abound in images of this nature. From Homer down to Dr. Young, the whole inspired tribe have ever been sensible that no other representation of things would suit the feeling and observation of each individual.

As to authorities, replied Demea, you need not seek them. Look round this library of Cleanthes. I shall venture to affirm that, except authors of particular sciences, such as chemistry or botany, who have no occasion to treat of human life, there is scarce one of those innumerable writers from whom the sense of human misery has not, in some passage or other, extorted a complaint and confession of it. At least, the chance is entirely on that side; and no one author has ever, so far as I can recollect, been so extravagant as to deny it.

There you must excuse me, said Philo: Leibniz has denied it, and is perhaps the first[1] who ventured upon so bold and paradoxical an opinion; at least, the first who made it essential to his philosophical system.

And by being the first, replied Demea, might he not have been sensible of his error? For is this a subject in which philosophers can propose to make discoveries especially in so late an age? And can any man hope by a simple denial (for the subject scarcely admits of reasoning) to bear down the united testimony of mankind, founded on sense and consciousness?

And why should man, added he, pretend to an exemption from the lot of all other animals? The whole earth, believe me, Philo, is cursed and polluted. A perpetual war is kindled amongst all living creatures. Necessity, hunger, want stimulate the strong and courageous; fear, anxiety, terror agitate the weak and infirm. The first entrance into life gives anguish to the new-born infant and to its wretched parent; weakness, impotence, distress attend each stage of that life, and it is, at last, finished in agony and horror.

Observe, too, says Philo, the curious artifices of nature in order to embitter the life of every living being. The stronger prey upon the weaker and keep them in perpetual terror and anxiety. The weaker, too, in their turn, often prey upon the stronger, and vex and molest them without relaxation. Consider that innumerable race of insects, which either are bred on the body of each animal or, flying about, infix their stings in him. These insects have others still less than themselves which torment them. And thus on each hand, before and behind, above and below, every animal is surrounded with enemies which incessantly seek his misery and destruction.

Man alone, said Demea, seems to be, in part, an exception to this rule. For by combination in society he can easily master lions, tigers, and bears, whose greater strength and agility naturally enable them to prey upon him.

On the contrary, it is here chiefly, cried Philo, that the uniform and equal maxims of nature are most apparent. Man, it is true, can, by combination, surmount all his *real* enemies and become master of the whole animal creation; but does he not immediately raise up to himself *imaginary* enemies, the demons of his fancy, who haunt him with super-stitious terrors and blast every enjoyment of life? His pleasure, as he imagines, becomes in their eyes a crime; his food and repose give them umbrage and offence; his very sleep and dreams furnish new materials to anxious fear; and even death, his refuge from every other ill, presents only the dread of endless and innumerable woes. Nor does the wolf molest more the timid flock than superstition does the anxious breast of wretched mortals.

Besides, consider, Demea: This very society by which we surmount those wild beasts, our natural enemies, what new enemies does it not raise to us? What woe and misery does it not occasion? Man is the greatest enemy of man. Oppression, injustice, contempt, contumely, violence, sedition, war, calumny, treachery, fraud – by these they mutually torment each other, and they would soon dissolve that society which they had formed were it not for the dread of still greater ills which must attend their separation.

But though these external insults, said Demea, from animals, from men, from all the elements, which assault us form a frightful catalogue of woes, they are nothing in comparison of those which arise within ourselves, from the distempered condition of our mind and body. How many lie under the lingering torment of diseases? Hear the pathetic enumeration of the great poet.

> Intestine stone and ulcer, colic-pangs,
> Demoniac frenzy, moping melancholy,

And moon-struck madness, pining atrophy,
Marasmus, and wide-wasting pestilence.
Dire was the tossing, deep the groans: *Despair*
Tended the sick, busiest from couch to couch.
And over them triumphant *Death* his dart
Shook: but delay'd to strike, though oft invok'd
With vows, as their chief good and final hope.[2]

The disorders of the mind, continued Demea, though more secret, are not perhaps less dismal and vexatious. Remorse, shame, anguish, rage, disappointment, anxiety, fear, dejection, despair – who has ever passed through life without cruel inroads from these tormentors? How many have scarcely ever felt any better sensations? Labour and poverty, so abhorred by everyone, are the certain lot of the far greater number; and those few privileged persons who enjoy ease and opulence never reach contentment or true felicity. All the goods of life united would not make a very happy man, but all the ills united would make a wretch indeed; and any one of them almost (and who can be free from every one?), nay, often the absence of one good (and who can possess all?) is sufficient to render life in-eligible.

Were a stranger to drop on a sudden into this world, I would show him, as a specimen of its ills, an hospital full of diseases, a prison crowded with malefactors and debtors, a field of battle strewed with carcases, a fleet foundering in the ocean, a nation languishing under tyranny, famine, or pestilence. To turn the gay side of life to him and give him a notion of its pleasures – whether should I conduct him? To a ball, to an opera, to court? He might justly think that I was only showing him a diversity of distress and sorrow.

There is no evading such striking instances, said Philo, but by apologies which still further aggravate the charge. Why have all men, I ask, in all ages, complained incessantly of the miseries of life? . . . They have no just reason, says one: these complaints proceed only from their discontented, repining, anxious disposition. . . . And can there possibly, I reply, be a more certain foundation of misery than such a wretched temper?

But if they were really as unhappy as they pretend, says my antago-nist, why do they remain in life? . . .

Not satisfied with life, afraid of death –

this is the secret chain, say I, that holds us. We are terrified, not bribed to the continuance of our existence.

It is only a false delicacy, he may insist, which a few refined spirits indulge, and which has spread these complaints among the whole race of mankind.... And what is this delicacy, I ask, which you blame? Is it anything but a greater sensibility to all the pleasures and pains of life? And if the man of a delicate, refined temper, by being so much more alive than the rest of the world, is only so much more unhappy, what judgment must we form in general of human life?

Let men remain at rest, says our adversary, and they will be easy. They are willing artificers of their own misery.... No! reply I: an anxious languor follows their repose; disappointment, vexation, trouble, their activity and ambition.

I can observe something like what you mention in some others, replied Cleanthes, but I confess I feel little or nothing of it in myself, and hope that it is not so common as you represent it.

If you feel not human misery yourself, cried Demea, I congratulate you on so happy a singularity. Others, seemingly the most prosperous, have not been ashamed to vent their complaints in the most melancholy strains. Let us attend to the great, the fortunate emperor, Charles V, when, tired with human grandeur, he resigned all his extensive dominions into the hands of his son. In the last harangue which he made on that memorable occasion, he publicly avowed *that the greatest prosperities which he had ever enjoyed had been mixed with so many adversities that he might truly say he had never enjoyed any satisfaction or contentment.* But did the retired life in which he sought for shelter afford him any greater happiness? If we may credit his son's account, his repentance commenced the very day of his resignation.

Cicero's fortune, from small beginnings, rose to the greatest lustre and renown; yet what pathetic complaints of the ills of life do his familiar letters, as well as philosophical discourses, contain? And suitably to his own experience, he introduces Cato, the great, the fortunate Cato protesting in his old age that had he a new life in his offer he would reject the present.

Ask yourself, ask any of your acquaintance, whether they would live over again the last ten or twenty years of their life. No! but the next twenty, they say, will be better:

And from the dregs of life, hope to receive
What the first sprightly running could not give.[3]

Thus, at last, they find (such is the greatness of human misery, it reconciles even contradictions) that they complain at once of the shortness of life and of its vanity and sorrow.

And is it possible, Cleanthes, said Philo, that after all these reflections, and infinitely more which might be suggested, you can still persevere in your anthropomorphism, and assert the moral attributes of the Deity, his justice, benevolence, mercy, and rectitude, to be of the same nature with these virtues in human creatures? His power, we allow, is infinite; whatever he wills is executed; but neither man nor any other animal is happy; therefore, he does not will their happiness. His wisdom is infinite; he is never mistaken in choosing the means to any end; but the course of nature tends not to human or animal felicity; therefore, it is not established for that purpose. Through the whole compass of human knowledge there are no inferences more certain and infallible than these. In what respect, then, do his benevolence and mercy resemble the benevolence and mercy of men?

Epicurus' old questions are yet unanswered.

Is he willing to prevent evil, but not able? then is he impotent. Is he able, but not willing? then is he malevolent. Is he both able and willing? whence then is evil?

You ascribe, Cleanthes, (and I believe justly) a purpose and intention to nature. But what, I beseech you, is the object of that curious artifice and machinery which she has displayed in all animals – the preservation alone of individuals, and propagation of the species? It seems enough for her purpose, if such a rank be barely upheld in the universe, without any care or concern for the happiness of the members that compose it. No resource for this purpose: no machinery in order merely to give pleasure or ease; no fund of pure joy and contentment; no indulgence without some want or necessity accompanying it. At least, the few phenomena of this nature are overbalanced by opposite phenomena of still greater importance.

Our sense of music, harmony, and indeed beauty of all kinds, gives satisfaction, without being absolutely necessary to the preservation and propagation of the species. But what racking pains, on the other hand, arise from gouts, gravels, megrims, toothaches, rheumatisms, where the injury to the animal machinery is either small or incurable? Mirth, laughter, play, frolic seem gratuitous satisfactions which have no further tendency; spleen, melancholy, discontent, superstition are pains of the same nature. How then does the Divine benevolence display itself, in the sense of you anthropomorphites? None but we mystics, as you were pleased to call us, can account for this strange mixture of phenomena, by deriving it from attributes infinitely perfect but incomprehensible.

And have you, at last, said Cleanthes smiling, betrayed your intentions, Philo? Your long agreement with Demea did indeed a little surprise me, but I find you were all the while erecting a concealed battery against me. And I must confess that you have now fallen upon a subject worthy of your noble spirit of opposition and controversy. If you can make out the present point, and prove mankind to be unhappy or corrupted, there is an end at once of all religion. For to what purpose establish the natural attributes of the Deity, while the moral are still doubtful and uncertain?

You take umbrage very easily, replied Demea, at opinions the most innocent and the most generally received, even amongst the religious and devout themselves; and nothing can be more surprising than to find a topic like this – concerning the wickedness and misery of man – charged with no less than atheism and profaneness. Have not all pious divines and preachers who have indulged their rhetoric on so fertile a subject, have they not easily, I say, given a solution of any difficulties which may attend it? This world is but a point in comparison of the universe; this life but a moment in comparison of eternity. The present evil phenomena, therefore, are rectified in other regions, and in some future period of existence. And the eyes of men, being then opened to larger views of things, see the whole connection of general laws, and trace, with adoration, the benevolence and rectitude of the Deity through all the mazes and intricacies of his providence.

No! replied Cleanthes, no! These arbitrary suppositions can never be admitted, contrary to matter of fact, visible and uncontroverted. Whence can any cause be known but from its known effects? Whence can any hypothesis be proved but from the apparent phenomena? To establish one hypothesis upon another is building entirely in the air; and the utmost we ever attain by these conjectures and fictions is to ascertain the bare possibility of our opinion, but never can we, upon such terms, establish its reality.

The only method of supporting Divine benevolence – and it is what I willingly embrace – is to deny absolutely the misery and wickedness of man. Your representations are exaggerated; your melancholy views mostly fictitious; your inferences contrary to fact and experience. Health is more common than sickness; pleasure than pain; happiness than misery. And for one vexation which we meet with, we attain, upon computation, a hundred enjoyments.

Admitting your position, replied Philo, which yet is extremely doubtful, you must at the same time allow that, if pain be less frequent than pleasure, it is infinitely more violent and durable. One hour of it is often able to outweigh a day, a week, a month of our common insipid enjoyments; and how many days, weeks, and months are passed by several in the most acute torments? Pleasure, scarcely in one instance, is ever able to reach ecstasy and rapture; and in no one instance can it continue for any time at its highest pitch and altitude. The spirits evaporate, the nerves relax, the fabric is disordered, and the enjoyment quickly degenerates into fatigue and uneasiness. But pain often, good God, how often! rises to torture and agony; and the longer it continues, it becomes still more genuine agony and torture. Patience is exhausted, courage languishes, melancholy seizes us, and nothing terminates our misery but the removal of its cause or another event which is the sole cure of all evil, but which, from our natural folly, we regard with still greater horror and consternation.

But not to insist upon these topics, continued Philo, though most obvious, certain, and important, I must use the freedom to admonish you, Cleanthes, that you have put the controversy upon a most dangerous issue, and are unawares introducing a total scepticism into the most essential articles of natural and revealed theology. What! no method of fixing a just foundation for religion unless we allow the happiness of human life, and maintain a continued existence even in this world, with all our present pains, infirmities, vexations, and follies, to be eligible and desirable! But this is contrary to everyone's feeling and experience; it is contrary to an authority so established as nothing can subvert. No decisive proofs can ever be produced against this authority; nor is it possible for you to compute, estimate, and compare all the pains and all the pleasures in the lives of all men and of all animals; and thus, by your resting the whole system of religion on a point which, from its very nature, must for ever be uncertain, you tacitly confess that that system is equally uncertain.

But allowing you what never will be believed, at least, what you never possibly can prove, that animal or, at least, human happiness in this life exceeds its misery, you have yet done nothing; for this is not, by any means, what we expect from infinite power, infinite wisdom, and infinite goodness. Why is there any misery at all in the world? Not by chance, surely. From some cause then. Is it from the intention of the Deity?

But he is perfectly benevolent. Is it contrary to his intention? But he is almighty. Nothing can shake the solidity of this reasoning, so short, so clear, so decisive, except we assert that these subjects exceed all human capacity, and that our common measures of truth and falsehood are not applicable to them – a topic which I have all along insisted on, but which you have, from the beginning, rejected with scorn and indignation.

But I will be contented to retire still from this intrenchment, for I deny that you can ever force me in it. I will allow that pain or misery in man is *compatible* with infinite power and goodness in the Deity, even in your sense of these attributes: what are you advanced by all these concessions? A mere possible compatibility is not sufficient. You must *prove* these pure, unmixt, and uncontrollable attributes from the present mixed and confused phenomena, and from these alone. A hopeful undertaking! Were the phenomena ever so pure and unmixed, yet, being finite, they would be insufficient for that purpose. How much more, where they are also so jarring and discordant!

Here, Cleanthes, I find myself at ease in my argument. Here I triumph. Formerly, when we argued concerning the natural attributes of intelligence and design, I needed all my sceptical and metaphysical subtilty to elude your grasp. In many views of the universe and of its parts, particularly the latter, the beauty and fitness of final causes strike us with such irresistible force that all objections appear (what I believe they really are) mere cavils and sophisms; nor can we then imagine how it was ever possible for us to repose any weight on them. But there is no view of human life or of the condition of mankind from which, without the greatest violence, we can infer the moral attributes or learn that infinite benevolence, conjoined with infinite power and infinite wisdom, which we must discover by the eyes of faith alone. It is your turn now to tug the labouring oar, and to support your philosophical subtilties against the dictates of plain reason and experience.

PART XI

I scruple not to allow, said Cleanthes, that I have been apt to suspect the frequent repetition of the word *infinite*, which we meet with in all theological writers, to savour more of panegyric than of philosophy, and that any purposes of reasoning, and even of religion, would be better served were we to rest contented with more accurate and more moderate expressions. The terms *admirable, excellent, superlatively great,* wise, and *holy* – these sufficiently fill the imaginations of men, and anything beyond, besides that it leads into absurdities, has no influence on the affections or sentiments. Thus, in the present subject, if we abandon all human analogy, as seems your intention, Demea, I am afraid we abandon all religion and retain no conception of the great object of our adoration. If we preserve human analogy, we must forever find it impossible to reconcile any mixture of evil in the universe with infinite attributes; much less can we ever prove the latter from the former. But supposing the Author of nature to be finitely perfect, though far exceeding mankind, a satisfactory account may then be given of natural and moral evil, and every untoward phenomenon be explained and adjusted. A less evil may then be chosen in order to avoid a greater; inconveniences be submitted to in order to reach a desirable end; and, in a word, benevolence, regulated by wisdom and limited by necessity, may produce just such a world as the present. You, Philo, who are so prompt at starting views and reflections and analogies, I would gladly hear, at length, without interruption, your opinion of this new theory; and if it deserve our attention, we may afterwards, at more leisure, reduce it into form.

My sentiments, replied Philo, are not worth being made a mystery of; and, therefore, without any ceremony, I shall deliver what occurs to me with regard to the present subject. It must, I think, be allowed that, if a very limited intelligence whom we shall suppose utterly unacquainted with the universe were assured that it were the production of a very good, wise, and powerful Being, however finite, he would, from his conjectures, form *beforehand* a different notion of it from what we find it to be by experience; nor would he ever imagine, merely from these attributes of the cause of which he is informed, that the effect could be so full of vice and misery and disorder, as it appears in this life. Supposing now that this person were brought into the world, still assured that it was the workmanship of such a sublime and benevolent Being, he might, perhaps, be surprised at the disappointment, but would never retract his former belief if founded on any very solid argument, since such a limited intelligence must be sensible of his own blindness and ignorance, and must allow that there may be many solutions of those phenomena which will for ever escape his comprehension. But supposing, which is the real case with regard to man, that this creature is not antecedently convinced of a supreme intelligence, benevolent, and powerful, but is left to gather such a belief from the appearances of things – this entirely alters the case, nor will he ever find any reason for such a conclusion. He may be fully convinced of the narrow limits of his understanding, but this will not help him in forming an inference concerning the goodness of superior powers, since he must form that inference from what he knows, not from what he is ignorant of. The more you exaggerate his weakness and ignorance, the more diffident you render him, and give him the greater suspicion that such subjects are beyond the reach of his faculties. You are obliged, therefore, to reason with him merely from the known phenomena, and to drop every arbitrary supposition or conjecture.

Did I show you a house or palace where there was not one apartment convenient or agreeable, where the windows, doors, fires, passages, stairs, and the whole economy of the building were the source of noise, confusion, fatigue, darkness, and the extremes of heat and cold, you would certainly blame the contrivance, without any further examination. The architect would in vain display his subtilty, and prove to you that, if this door or that window were altered, greater ills would ensue. What he says may be strictly true: the alteration of one particular, while the other parts of the building remain, may only augment the inconveniences. But still you would assert in general that, if the architect had had skill and good intentions, he might have formed such a plan of the whole, and might have adjusted the parts in such a manner as would have remedied all or most of these inconveniences. His ignorance, or even your own ignorance of such a plan, will never convince you of the impossibility of it. If you find any inconveniences and deformities in the building, you will always, without entering into any detail, condemn the architect.

In short, I repeat the question: Is the world, considered in general and as it appears to us in this life, different from what a man or such a limited being would, *beforehand*, expect from a very powerful, wise, and benevolent Deity? It must be strange prejudice to assert the contrary. And from thence I conclude that, however consistent the world may be, allowing certain suppositions and conjectures with the idea of such a Deity, it can never afford us an inference concerning his existence. The consistency is not absolutely denied, only the inference. Conjectures, especially where infinity is excluded from the Divine attributes, may perhaps be sufficient to prove a consistency, but can never be foundations for any inference.

There seem to be *four* circumstances on which depend all or the greatest part of the ills that molest sensible creatures; and it is not impossible but all these circumstances may be necessary and unavoidable. We know so little beyond common life, or even of common life, that, with regard to the economy of a universe, there is no conjecture, however wild, which may not be just, nor any one, however plausible, which may not be erroneous. All that belongs to human understanding, in this deep ignorance and obscurity, is to be sceptical or at least cautious, and not to admit of any hypothesis whatever, much less of any which is supported by no appearance of probability. Now this I assert to be the case with regard to all the causes of evil and the circumstances on which it depends. None of them appear to human reason in the least degree necessary or unavoidable, nor can we suppose them such, without the utmost license of imagination.

The *first* circumstance which introduces evil is that contrivance or economy of the animal creation by which pains, as well as pleasures, are employed to excite all creatures to action, and make them vigilant in the great work of self-preservation. Now pleasure alone, in its various degrees, seems to human understanding sufficient for this purpose. All animals might be constantly in a state of enjoyment; but when urged by any of the necessities of nature, such as thirst, hunger, weariness, instead of pain, they might feel a diminution of pleasure by which they might be prompted to seek that object which is necessary to their subsistence. Men pursue pleasure as eagerly as they avoid pain; at least, they might have been so constituted. It seems, therefore, plainly possible to carry on the business of life without any pain. Why then is any animal ever rendered susceptible of such a sensation? If animals can be free from it an hour, they might enjoy a perpetual exemption from it, and it required as particular a contrivance of their organs to produce that feeling as to endow them with sight, hearing, or any of the senses. Shall we conjecture that such a contrivance was necessary, without any appearance of reason, and shall we build on that conjecture as on the most certain truth?

But a capacity of pain would not alone produce pain were it not for the *second* circumstance, viz., the conducting of the world by general laws; and this seems nowise necessary to a very perfect Being. It is true, if everything were conducted by particular volitions, the course of nature would be perpetually broken, and no man could employ his reason in the conduct of life. But might not other particular volitions remedy this inconvenience? In short, might not the Deity exterminate all ill, wherever it were to be found, and produce all good, without any preparation or long progress of causes and effects?

Besides, we must consider that, according to the present economy of the world, the course of nature, though supposed exactly regular, yet to us appears not so, and many events are uncertain, and many disappoint our expectations. Health and sickness, calm and tempest, with an infinite number of other accidents whose causes are unknown and variable, have a great influence both on the fortunes of particular persons and on the prosperity of public societies; and indeed all human life, in a manner, depends on such accidents. A being, there-fore, who knows the secret springs of the universe might easily, by particular volitions, turn all these accidents to the good of mankind and render the whole world happy, without discovering himself in any operation. A fleet whose purposes were salutary to society might always meet with a fair wind. Good princes enjoy sound health and long life. Persons born to power and authority be framed with good tempers and virtuous dispositions. A few such events as these, regularly and wisely conducted, would change the face of the world, and yet would no more seem to disturb the course of nature or confound human conduct than the present economy of things where the causes are secret and variable and compounded. Some small touches given to Caligula's brain in his infancy might have converted him into a Trajan. One wave, a little higher than the rest, by burying Caesar and his fortune in the bottom of the ocean, might have restored liberty to a considerable part of man-kind. There may, for aught we know, be good reasons why Providence interposes not in this manner, but they are unknown to us; and, though the mere supposition that such reasons exist may be sufficient to *save* the conclusion concerning the Divine attributes, yet surely it can never be sufficient to *establish* that conclusion.

If everything in the universe be conducted by general laws, and if animals be rendered susceptible of pain, it scarcely seems possible but some ill must arise in the various shocks of matter and the various concurrence and opposition of general laws; but this ill would be very rare were it not for the *third* circumstance which I proposed to mention, viz., the great frugality with which all powers and faculties are distrib-uted to every particular being. So well adjusted are the organs and capacities of all animals, and so well fitted to their preservation, that, as far as history or tradition reaches, there appears not to be any single species which has yet been extinguished in the universe. Every animal has the requisite endowments, but these endowments are bestowed with so scrupulous an economy that any considerable diminution must entirely destroy the creature. Wherever one power is increased, there is a proportional abatement in the others. Animals which excel in swiftness are commonly defective in force. Those which possess both are either imperfect in some of their senses or are oppressed with the most craving wants. The human species, whose chief excellence is reason and sagacity, is of all others the most necessitous, and the most deficient in bodily advantages, without clothes, without arms, without food, without lodging, without any convenience of life, except what they owe to their own skill and industry. In short, nature seems to have formed an exact calculation of the necessities of her creatures, and, like a *rigid master,* has afforded them little more powers or endowments than what are strictly sufficient to supply those necessities. An *indulgent parent* would have bestowed a large stock in order to guard against accidents, and secure the happiness and welfare of the creature in the most unfortunate concurrence of circumstances. Every course of life would not have been so surrounded with precipices that the least departure from the true path, by mistake or necessity, must involve us in misery and ruin. Some reserve, some fund, would have been provided to ensure happiness, nor would the powers and the necessities have been adjusted with so rigid an economy. The Author of nature is inconceivably powerful; his force is supposed great, if not altogether inexhaustible, nor is there any reason, as far as we can judge, to make him observe this strict frugality in his dealings with his creatures. It would have been better, were his power extremely limited, to have created fewer animals, and to have endowed these with more faculties for their happiness and preservation. A builder is never esteemed prudent who undertakes a plan beyond what his stock will enable him to finish.

In order to cure most of the ills of human life, I require not that man should have the wings of the eagle, the swiftness of the stag, the force of the ox, the arms of the lion, the scales of the crocodile or rhinoceros; much less do I demand the sagacity of an angel or cherubim. I am contented to take an increase in one single power or faculty of his soul. Let him be endowed with a greater propensity to industry and labour, a more vigorous spring and activity of mind, a more constant bent to business and application. Let the whole species possess naturally an equal diligence with that which many individuals are able to attain by habit and reflection, and the most beneficial consequences, without any allay of ill, is the immediate and necessary result of this endowment. Almost all the moral as well as natural evils of human life arise from idleness; and were our species, by the original constitution of their frame, exempt from this vice or infirmity, the perfect cultivation of land, the improvement of arts and manufactures, the exact execution of every office and duty, immediately follow; and men at once may fully reach that state of society which is so imperfectly attained by the best regulated government. But as industry is a power, and the most valuable of any, nature seems determined, suitably to her usual maxims, to bestow it on men with a very sparing hand, and rather to punish him severely for his deficiency in it than to reward him for his attainments. She has so contrived his frame that nothing but the most violent necessity can oblige him to labour; and she employs all his other wants to overcome, at least in part, the want of diligence, and to endow him with some share of a faculty of which she has thought fit naturally to bereave him. Here our demands may be allowed very humble, and therefore the more reasonable. If we required the endowments of superior penetration and judgment, of a more delicate taste of beauty, of a nicer sensibility to benevolence and friendship, we might be told that we impiously pretend to break the order of nature, that we want to exalt ourselves into a higher rank of being, that the presents which we require, not being suitable to our state and condition, would only be pernicious to us. But it is hard, I dare to repeat it, it is hard that, being placed in a world so full of wants and necessities, where almost every being and element is either our foe or refuses its assistance . . . we should also have our own temper to struggle with, and should be deprived of that faculty which can alone fence against these multiplied evils.

The *fourth* circumstance whence arises the misery and ill of the universe is the inaccurate workmanship of all the springs and principles of the great machine of nature. It must be acknowledged that there are few parts of the universe which seem not to serve some purpose, and whose removal would not produce a visible defect and disorder in the whole. The parts hang all together, nor can one be touched without affecting the rest, in a greater or less degree. But at the same time, it must be observed that none of these parts or principles, however useful, are so accurately adjusted as to keep precisely within those bounds in which their utility consists; but they are, all of them, apt, on every occasion, to run into the one extreme or the other. One would imagine that this grand production had not received the last hand of the maker – so little finished is every part, and so coarse are the strokes with which it is executed. Thus the winds are requisite to convey the vapours along the surface of the globe, and to assist men in navigation; but how often, rising up to tempests and hurricanes, do they become pernicious? Rains are necessary to nourish all the plants and animals of the earth; but how often are they defective? how often excessive? Heat is requisite to all life and vegetation, but is not always found in the due proportion. On the mixture and secretion of the humours and juices of the body depend the health and prosperity of the animal; but the parts perform not regularly their proper function. What more useful than all the passions of the mind, ambition, vanity, love, anger? But how often do they break their bounds and cause the greatest convulsions in society? There is nothing so advantageous in the universe but what frequently becomes pernicious, by its excess or defect; nor has nature guarded, with the requisite accuracy, against all disorder or confusion. The irregularity is never perhaps so great as to destroy any species, but is often sufficient to involve the individuals in ruin and misery.

On the concurrence, then, of these *four* circumstances does all or the greatest part of natural evil depend. Were all living creatures incapable of pain, or were the world administered by particular volitions, evil never could have found access into the universe; and were animals endowed with a large stock of powers and faculties, beyond what strict necessity requires, or were the several springs and principles of the universe so accurately framed as to preserve always the just temperament and medium, there must have been very little ill in comparison of what we feel at present. What then shall we pronounce on this occasion? Shall we say that these circumstances are not necessary, and that they might easily have been altered in the contrivance of the universe? This decision seems too presumptuous for creatures so blind and ignorant. Let us be more modest in our conclusions. Let us allow that, if the goodness of the Deity (I mean a goodness like the human) could be established on any tolerable reasons *a priori*, these phenomena, however untoward, would not be sufficient to subvert that principle, but might easily, in some unknown manner, be reconcilable to it. But let us still assert that, as this goodness is not antecedently established but must be inferred from the phenomena, there can be no grounds for such an inference while there are so many ills in the universe, and while these ills might so easily have been remedied, as far as human understanding can be allowed to judge on such a subject. I am sceptic enough to allow that the bad appearances, notwithstanding all my reasonings, may be compatible with such attributes as you suppose, but surely they can never prove these attributes. Such a conclusion cannot result from scepticism, but must arise from the phenomena, and from our confidence in the reasonings which we deduce from these phenomena.

Look round this universe. What an immense profusion of beings, animated and organized, sensible and active! You admire this prodigious variety and fecundity. But inspect a little more narrowly these living existences, the only beings worth regarding. How hostile and destructive to each other! How insufficient all of them for their own happiness! How contemptible or odious to the spectator! The whole presents nothing but the idea of a blind nature, impregnated by a great vivifying principle, and pouring forth from her lap, without discernment or parental care, her maimed and abortive children!

Here the Manichaean system occurs as a proper hypothesis to solve the difficulty; and, no doubt, in some respects it is very specious and has more probability than the common hypothesis, by giving a plausible account of the strange mixture of good and ill which appears in life. But if we consider, on the other hand, the perfect uniformity and agreement of the parts of the universe, we shall not discover in it any marks of the combat of a malevolent with a benevolent being. There is indeed an opposition of pains and pleasures in the feelings of sensible creatures; but are not all the operations of nature carried on by an opposition of principles, of hot and cold, moist and dry, light and heavy? The true conclusion is that the original Source of all things is entirely indifferent to all these principles, and has no more regard to good above ill than to heat above cold, or to drought above moisture, or to light above heavy.

There may *four* hypotheses be framed concerning the first causes of the universe: that they are endowed with perfect goodness; that they have perfect malice; that they are opposite and have both goodness and malice; that they have neither goodness nor malice. Mixed phenomena can never prove the two former unmixed principles; and the uniformity and steadiness of general laws seem to oppose the third. The fourth, therefore, seems by far the most probable.

What I have said concerning natural evil will apply to moral with little or no variation; and we have no more reason to infer that the rectitude of the Supreme Being resembles human rectitude than that his benevolence resembles the human. Nay, it will be thought that we have still greater cause to exclude from him moral sentiments, such as we feel them, since moral evil, in the opinion of many, is much more predominant above moral good than natural evil above natural good.

But even though this should not be allowed, and though the virtue which is in mankind should be acknowledged much superior to the vice, yet, so long as there is any vice at all in the universe, it will very much puzzle you anthropomorphites how to account for it. You must assign a cause for it, without having recourse to the first cause. But as every effect must have a cause, and that cause another, you must either carry on the progression *in infinitum* or rest on that original principle, who is the ultimate cause of all things....

Hold! hold! cried Demea: Whither does your imagination hurry you? I joined in alliance with you in order to prove the incomprehensible nature of the Divine Being, and refute the principles of Cleanthes, who would measure everything by human rule and standard. But I now find you running into all the topics of the greatest libertines and infidels, and betraying that holy cause which you seemingly espoused. Are you secretly, then, a more dangerous enemy than Cleanthes himself?

And are you so late in perceiving it? replied Cleanthes. Believe me, Demea, your friend Philo, from the beginning, has been amusing himself at both our expense; and it must be confessed that the injudicious reasoning of our vulgar theology has given him but too just a handle of ridicule. The total infirmity of human reason, the absolute incomprehensibility of the Divine Nature, the great and universal misery, and still greater wickedness of men – these are strange topics, surely, to be so fondly cherished by orthodox divines and doctors. In ages of stupidity and ignorance, indeed, these principles may safely be espoused; and perhaps no views of things are more proper to promote superstition than such as encourage the blind amazement, the diffidence, and melancholy of mankind. But at present...

Blame not so much, interposed Philo, the ignorance of these reverend gentlemen. They know how to change their style with the times. Formerly, it was a most popular theological topic to maintain that human life was vanity and misery, and to exaggerate all the ills and pains which are incident to men. But of late years, divines, we find, begin to retract this position and maintain, though still with some hesitation, that there are more goods than evils, more pleasures than pains, even in this life. When religion stood entirely upon temper and education, it was thought proper to encourage melancholy, as, indeed, mankind never have recourse to superior powers so readily as in that disposition. But as men have now learned to form principles and to draw consequences, it is necessary to change the batteries, and to make use of such arguments as will endure at least some scrutiny and examination. This variation is the same (and from the same causes) with that which I formerly remarked with regard to scepticism.

Thus Philo continued to the last his spirit of opposition, and his censure of established opinions. But I could observe that Demea did not at all relish the latter part of the discourse; and he took occasion soon after, on some pretence or other, to leave the company.

NOTES

1   That sentiment had been maintained by Dr. King and some few others before Leibniz, though by none of so great fame as that German philosopher.
2   Milton: *Paradise Lost*, Bk. XI.
3   John Dryden, *Aureng-Zebe*, Act IV, sc. 1.

4

NELSON PIKE

Hume on Evil

In Parts X and XI of the *Dialogues Concerning Natural Religion*, Hume sets forth his views on the traditional theological problem of evil. Hume's remarks on this topic seem to me to contain a rich mixture of insight and oversight. It will be my purpose in this essay to disentangle these contrasting elements of his discussion.[1]

PHILO'S FIRST POSITION

(1) God, according to the traditional Christian view put forward by Cleanthes in the *Dialogues*, is all-powerful, all-knowing, and perfectly good. And it is clear that for Cleanthes, the terms "powerful," "knowing," and "good" apply to God in exactly the same sense in which these terms apply to men. Philo argues as follows (pp. 61–9): If God is to be all-powerful, all-knowing, and perfectly good (using all key terms in their ordinary sense), then to claim that God exists is to preclude the possibility of admitting that there occur instances of evil; that is, is to preclude the possibility of admitting that there occur instances of suffering, pain, superstition, wickedness, and so forth.[2] The statements "God exists" and "There occur instances of suffering" are logically incompatible. Of course, no one could deny that there occur instances of suffering. Such a denial would plainly conflict with common experience.[3] Thus it follows from obvious fact that God (having the attributes assigned to him by Cleanthes) does not exist.

Original publication: Nelson Pike, "Hume on Evil," *The Philosophical Review* 72 (2) (1963): 180–97.

This argument against the existence of God has enjoyed considerable popularity since Hume wrote the *Dialogues*. Concerning the traditional theological problem of evil, F. H. Bradley comments as follows:

> The trouble has come from the idea that the Absolute is a moral person. If you start from that basis, then the relation of evil to the Absolute presents at once an irreducible dilemma. The problem then becomes insoluble, but not because it is obscure or in any way mysterious. To any one who has the sense and courage to see things as they are, and is resolved not to mystify others or himself, *there is really no question to discuss. The dilemma is plainly insoluble because it is based on a clear self-contradiction.*[4]

John Stuart Mill,[5] J. E. McTaggart,[6] Antony Flew,[7] H. D. Aiken,[8] J. L. Mackie,[9] C. J. Ducasse,[10] and H. J. McCloskey[11] are but a very few of the many others who have echoed Philo's finalistic dismissal of traditional theism after making reference to the logical incompatibility of "God exists" and "There occur instances of suffering." W. T. Stace refers to Hume's discussion of the matter as follows:

> (Assuming that "good" and "powerful" are used in theology as they are used in ordinary discourse), we have to say that Hume was right. The change has never been answered and never will be. The simultaneous attribution of all-power and all-goodness to the Creator of the whole world is logically incompatible with the existence of evil and pain in the world, for which reason the conception of a finite God, who is not all-powerful . . . has become popular in some quarters.[12]

In the first and second sections of this essay, I shall argue that the argument against the existence of God presented in Part X of the *Dialogues* is quite unconvincing. It is not at all clear that "God exists" and "There occur instances of suffering" are logically incompatible statements.

(2) Moving now to the details of the matter, we may, I think, formulate Philo's first challenge to Cleanthes as follows:

(1) The world contains instances of suffering.
(2) God exists – and is omnipotent and omniscient.
(3) God exists – and is perfectly good.

According to the view advanced by Philo, these three statements constitute an "inconsistent triad" (p. 66). Any two of them might be held
together. But if any two of them are endorsed, the third must be denied.
Philo argues that to say of God that he is omnipotent and omniscient is
to say that he *could* prevent suffering if he wanted to. Unless God could
prevent suffering, he would not qualify as both omnipotent and omniscient. But, Philo continues, to say of God that he is perfectly good is to
say that God *would* prevent suffering if he could. A being who would not
prevent suffering when it was within his power to do so would not
qualify as perfectly good. Thus, to affirm propositions (2) and (3) is to
affirm the existence of a being who both could prevent suffering if he
wanted to and who would prevent suffering if he could. This, of course,
is to deny the truth of proposition (1). By similar reasoning, Philo would
insist, to affirm (1) and (2) is to deny the truth of (3). And to affirm (1)
and (3) is to deny the truth of (2). But, as conceived by Cleanthes, God
is both omnipotent–omniscient and perfectly good. Thus, as understood by Cleanthes, "God exists" and "There occur instances of suffering" are logically incompatible statements. Since the latter of these
statements is obviously true, the former must be false. Philo reflects:
"Nothing can shake the solidarity of this reasoning, so short, so clear
(and) so decisive" (p. 69).

It seems to me that this argument is deficient. I do not think it follows
from the claim that a being is perfectly good that he would prevent
suffering if he could.

Consider this case. A parent forces a child to take a spoonful of bitter
medicine. The parent thus brings about an instance of discomfort –
suffering. The parent could have refrained from administering the
medicine; and he knew that the child would suffer discomfort if he
did administer it. Yet, when we are assured that the parent acted in the
interest of the child's health and happiness, the fact that he knowingly
caused discomfort is not sufficient to remove the parent from the class
of perfectly good beings. If the parent fails to fit into this class, it is not
because he caused *this* instance of suffering.

Given only that the parent knowingly caused an instance of discomfort, we are tempted to *blame* him for his action – that is, to exclude
him from the class of perfectly good beings. But when the full circumstances are known, blame becomes inappropriate. In this case, there
is what I shall call a "morally sufficient reason" for the parent's
action. To say that there is a morally sufficient reason for his action
is simply to say that there is a circumstance or condition which, when

known, renders *blame* (though, of course, not *responsibility*) for the action inappropriate. As a general statement, a being who permits (or brings about) an instance of suffering might be perfectly good providing only that there is a morally sufficient reason for his action. Thus, it does not follow from the claim that God is perfectly good that he would prevent suffering if he could. God might fail to prevent suffering, or himself bring about suffering, while remaining perfectly good. It is required only that there be a morally sufficient reason for his action.

(3) In the light of these reflections, let us now attempt to put Philo's challenge to Cleanthes in sharper form.

(4) The world contains instances of suffering.
(5) God exists – and is omnipotent, omniscient, and perfectly good.
(6) An omnipotent and omniscient being would have no morally sufficient reason for allowing instances of suffering.

Unlike the first, this sequence is logically tight. Suppose (6) and (4) true. If an omnipotent and omniscient being would have no morally sufficient reason for allowing instances of suffering, then, in a world containing such instances, either there would be no omnipotent and omniscient being or that being would be blameworthy. On either of these last alternatives, proposition (5) would be false. Thus, if (6) and (4) are true, (5) must be false. In similar fashion, suppose (6) and (5) true. If an omnipotent and omniscient being would have no morally sufficient reason for allowing suffering, then, if there existed an omnipotent and omniscient being who was also perfectly good, there would occur no suffering. Thus, if (6) and (5) are true, (4) must be false. Lastly, suppose (5) and (4) true. If there existed an omnipotent and omniscient being who was also perfectly good, then if there occurred suffering, the omnipotent and omniscient being (being also perfectly good) would have to have a morally sufficient reason for permitting it. Thus, if (5) and (4) are true, (6) must be false.

Now, according to Philo (and all others concerned), proposition (4) is surely true. And proposition (6) – well, what about proposition (6)? At this point, two observations are needed.

First, it would not serve Philo's purpose were he to argue the truth of proposition (6) by enumerating a number of reasons for permitting suffering (which might be assigned to an omnipotent and omniscient being) and then by showing that in each case the reason offered is not a morally sufficient reason (when assigned to an omnipotent and omniscient being). Philo could never claim to have examined all of the possibilities. And at any given point in the argument, Cleanthes could always claim that God's reason for permitting suffering is one which Philo has not yet considered. A retreat to unexamined reasons would remain open to Cleanthes regardless of how complete the list of examined reasons seemed to be.

Second, the position held by Philo in Part X of the *Dialogues* demands that he affirm proposition (6) as a *necessary truth*. If this is not already clear, consider the following inconsistent triad.

(7)   All swans are white.
(8)   Some swans are not large.
(9)   All white things are large.

Suppose (9) true, but not necessarily true. Either (7) or (8) must be false. But the conjunction of (7) and (8) is not contradictory. If the conjunction of (7) and (8) were contradictory, then (9) would be a necessary truth. Thus, unless (9) is a necessary truth, the conjunction of (7) and (8) is not contradictory. Note what happens to this antilogism when "colored" is substituted for "large." Now (9) becomes a necessary truth and, correspondingly, (7) and (8) become logically incompatible. The same holds for the inconsistent triad we are now considering. As already discovered, Philo holds that "There are instances of suffering" (proposition 4) and "God exists" (proposition 5) are logically incompatible. But (4) and (5) will be logically incompatible only if (6) is a necessary truth. Thus, if Philo is to argue that (4) and (5) are logically incompatible, he must be prepared to affirm (6) as a necessary truth.

We may now reconstitute Philo's challenge to the position held by Cleanthes.

Proposition (4) is obviously true. No one could deny that there occur instances of suffering. But proposition (6) is a necessary truth. An omnipotent and omniscient being would have no morally sufficient reason for allowing instances of suffering – just as a bachelor would have no wife. Thus, there exists no being who is, at once, omnipotent, omniscient, and perfectly good. Proposition (5) must be false.

(4)   This is a formidable challenge to Cleanthes' position. Its strength can best be exposed by reflecting on some of the circumstances or

conditions which, in ordinary life, and with respect to ordinary agents, are usually counted as morally sufficient reasons for failing to prevent (or relieve) some given instance of suffering. Let me list five such reasons.

First, consider an agent who lacked physical ability to prevent some instance of suffering. Such an agent could claim to have had a morally sufficient reason for not preventing the instance in question.

Second, consider an agent who lacked knowledge of (or the means of knowing about) a given instance of suffering. Such an agent could claim to have had a morally sufficient reason for not preventing the suffering, even if (on all other counts) he had the ability to prevent it.

Third, consider an agent who knew of an instance of suffering and had the physical ability to prevent it, but did not *realize* that he had this ability. Such an agent could usually claim to have had a morally sufficient reason for not preventing the suffering. Example: if I push the button on the wall, the torment of the man in the next room will cease. I have the physical ability to push the button. I know that the man in the next room is in pain. But I do not know that pushing the button will relieve the torment. I do not push the button and thus do not relieve the suffering.

Fourth, consider an agent who had the ability to prevent an instance of suffering, knew of the suffering, knew that he had the ability to prevent it, but did not prevent it because he believed (rightly or wrongly) that to do so would be to fail to effect some future good which would outweigh the negative value of the suffering. Such an agent might well claim to have had a morally sufficient reason for not preventing the suffering. Example: go back to the case of the parent causing discomfort by administering bitter medicine to the child.

Fifth, consider an agent who had the ability to prevent an instance of suffering, knew of the suffering, knew that he had the ability to prevent it, but failed to prevent it because to do so would have involved his preventing a prior good which outweighed the negative value of the suffering. Such an agent might claim to have had a morally sufficient reason for not preventing the suffering. Example: a parent permits a child to eat some birthday cake knowing that his eating the cake will result in the child's feeling slightly ill later in the day. The parent estimates that the child's pleasure of the moment outweighs the discomfort which will result.

Up to this point, Philo would insist, we have not hit on a circumstance or condition which could be used by Cleanthes when constructing a "theodicy," that is, when attempting to identify the morally sufficient reason God has for permitting instances of suffering.

The first three entries on the list are obviously not available. Each makes explicit mention of some lack of knowledge or power on the part of the agent. Nothing more need be said about them.

A theologian might, however, be tempted to use a reason for the fourth type when constructing a theodicy. He might propose that suffering *results in goods* which outweigh the negative value of the suffering. Famine (hunger) leads man to industry and progress. Disease (pain) leads man to knowledge and understanding. Philo suggests that no theodicy of this kind can be successful (pp. 73–4 and 76). An omnipotent and omniscient being could find other means of bringing about the same results. The mere fact that evils give rise to goods cannot serve as a morally sufficient reason for an omnipotent and omniscient being to permit suffering.

A theologian might also be tempted to use reasons of the fifth type when constructing a theodicy. He might propose that instances of suffering *result from goods* which outweigh the negative value of the suffering. That the world is run in accordance with natural law is good. But any such regular operation will result in suffering. That men have the ability to make free choices is good. But free choice will sometimes result in wrong choice and suffering. Philo argues that it is not at all clear that a world run in accordance with natural law is better than one not so regulated (p. 74). And one might issue a similar challenge with respect to free will. But a more general argument has been offered in the contemporary literature on evil which is exactly analogous to the one suggested by Philo above. According to H. J. McCloskey, an omnipotent and omniscient being could devise a law-governed world which would not include suffering.[13] And according to J. L. Mackie, an omnipotent and omniscient being could create a world containing free agents which would include no suffering or wrong-doing.[14] The import of both of these suggestions is that an omnipotent and omniscient being could create a world containing whatever is good (regularity, free will, and so on) without allowing the suffering which (only factually) results from these goods. The mere fact that suffering results from good cannot serve as a morally sufficient reason for an omnipotent and omniscient being to allow suffering.

Though the above reflections may be far from conclusive, let us grant that, of the morally sufficient reasons so far considered, none could be assigned to an omnipotent and omniscient being. This, of course, is not to say that proposition (6) is true – let alone necessarily true. As mentioned earlier, proposition (6) will not be shown true by an enumerative procedure of the above kind. But consider the matter less rigorously. If none of the reasons so far considered could be assigned to an omnipotent and omniscient being, ought this not to raise a suspicion? Might there not be a principle operating in each of these reasons which guarantees that *no* morally sufficient reason for permitting suffering *could* be assigned to an omnipotent and omniscient being? Such a principle immediately suggests itself. Men are sometimes excused for allowing suffering. But in these cases, men are excused only because they lack the knowledge or power to prevent suffering, or because they lack the knowledge or power to bring about goods (which are causally related to suffering) without also bringing about suffering. In other words, men are excusable only because they are limited. Having a morally sufficient reason for permitting suffering *entails* having some lack of knowledge or power. If this principle is sound (and, indeed, it is initially plausible) then proposition (6) must surely be listed as a necessary truth.

DEMEA'S THEODICY

But the issue is not yet decided. Demea has offered a theodicy which does not fit any of the forms outlined above. And Philo must be willing to consider all proposals if he is to claim "decisiveness" for his argument against Cleanthes.

Demea reasons as follows:

> This world is but a point in comparison of the universe; this life but a moment in comparison of eternity. The present evil phenomena, therefore, are rectified in other regions, and in some future period of existence. And the eyes of men, being then opened to larger views of things, see the whole connection of general laws, and trace, with adoration, the benevolence and rectitude of the Deity through all mazes and intricacies of his providence. (p. 67)

It might be useful if we had a second statement of this theodicy, one taken from a traditional theological source. In Chapter LXXI of the *Summa Contra Gentiles*, St. Thomas argues as follows:

The good of the whole is of more account than the good of the part. Therefore, it belongs to a prudent governor to overlook a lack of goodness in a part, that there may be an increase of goodness in the whole. Thus, the builder hides the foundation of a house underground, that the whole house may stand firm. Now, if evil were taken away from certain parts of the universe, the perfection of the universe would be much diminished, since its beauty results from the ordered unity of good and evil things, seeing that evil arises from the failure of good, and yet certain goods are occasioned from those very evils through the providence of the governor, even as the silent pause gives sweetness to the chant. Therefore, evil should not be excluded from things by the divine providence.

Neither of these statements seems entirely satisfactory. Demea might be suggesting that the world is good on the whole – that the suffering we discover in our world is, as it were, made up for in other regions of creation. God here appears as the husband who beats his wife on occasion but makes up for it with favors at other times. In St. Thomas' statement, there are unmistakable hints of causal reasoning. Certain goods are "occasioned" by evils, as the foundation of the house permits the house to stand firm. But in both of these statements another theme occurs. Let me state it in my own way without pretense of historical accuracy.

I have a set of ten wooden blocks. There is a T-shaped block, an L-shaped block, an F-shaped block, and so on. No two blocks have the same shape. Let us assign each block a value – say an aesthetic value – making the T-shaped block most valuable and the L-shaped block least valuable. Now the blocks may be fitted together into formations. And let us suppose that the blocks are so shaped that there is one and only one subset of the blocks which will fit together into a square. The L-shaped block is a member of that subset. Further, let us stipulate that any formation of blocks (consisting of two or more blocks fitted together) will have more aesthetic value than any of the blocks taken individually or any subset of the blocks taken as a mere collection. And, as a last assumption, let us say that the square formation has greater aesthetic value than any other logically possible block formation. The L-shaped block is a necessary component of the square formation; that is, the L-shaped block is logically indispensable to the square formation. Thus the L-shaped block is a necessary component of the best of all possible block formations. Hence, the block with the least aesthetic value is logically indispensable to the best of all possible block formations. Without this very block, it would be logically impossible to create the best of all possible block formations.

Working from this model, let us understand Demea's theodicy as follows. Put aside the claim that instances of suffering are *de facto* causes or consequences of greater goods. God, being a perfectly good, omniscient, and omnipotent being, would create the best of all possible worlds. But the best of all possible worlds must contain instances of suffering: they are logically indispensable components. This is why there are instances of suffering in the world which God created.

What shall we say about this theodicy? Philo expresses no opinion on the subject.

Consider this reply to Demea's reasonings. A world containing instances of suffering as necessary components might be the best of all possible worlds. And if a world containing instances of suffering as necessary components were the best of all possible worlds, an omnipotent and omniscient being would have a morally sufficient reason for permitting instances of suffering. But how are we to know that, in fact, instances of suffering are logically indispensable components of the best of all possible worlds? There would appear to be no way of establishing this claim short of assuming that God does in fact exist and then concluding (as did Leibniz) that the world (containing suffering) which he did in fact create is the best of all possible worlds. But, this procedure assumes that God exists. And this latter is precisely the question now at issue.

It seems to me that this reply to Demea's theodicy has considerable merit. First, my hypothetical objector is probably right in suggesting that the only way one could show that the best of all possible worlds must contain instances of suffering would be via the above argument in which the existence of God is assumed. Second, I think my objector is right in allowing that if instances of suffering were logically indispensable components of the best of all possible worlds, this would provide a morally sufficient reason for an omnipotent and omniscient being to permit instances of suffering. And, third, I think that my objector exhibits considerable discretion in not challenging the claim that the best of all possible worlds *might* contain instances of suffering as necessary components. I know of no argument which will show this claim to be true. But on the other hand, I know of no argument which will show this claim to be false. (I shall elaborate this last point directly.)

Thus, as I have said, the above evaluation of the theodicy advanced by Demea seems to have considerable merit. But this evaluation, *if correct*, seems to be sufficient to refute Philo's claim that "God exists" and "There occur instances of suffering" are logically incompatible statements. If instances of suffering were necessary components of the best of all possible worlds, then an omnipotent and omniscient being would have a morally sufficient reason for permitting instances of suffering. Thus, if it is *possible* that instances of suffering are necessary components of the best of all possible worlds, then there *might be* a morally sufficient reason for an omnipotent and omniscient being to permit instances of suffering. Thus if the statement "Instances of suffering are necessary components of the best of all possible worlds" is not contradictory, then proposition (6) is not a necessary truth. And, as we have seen, if proposition (6) is not a necessary truth, then "God exists" and "There occur instances of suffering" are not logically incompatible statements.

What shall we say? Is the statement "Instances of suffering are logically indispensable components of the best of all possible worlds" contradictory? That it is is simply assumed in Philo's first position. But, surely, this is not a trivial assumption. If it is correct, it must be shown to be so; it is not *obviously* correct. And how shall we argue that it is correct? Shall we, for example, assume that any case of suffering contained in any complex of events detracts from the value of the complex? If this principle were analytic, then a world containing an instance of suffering could not be the best of all possible worlds. But G. E. Moore has taught us to be suspicious of any such principle.[15] And John Wisdom has provided a series of counterexamples which tend to show that this very principle is, in fact, not analytic. Example: if I believe (rightly or wrongly) that you are in pain and become unhappy as a result of that belief. The resulting complex would appear to be better by virtue of my unhappiness (suffering) than it would have been had I believed you to be in pain but had not become unhappy (or had become happy) as a result.[16] Philo's argument against the existence of God is not finished. And it is not at all obvious that it is *capable* of effective completion. It is, I submit, far from clear that God and evil could not exist together in the same universe.

PHILO'S SECOND POSITION

At the end of Part X, Philo agrees to "retire" from his first position. He now concedes that "God exists" and "There occur instances of suffering" are not logically incompatible statements (p. 69). (It is clear from the context that this adjustment in Philo's thinking is made only for purposes of argument and not because Hume senses any inadequacy in Philo's first position.) Most contemporary philosophers think that Hume's major contribution to the literature on evil was made in Part X of the *Dialogues*. But it seems to me that what is of really lasting value in Hume's reflections on this subject is to be found not in Part X, but in the discussion in Part XI which follows Philo's "retirement" from his first position.

(1) Consider, first of all, a theology in which the existence of God is accepted on the basis of what is taken to be a conclusive (*a priori*) demonstration. (A theology in which the existence of God is taken as an item of faith can be considered here as well.) On this view, that God exists is a settled matter, not subject to review or challenge. It is, as it were, axiomatic to further theological debate. According to Philo, evil in the world presents no special problem for a theology of this sort:

> Let us allow that, if the goodness of the Deity (I mean a goodness like the human) could be established on any tolerable reasons *a priori*, these (evil) phenomena, however untoward, would not be sufficient to subvert that principle, but might easily, in some unknown manner, be reconcilable to it. (p. 78)

This point, I think, is essentially correct, but it must be put more firmly.

Recalling the remarks advanced when discussing the inconsistent nature of propositions (4) through (6) above, a theologian who accepts the existence of God (either as an item of faith or on the basis of an *a priori* argument) must conclude either that there is some morally sufficient reason for God's allowing suffering in the world, or that there are no instances of suffering in the world. He will, of course, choose the first alternative. Thus, in a theology of the sort now under consideration, the theologian begins by affirming the existence of God and by acknowledging the occurrence of suffering. It follows *logically* that God has some morally sufficient reason for allowing instances of suffering. The conclusion is not, as Philo suggests, that there *might be* a morally sufficient reason for evil. The conclusion is, rather, that there *must be* such a reason. It *could* not be otherwise.

What then of the traditional theological problem of evil? Within a theology of the above type, the problem of evil can only be the problem of discovering a *specific* theodicy which is adequate – that is, of discovering which, if any, of the specific proposals which might be advanced really describes God's morally sufficient reason for allowing instances of suffering. This problem, of course, is not a major one for the theologian. If the problem of evil is simply the problem of uncovering the specific reason for evil – given assurance that there is (and must be) some such reason – it can hardly be counted as a critical problem. Once it is granted that there is some specific reason for evil, there is a sense in which it is no longer vital to find it. A theologian of the type we are now considering might never arrive at a satisfactory theodicy. (Philo's "unknown" reason might remain forever unknown.) He might condemn as erroneous all existing theodicies and might despair of ever discovering the morally sufficient reason in question. A charge of incompleteness would be the worst that could be leveled at his world view.

(2) Cleanthes is not, of course, a theologian of the sort just described. He does not accept the existence of God as an item of faith, nor on the basis of an *a priori* argument. In the *Dialogues*, Cleanthes supports his theological position with an *a posteriori* argument from design. He argues that "order" in the universe provides sufficient evidence that the world was created by an omnipotent, omniscient, and perfectly good being.[17] He proposes the existence of God as a quasi-scientific explanatory hypothesis, arguing its truth via the claim that it provides an adequate explanation for observed facts.

Philo has two comments to make regarding the relevance of suffering in the world for a theology of this kind.

The first is a comment with which Philo is obviously well pleased. It is offered at the end of Part X and is repeated no less than three times in Part XI. It is this: even if the existence of God and the occurrence of suffering in the world are logically compatible, one cannot argue from a world containing suffering to the existence of an omnipotent, omniscient, and perfectly good creator. This observation, I think all would agree, is correct. Given only a painting containing vast areas of green, one could not effectively argue that its creator disliked using green. There would be no *logical* conflict in holding that a painter who disliked using green painted a picture containing vast areas of green. But given *only* the picture (and no further information), the hypothesis that its creator disliked using green would be poorly supported indeed.

It is clear that in this first comment Philo has offered a criticism of Cleanthes' *argument* for the existence of God. He explicitly says that this complaint is against Cleanthes' *inference* from a world containing instances of suffering to the existence of an omnipotent, omniscient, and perfectly good creator (p. 73). Philo's second comment, however, is more forceful than this. It is a challenge of the *truth* of Cleanthes' *hypothesis*.

Philo argues as follows:

> Look round this universe. What an immense profusion of beings, animated and organized, sensible and active! You admire this prodigious variety and fecundity. But inspect a little more narrowly these living existences, the only beings worth regarding. How hostile and destructive to each other! How insufficient all of them for their own happiness!... There is indeed an opposition of pains and pleasures in the feelings of sensible creatures; but are not all the operations of nature carried on by an opposition of principles, of hot and cold, moist and dry, light and heavy! The true conclusion is that the original Source of all things is entirely indifferent to all these principles, and has no more regard to good above ill than to heat above cold, or to drought above moisture, or to light above heavy. (p. 79)

Philo claims that *there is* an "original Source of all things" and that this source is indifferent with respect to matters of good and evil. He pretends to be inferring this conclusion from observed data. This represents a departure from Philo's much professed skepticism in the *Dialogues*. And, no doubt, many of the criticisms of Cleanthes' position which Philo advanced earlier in the *Dialogues* would apply with equal force to the inference Philo has just offered. But I shall not dwell on this last point. I think the center of Philo's remarks in this passage must be located in their skeptical rather than their metaphysical import. Philo has proposed a hypothesis which is counter to the one offered by Cleanthes. And he claims that his hypothesis is the "true conclusion" to be drawn from the observed data. But the point is not, I think, that Philo's new hypothesis is true, or even probable. The conclusion is, rather, that the hypothesis advanced by Cleanthes is false, or very improbable. When claiming that evil in the world *supports* a hypothesis which is counter to the one offered by Cleanthes, I think Philo simply means to be calling attention to the fact that evil in the world provides *evidence against* Cleanthes' theological position.

Consider the following analogy which, I think, will help expose this point. I am given certain astronomical data. In order to explain the data, I introduce the hypothesis that there exists a planet which has not yet been observed but which will be observable at such and such a place in the sky at such and such a time. No other hypothesis seems as good. The anticipated hour arrives and the telescopes are trained on the designated area. No planet appears. Now, either one of two conclusions may be drawn. First, I might conclude that there is no planet there to be seen. This requires either that I reject the original astronomical data or that I admit that what seemed the best explanation of the data is not, in fact, the true explanation. Second, I might conclude that there is a planet there to be seen, but that something in the observational set-up went amiss. Perhaps the equipment was faulty, perhaps there were clouds, and so on. Which conclusion is correct? The answer is not straightforward. I must check both possibilities.

Suppose I find nothing in the observational set-up which is in the least out of order. My equipment is in good working condition, I find no clouds, and so on. To decide to retain the planet hypothesis in the face of the recalcitrant datum (my failure to observe the planet) is, in part, to decide that there is some circumstance (as yet unknown) which explains the datum *other* than the nonexistence of the planet in question. But a decision to retain the planet hypothesis (in the face of my failure to observe the planet and in the absence of an explicit explanation which "squares" this failure with the planet hypothesis) is made correctly *only* when the *evidence for* the planet hypothesis is such as to render its negation less plausible than would be the assumption of a (as yet unknown) circumstance which explains the observation failure. This, I think, is part of the very notion of dealing reasonably with an explanatory hypothesis.

Now Cleanthes has introduced the claim that there exists an omnipotent, omniscient, and perfectly good being as a way of explaining "order" in the world. And Philo, throughout the *Dialogues* (up to and including most of Part XI), has been concerned to show that this procedure provides very little (if any) solid evidence for the existence of God. The inference from the data to the hypothesis is extremely tenuous. Philo is now set for his final thrust at Cleanthes' position. Granting that God and evil are not logically incompatible, the existence of human suffering in the world must still be taken as a recalcitrant datum with respect to Cleanthes' hypothesis. Suffering, as Philo says, is not what we should antecedently expect in a world created by an omnipotent, omniscient, and perfectly good being (pp. 71–2). Since Cleanthes has offered nothing in the way of an explicit theodicy (that is, an explanation of the recalcitrant datum which would "square" it with his hypothesis) and since the *evidence for* his hypothesis is extremely weak and generally ineffective, there is pretty good reason for thinking that Cleanthes' hypothesis is false.

This, I think, is the skeptical import of Philo's closing remarks in Part XI. On this reading nothing is said about an "original Source of all things" which is indifferent with respect to matters of good and evil. Philo is simply making clear the negative force of the fact of evil in the world for a hypothesis such as the one offered by Cleanthes.

It ought not to go unnoticed that Philo's closing attack on Cleanthes' position has extremely limited application. Evil in the world has central negative importance for theology only when theology is approached as a quasi-scientific subject, as by Cleanthes. That it is seldom approached in this way will be evident to anyone who has studied the history of theology. Within most theological positions, the existence of God is taken as an item of faith or embraced on the basis of an *a priori* argument. Under these circumstances, where there is nothing to qualify as a "hypothesis" capable of having either negative or positive "evidence," the fact of evil in the world presents no special problem for theology. As Philo himself has suggested, when the existence of God is accepted prior to any rational consideration of the status of evil in the world, the traditional problem of evil reduces to a noncrucial perplexity of relatively minor importance.

NOTES

1 All references to Hume's *Dialogues Concerning Natural Religion* will be to the Hafner Library of Classics edition, ed. by H. D. Aiken (New York, 1955).

2 It is clear that, for Philo, the term "evil" is used simply as a tag for the class containing all instances of suffering, pain, and so on. Philo offers no analysis of "evil" nor does his challenge to Cleanthes rest in the least on the particularities of the logic of this term. On p. 69, e.g., Philo formulates his challenge to Cleanthes without using "evil." Here he speaks only of *misery*. In what is to follow, I shall (following Hume) make little use of "evil." Also, I shall use "suffering" as short for "suffering, pain, superstition, wickedness, and so on."

3 Had Philo been dealing with "evil" (defined in some special way) instead of "suffering," this move in the argument might not have been open to him.

4 *Appearance and Reality* (Oxford, 1930), p. 174. Italics mine.

5   *Theism* (New York, 1957), p. 40. See also *The Utility of Religion* (New York, 1957), pp. 73ff.

6   *Some Dogmas of Religion* (London, 1906), p. 212–13.

7   "Theology and Falsification," in Flew and MacIntyre (eds.), *New Essays in Philosophical Theology* (New York, 1955), p. 108.

8   "God and Evil: Some Relations between Faith and Morals," *Ethics*, LXVIII (1958), 77–97.

9   "Evil and Omnipotence," *Mind*, LXIV (1955), 201.

10 *A Philosophical Scrutiny of Religion* (New York, 1953), ch. 16.

11 "God and Evil," *Philosophical Quarterly*, X (1960), 97–114.

12 *Time and Eternity* (Princeton, 1952), p. 56.

13 "God and Evil," pp. 103–4.

14 "Evil and Omnipotence," pp. 208–10.

15 I refer here to Moore's discussion of "organic unities" in *Principia Ethica* (Cambridge, 1903), pp. 28ff.

16 "God and Evil," *Mind*, XLIV (1935), 13–14. I have modified Wisdom's example slightly.

17 It is interesting to notice that, in many cases, theologians who have used an argument from design have not attempted to argue that "order" in the world proves the existence of a perfectly moral being. For example, in St. Thomas' "fifth way" and in William Paley's *Natural Theology*, "order" is used to show only that the creator of the world was *intelligent*. There are, however, historical instances of the argument from design being used to prove the goodness as well as the intelligence of a creator. For example, Bishop Berkeley argues this way in the second of the *Dialogues Between Hylas and Philonous*.

PART II

THE LOGICAL PROBLEM OF EVIL

Two statements are logically inconsistent provided it is logically impossible for both of them to be true. If we can prove that GOD EXISTS and EVIL EXISTS are logically inconsistent, we will have proved that God does not exist, for it is obvious to any rational person that evil exists in the world. But can it be *proved* that GOD EXISTS and EVIL EXISTS are logically inconsistent? To prove that GOD EXISTS and EVIL EXISTS are logically inconsistent one must find another proposition that is necessarily true and use it along with one of the original pair to deduce the explicit denial of the other member of that pair. For example, to prove that THIS OBJECT IS RED and THIS OBJECT IS NOT COLORED are logically inconsistent we can use the necessarily true statement that WHATEVER IS RED IS COLORED with THIS OBJECT IS RED to deduce THIS OBJECT IS COLORED, which is the explicit denial of THIS OBJECT IS NOT COLORED. Of course, one wouldn't have to go to the trouble of proving that THIS OBJECT IS RED and THIS OBJECT IS NOT COLORED are logically inconsistent because we all can see that they are. But in the case of GOD EXISTS and EVIL EXISTS it can be doubted that they are logically inconsistent. So, as J. L. Mackie realizes, one needs to find a *necessarily true* statement that along with GOD EXISTS, enables us to deduce the explicit denial of EVIL EXISTS. He suggests using A GOOD BEING ALWAYS ELIMINATES EVIL AS FAR AS IT CAN. But as Plantinga points out, A GOOD BEING ALWAYS ELIMINATES EVIL AS FAR AS IT CAN does not seem to be *necessarily* true. For a good being might have a morally sufficient reason to permit an evil to occur. (Perhaps the evil is logically required for the existence of a far greater good.) We might then revise Mackie's added statement to read: A GOOD BEING WOULD ELIMINATE EVIL

UNLESS IT HAD A MORALLY SUFFICIENT REASON FOR PERMITTING IT. But even if this revision is necessarily true, its conjunction with GOD EXISTS won't enable us to deduce NO EVIL EXISTS. All that we would be able to deduce is that God has a morally sufficient reason to permit any evils that exist. And, as Plantinga points out, this result seems to be the problem with any attempt to *prove* that our original pair of statements cannot, logically speaking, both be true.

It would be a mistake to conclude from what has just been said that GOD EXISTS and EVIL EXISTS are logically consistent. Failure to *prove* that two statements are logically inconsistent might be due to our limitations. So, failure to prove that GOD EXISTS and EVIL EXISTS are inconsistent won't show that they are consistent. Can it be established that GOD EXISTS and EVIL EXISTS are logically consistent? Suppose there is some proposition, *p*, from which both GOD EXISTS and EVIL EXISTS can be deduced. If so, and if it is *logically possible* that *p* is true, it will follow that GOD EXISTS and EVIL EXISTS are logically consistent. And, of course, if they are logically consistent, then the fact that there is evil in the world does not logically preclude the existence of God. Having pointed out the failure of arguments for the inconsistency of GOD EXISTS and EVIL EXISTS, Plantinga develops an ingenious argument in support of the logical consistency of GOD EXISTS and EVIL EXISTS. His argument makes use of the idea, found in Leibniz, of a possible world, a way in which things might be. The pivotal notion in Plantinga's argument, however, is the freedom of rational creatures to do or not do various actions, a freedom God may give but, once given, is beyond God's direct control. It then turns out that there are possible worlds that God cannot create. For although God can create me in a world where I am free to do X and free to refrain from doing X, in the end it will be up to me and not God whether that created world contains my freely doing X or my freely refraining from doing X. On Plantinga's view God can know in advance which world will result, and he may base his decision to create on that knowledge. But since God is limited by how we will use our freedom should he create us, it may be that God simply cannot create a world in which we in fact always use our freedom to do what is right. Of course, there is such a possible world. But whether God can create it (i.e., actualize it) depends on how we will use our freedom. And it is possible that no world in which free creatures are sinless can be created by God. The result of Plantinga's work, then, is that the logical problem of evil has been severely diminished, if not entirely resolved.

5

J. L. MACKIE

Evil and Omnipotence

The traditional arguments for the existence of God have been fairly thoroughly criticised by philosophers. But the theologian can, if he wishes, accept this criticism. He can admit that no rational proof of God's existence is possible. And he can still retain all that is essential to his position, by holding that God's existence is known in some other, non-rational way. I think, however, that a more telling criticism can be made by way of the traditional problem of evil. Here it can be shown, not that religious beliefs lack rational support, but that they are positively irrational, that the several parts of the essential theological doctrine are inconsistent with one another, so that the theologian can maintain his position as a whole only by a much more extreme rejection of reason than in the former case. He must now be prepared to believe, not merely what cannot be proved, but what can be *disproved* from other beliefs that he also holds.

The problem of evil, in the sense in which I shall be using the phrase, is a problem only for someone who believes that there is a God who is both omnipotent and wholly good. And it is a logical problem, the problem of clarifying and reconciling a number of beliefs: it is not a scientific problem that might be solved by further observations, or a practical problem that might be solved by a decision or an action. These points are obvious; I mention them only because they are sometimes ignored by theologians, who sometimes parry a statement of the problem with such remarks as "Well, can you solve the problem yourself?" or "This is a mystery which may be revealed to us later" or "Evil is something to be faced and overcome, not to be merely discussed".

Original publication: J. L. Mackie, "Evil and Omnipotence," *Mind* 64 (1955): 200–12.

In its simplest form the problem is this: God is omnipotent; God is wholly good; and yet evil exists. There seems to be some contradiction between these three propositions, so that if any two of them were true the third would be false. But at the same time all three are essential parts of most theological positions: the theologian, it seems, at once *must* adhere and *cannot consistently* adhere to all three. (The problem does not arise only for theists, but I shall discuss it in the form in which it presents itself for ordinary theism.)

However, the contradiction does not arise immediately; to show it we need some additional premises, or perhaps some quasi-logical rules connecting the terms 'good', 'evil', and 'omnipotent'. These additional principles are that good is opposed to evil, in such a way that a good thing always eliminates evil as far as it can, and that there are no limits to what an omnipotent thing can do. From these it follows that a good omnipotent thing eliminates evil completely, and then the propositions that a good omnipotent thing exists, and that evil exists, are incompatible.

A. ADEQUATE SOLUTIONS

Now once the problem is fully stated it is clear that it can be solved, in the sense that the problem will not arise if one gives up at least one of the propositions that constitute it. If you are prepared to say that God is not wholly good, or not quite omnipotent, or that evil does not exist, or that good is not opposed to the kind of evil that exists, or that there are limits to what an omnipotent thing can do, then the problem of evil will not arise for you.

There are, then, quite a number of adequate solutions of the problem of evil, and some of these have been adopted, or almost adopted, by various thinkers. For example, a few have been prepared to deny God's omnipotence, and rather more have been prepared to keep the term 'omnipotence' but severely to restrict its meaning, recording quite a number of things that an omnipotent being cannot do. Some have said that evil is an illusion, perhaps because they held that the whole world of temporal, changing things is an illusion, and that what we call evil belongs only to this world, or perhaps because they held that although temporal things *are* much as we see them, those that we call evil are not really evil. Some have said that what we call evil is merely the privation of good, that evil in a positive sense, evil that would really be opposed to good, does not exist. Many have agreed with Pope that disorder is harmony not understood, and that partial evil is universal good. Whether any of these views is *true* is, of course, another question. But each of them gives an adequate solution of the problem of evil in the sense that if you accept it this problem does not arise for you, though you may, of course, have *other* problems to face.

But often enough these adequate solutions are only *almost* adopted. The thinkers who restrict God's power, but keep the term 'omnipotence', may reasonably be suspected of thinking, in other contexts, that his power is really unlimited. Those who say that evil is an illusion may also be thinking, inconsistently, that this illusion is itself an evil. Those who say that "evil" is merely privation of good may also be thinking, inconsistently, that privation of good is an evil. (The fallacy here is akin to some forms of the "naturalistic fallacy" in ethics, where some think, for example, that "good" is just what contributes to evolutionary progress, and that evolutionary progress is itself good.) If Pope meant what he said in the first line of his couplet, that "disorder" is only harmony not understood, the "partial evil" of the second line must, for consistency, mean "that which, taken in isolation, falsely appears to be evil", but it would more naturally mean "that which, in isolation, really is evil". The second line, in fact, hesitates between two views, that "partial evil" isn't really evil, since only the universal quality is real, and that "partial evil" is really an evil, but only a little one.

In addition, therefore, to adequate solutions, we must recognise unsatisfactory inconsistent solutions, in which there is only a half-hearted or temporary rejection of one of the propositions which together constitute the problem. In these, one of the constituent propositions is explicitly rejected, but it is covertly re-asserted or assumed elsewhere in the system.

B. FALLACIOUS SOLUTIONS

Besides these half-hearted solutions, which explicitly reject but implicitly assert one of the constituent propositions, there are definitely fallacious solutions which explicitly maintain all the constituent propositions, but implicitly reject at least one of them in the course of the argument that explains away the problem of evil.

There are, in fact, many so-called solutions which purport to remove the contradiction without abandoning any of its constituent propositions. These must be fallacious, as we can see from the very statement of the problem, but it is not so easy to see in each case precisely where the fallacy lies. I suggest that in all cases the fallacy has the general form suggested above: in order to solve the problem one (or perhaps more) of its constituent propositions is given up, but in such a way that it appears to have been retained, and can therefore be asserted without qualification in other contexts. Sometimes there is a further complication: the supposed solution moves to and fro between, say, two of the constituent propositions, at one point asserting the first of these but covertly abandoning the second, at another point asserting the second but covertly abandoning the first. These fallacious solutions often turn upon some equivocation with the words 'good' and 'evil', or upon some vagueness about the way in which good and evil are opposed to one another, or about how much is meant by 'omnipotence'. I propose to examine some of these so-called solutions, and to exhibit their fallacies in detail. Incidentally, I shall also be considering whether an adequate solution could be reached by a minor modification of one or more of the constituent propositions, which would, however, still satisfy all the essential requirements of ordinary theism.

(1)   "Good cannot exist without evil" or "Evil is necessary as a counterpart to good."

It is sometimes suggested that evil is necessary as a counterpart to good, that if there were no evil there could be no good either, and that this solves the problem of evil. It is true that it points to an answer to the question "Why should there be evil?" But it does so only by qualifying some of the propositions that constitute the problem.

First, it sets a limit to what God can do, saying that God *cannot* create good without simultaneously creating evil, and this means either that God is not omnipotent or that there are *some* limits to what an omnipotent thing can do. It may be replied that these limits are always presupposed, that omnipotence has never meant the power to do what is logically impossible, and on the present view the existence of good without evil would be a logical impossibility. This interpretation of omnipotence may, indeed, be accepted as a modification of our original account which does not reject anything that is essential to theism, and I shall in general assume it in the subsequent discussion. It is, perhaps, the most common theistic view, but I think that some theists at least have maintained that God can do what is logically impossible. Many theists, at any rate, have held that logic itself is created or laid down by God, that logic is the way in which God arbitrarily chooses to think. (This is, of course, parallel to the ethical view that morally right actions are those which God arbitrarily chooses to command, and the two views encounter similar difficulties.) And *this* account of logic is clearly inconsistent with the view that God is bound by logical necessities – unless it is possible for an omnipotent being to bind himself, an issue which we shall consider later, when we come to the Paradox of Omnipotence. This solution of the problem of evil cannot, therefore, be consistently adopted along with the view that logic is itself created by God.

But, secondly, this solution denies that evil is opposed to good in our original sense. If good and evil are counterparts, a good thing will not "eliminate evil as far as it can". Indeed, this view suggests that good and evil are not strictly qualities of things at all. Perhaps the suggestion is that good and evil are related in much the same way as great and small. Certainly, when the term 'great' is used relatively as a condensation of 'greater than so-and-so', and 'small' is used correspondingly, greatness and smallness are counterparts and cannot exist without each other. But in this sense greatness is not a quality, not an intrinsic feature of anything; and it would be absurd to think of a movement in favour of greatness and against smallness in this sense. Such a movement would be self-defeating, since relative greatness can be promoted only by a simultaneous promotion of relative smallness. I feel sure that no theists would be content to regard God's goodness as analogous to this – as if what he supports were not the *good* but the *better*, and as if he had the paradoxical aim that all things should be better than other things.

This point is obscured by the fact that 'great' and 'small' seem to have an absolute as well as a relative sense. I cannot discuss here whether there is absolute magnitude or not, but if there is, there could be an absolute sense for 'great', it could mean of at least a certain size, and it would make sense to speak of all things getting bigger, of a universe that was expanding all over, and therefore it would make sense to speak of promoting greatness. But in *this* sense great and small are not logically necessary counterparts: either quality could exist without the other. There would be no logical impossibility in everything's being small or in everything's being great.

Neither in the absolute nor in the relative sense, then, of 'great' and 'small' do these terms provide an analogy of the sort that would be

needed to support this solution of the problem of evil. In neither case
are greatness and smallness *both* necessary counterparts *and* mutually
opposed forces or possible objects for support and attack.

It may be replied that good and evil are necessary counterparts in the
same way as any quality and its logical opposite: redness can occur, it is
suggested, only if non-redness also occurs. But unless evil is merely the
privation of good, they are not logical opposites, and some further
argument would be needed to show that they are counterparts in the
same way as genuine logical opposites. Let us assume that this could be
given. There is still doubt of the correctness of the metaphysical
principle that a quality must have a real opposite: I suggest that it is
not really impossible that everything should be, say, red, that the truth
is merely that if everything were red we should not notice redness, and
so we should have no word 'red'; we observe and give names to
qualities only if they have real opposites. If so, the principle that a
term must have an opposite would belong only to our language or to
our thought, and would not be an ontological principle, and, correspondingly, the rule that good cannot exist without evil would not state a
logical necessity of a sort that God would just have to put up with. God
might have made everything good, though *we* should not have noticed
it if he had.

But, finally, even if we concede that this *is* an ontological principle, it
will provide a solution for the problem of evil only if one is prepared to
say, "Evil exists, but only just enough evil to serve as the counterpart of
good". I doubt whether any theist will accept this. After all, the
ontological requirement that non-redness should occur would be satisfied
even if all the universe, except for a minute speck, were red, and, if
there were a corresponding requirement for evil as a counterpart to
good, a minute dose of evil would presumably do. But theists are not
usually willing to say, in all contexts, that all the evil that occurs is a
minute and necessary dose.

(2)   "Evil is necessary as a means to good."

It is sometimes suggested that evil is necessary for good not as a
counterpart but as a means. In its simple form this has little plausibility
as a solution of the problem of evil, since it obviously implies a severe
restriction of God's power. It would be a *causal* law that you cannot
have a certain end without a certain means, so that if God has to
introduce evil as a means to good, he must be subject to at least some

causal laws. This certainly conflicts with what a theist normally means by omnipotence. This view of God as limited by causal laws also conflicts with the view that causal laws are themselves made by God, which is more widely held than the corresponding view about the laws of logic. This conflict would, indeed, be resolved if it were possible for an omnipotent being to bind himself, and this possibility has still to be considered. Unless a favourable answer can be given to this question, the suggestion that evil is necessary as a means to good solves the problem of evil only by denying one of its constituent propositions, either that God is omnipotent or that 'omnipotent' means what it says.

(3) "The universe is better with some evil in it than it could be if there were no evil."

Much more important is a solution which at first seems to be a mere variant of the previous one, that evil may contribute to the goodness of a whole in which it is found, so that the universe as a whole is better as it is, with some evil in it, than it would be if there were no evil. This solution may be developed in either of two ways. It may be supported by an aesthetic analogy, by the fact that contrasts heighten beauty, that in a musical work, for example, there may occur discords which some-how add to the beauty of the work as a whole. Alternatively, it may be worked out in connexion with the notion of progress, that the best possible organisation of the universe will not be static, but progressive, that the gradual overcoming of evil by good is really a finer thing than would be the eternal unchallenged supremacy of good.

In either case, this solution usually starts from the assumption that the evil whose existence gives rise to the problem of evil is primarily what is called physical evil, that is to say, pain. In Hume's rather half-hearted presentation of the problem of evil, the evils that he stresses are pain and disease, and those who reply to him argue that the existence of pain and disease makes possible the existence of sympathy, benevolence, heroism, and the gradually successful struggle of doctors and reformers to over-come these evils. In fact, theists often seize the opportunity to accuse those who stress the problem of evil of taking a low, materialistic view of good and evil, equating these with pleasure and pain, and of ignoring the more spiritual goods which can arise in the struggle against evils.

But let us see exactly what is being done here. Let us call pain and misery 'first order evil' or 'evil (1)'. What contrasts with this, namely, pleasure and happiness, will be called 'first order good' or 'good (1)'.

Distinct from this is 'second order good' or 'good (2)' which somehow emerges in a complex situation in which evil (1) is a necessary component – logically, not merely causally, necessary. (Exactly *how* it emerges does not matter: in the crudest version of this solution good (2) is simply the heightening of happiness by the contrast with misery, in other versions it includes sympathy with suffering, heroism in facing danger, and the gradual decrease of first order evil and increase of first order good.) It is also being assumed that second order good is more important than first order good or evil, in particular that it more than outweighs the first order evil it involves.

Now this is a particularly subtle attempt to solve the problem of evil. It defends God's goodness and omnipotence on the ground that (on a sufficiently long view) this is the best of all logically possible worlds, because it includes the important second order goods, and yet it admits that real evils, namely first order evils, exist. But does it still hold that good and evil are opposed? Not, clearly, in the sense that we set out originally: good does not tend to eliminate evil in general. Instead, we have a modified, a more complex pattern. First order good (*e.g.* happiness) *contrasts with* first order evil (*e.g.* misery): these two are opposed in a fairly mechanical way; some second order goods (*e.g.* benevolence) try to maximise first order good and minimise first order evil; but God's goodness is not this, it is rather the will to maximise *second* order good. We might, therefore, call God's goodness an example of a third order goodness, or good (3). While this account is different from our original one, it might well be held to be an improvement on it, to give a more accurate description of the way in which good is opposed to evil, and to be consistent with the essential theist position.

There might, however, be several objections to this solution.

First, some might argue that such qualities as benevolence – and *a fortiori* the third order goodness which promotes benevolence – have a merely derivative value, that they are not higher sorts of good, but merely means to good (1), that is, to happiness, so that it would be absurd for God to keep misery in existence in order to make possible the virtues of benevolence, heroism, etc. The theist who adopts the present solution must, of course, deny this, but he can do so with some plausibility, so I should not press this objection.

Secondly, it follows from this solution that God is not in our sense benevolent or sympathetic: he is not concerned to minimise evil (1), but only to promote good (2); and this might be a disturbing conclusion for some theists.

But, thirdly, the fatal objection is this. Our analysis shows clearly the possibility of the existence of a *second* order evil, an evil (2) contrasting with good (2) as evil (1) contrasts with good (1). This would include malevolence, cruelty, callousness, cowardice, and states in which good (1) is decreasing and evil (1) increasing. And just as good (2) is held to be the important kind of good, the kind that God is concerned to promote, so evil (2) will, by analogy, be the important kind of evil, the kind which God, if he were wholly good and omnipotent, would eliminate. And yet evil (2) plainly exists, and indeed most theists (in other contexts) stress its existence more than that of evil (1). We should, therefore, state the problem of evil in terms of second order evil, and against this form of the problem the present solution is useless.

An attempt might be made to use this solution again, at a higher level, to explain the occurrence of evil (2): indeed the next main solution that we shall examine does just this, with the help of some new notions. Without any fresh notions, such a solution would have little plausibility: for example, we could hardly say that the really important good was a good (3), such as the increase of benevolence in proportion to cruelty, which logically required for its occurrence the occurrence of some second order evil. But even if evil (2) could be explained in this way, it is fairly clear that there would be third order evils contrasting with this third order good: and we should be well on the way to an infinite regress, where the solution of a problem of evil, stated in terms of evil (n), indicated the existence of an evil ($n + 1$), and a further problem to be solved.

(4)   "Evil is due to human freewill."

Perhaps the most important proposed solution of the problem of evil is that evil is not to be ascribed to God at all, but to the independent actions of human beings, supposed to have been endowed by God with freedom of the will. This solution may be combined with the preceding one: first order evil (*e.g.* pain) may be justified as a logically necessary component in second order good (*e.g.* sympathy) while second order evil (*e.g.* cruelty) is not *justified*, but is so ascribed to human beings that God cannot be held responsible for it. This combination evades my third criticism of the preceding solution.

The freewill solution also involves the preceding solution at a higher level. To explain why a wholly good God gave men freewill although it would lead to some important evils, it must be argued that it is better on the whole that men should act freely, and sometimes err, than that they should be innocent automata, acting rightly in a wholly determined way. Freedom, that is to say, is now treated as a third order good, and as being more valuable than second order goods (such as sympathy and heroism) would be if they were deterministically produced, and it is being assumed that second order evils, such as cruelty, are logically necessary accompaniments of freedom, just as pain is a logically necessary pre-condition of sympathy.

I think that this solution is unsatisfactory primarily because of the incoherence of the notion of freedom of the will: but I cannot discuss this topic adequately here, although some of my criticisms will touch upon it.

First I should query the assumption that second order evils are logically necessary accompaniments of freedom. I should ask this: if God has made men such that in their free choices they sometimes prefer what is good and sometimes what is evil, why could he not have made men such that they always freely choose the good? If there is no logical impossibility in a man's freely choosing the good on one, or on several, occasions, there cannot be a logical impossibility in his freely choosing the good on every occasion. God was not, then, faced with a choice between making innocent automata and making beings who, in acting freely, would sometimes go wrong: there was open to him the obviously better possibility of making beings who would act freely but always go right. Clearly, his failure to avail himself of this possibility is inconsistent with his being both omnipotent and wholly good.

If it is replied that this objection is absurd, that the making of some wrong choices is logically necessary for freedom, it would seem that 'freedom' must here mean complete randomness or indeterminacy, including randomness with regard to the alternatives good and evil, in other words that men's choices and consequent actions can be "free" only if they are not determined by their characters. Only on this assumption can God escape the responsibility for men's actions; for if he made them as they are, but did not determine their wrong choices, this can only be because the wrong choices are not determined by men as they are. But then if freedom is randomness, how can it be a characteristic of *will*? And, still more, how can it be the most important good? What value or merit would there be in free choices if these were random actions which were not determined by the nature of the agent?

I conclude that to make this solution plausible two different senses of 'freedom' must be confused, one sense which will justify the view that freedom is a third order good, more valuable than other goods would be without it, and another sense, sheer randomness, to prevent us from ascribing to God a decision to make men such that they sometimes go wrong when he might have made them such that they would always freely go right.

This criticism is sufficient to dispose of this solution. But besides this there is a fundamental difficulty in the notion of an omnipotent God creating men with free will, for if men's wills are really free this must mean that even God cannot control them, that is, that God is no longer omnipotent. It may be objected that God's gift of freedom to men does not mean that he *cannot* control their wills, but that he always *refrains* from controlling their wills. But why, we may ask, should God refrain from controlling evil wills? Why should he not leave men free to will rightly, but intervene when he sees them beginning to will wrongly? If God could do this, but does not, and if he is wholly good, the only explanation could be that even a wrong free act of will is not really evil, that its freedom is a value which outweighs its wrongness, so that there would be a loss of value if God took away the wrongness and the freedom together. But this is utterly opposed to what theists say about sin in other contexts. The present solution of the problem of evil, then, can be maintained only in the form that God has made men so free that he *cannot* control their wills.

This leads us to what I call the Paradox of Omnipotence: can an omnipotent being make things which he cannot subsequently control? Or, what is practically equivalent to this, can an omnipotent being make rules which then bind himself? (These are practically equivalent because any such rules could be regarded as setting certain things beyond his control, and *vice versa.*) The second of these formulations is relevant to the suggestions that we have already met, that an omnipotent God creates the rules of logic or causal laws, and is then bound by them.

It is clear that this is a paradox: the questions cannot be answered satisfactorily either in the affirmative or in the negative. If we answer "Yes", it follows that if God actually makes things which he cannot control, or makes rules which bind himself, he is not omnipotent once he has made them: there are *then* things which he cannot do. But if we answer "No", we are immediately asserting that there are things which he cannot do, that is to say that he is already not omnipotent.

It cannot be replied that the question which sets this paradox is not a proper question. It would make perfectly good sense to say that a human mechanic has made a machine which he cannot control: if there is any difficulty about the question it lies in the notion of omnipotence itself.

This, incidentally, shows that although we have approached this paradox from the free will theory, it is equally a problem for a theological determinist. No one thinks that machines have free will, yet they may well be beyond the control of their makers. The determinist might reply that anyone who makes anything determines its ways of acting, and so determines its subsequent behaviour: even the human mechanic does this by his *choice* of materials and structure for his machine, though he does not know all about either of these: the mechanic thus determines, though he may not foresee, his machine's actions. And since God is omniscient, and since his creation of things is total, he both determines and foresees the ways in which his creatures will act. We may grant this, but it is beside the point. The question is not whether God *originally* determined the future actions of his creatures, but whether he can *subsequently* control their actions, or whether he was able in his original creation to put things beyond his subsequent control. Even on determinist principles the answers "Yes" and "No" are equally irreconcilable with God's omnipotence.

Before suggesting a solution of this paradox, I would point out that there is a parallel Paradox of Sovereignty. Can a legal sovereign make a law restricting its own future legislative power? For example, could the British parliament make a law forbidding any future parliament to socialise banking, and also forbidding the future repeal of this law itself? Or could the British parliament, which was legally sovereign in Australia in, say, 1899, pass a valid law, or series of laws, which made it no longer sovereign in 1933? Again, neither the affirmative nor the negative answer is really satisfactory. If we were to answer "Yes", we should be admitting the validity of a law which, if it were actually made, would mean that parliament was no longer sovereign. If we were to answer "No", we should be admitting that there is a law, not logically absurd, which parliament cannot validly make, that is, that parliament is not now a legal sovereign. This paradox can be solved in the following way. We should distinguish between first order laws, that is laws governing the actions of individuals and bodies other than the legislature, and second order laws, that is laws about laws, laws governing the actions of the legislature itself. Correspondingly, we should distinguish two orders of sovereignty, first order sovereignty (sovereignty (1)) which is unlimited authority to make first order laws, and second order sovereignty (sovereignty (2)) which is unlimited authority to make second order laws. If we say that parliament is sovereign we might mean that any parliament at any time has sovereignty (1), or we might mean that parliament has both sovereignty (1) and sovereignty (2) at present, but we cannot without contradiction mean both that the present parliament has sovereignty (2) and that every parliament at every time has sovereignty (1), for if the present parliament has sovereignty (2) it may use it to take away the sovereignty (1) of later parliaments. What the paradox shows is that we cannot ascribe to any continuing institution legal sovereignty in an inclusive sense.

The analogy between omnipotence and sovereignty shows that the paradox of omnipotence can be solved in a similar way. We must distinguish between first order omnipotence (omnipotence (1)), that is unlimited power to act, and second order omnipotence (omnipotence (2)), that is unlimited power to determine what powers to act things shall have. Then we could consistently say that God all the time has omnipotence (1), but if so no beings at any time have powers to act independently of God. Or we could say that God at one time had omnipotence (2), and used it to assign independent powers to act to certain things, so that God thereafter did not have omnipotence (1). But what the paradox shows is that we cannot consistently ascribe to any continuing being omnipotence in an inclusive sense.

An alternative solution of this paradox would be simply to deny that God is a continuing being, that any times can be assigned to his actions at all. But on this assumption (which also has difficulties of its own) no meaning can be given to the assertion that God made men with wills so free that he could not control them. The paradox of omnipotence can be avoided by putting God outside time, but the freewill solution of the problem of evil cannot be saved in this way, and equally it remains impossible to hold that an omnipotent God *binds himself* by causal or logical laws.

CONCLUSION

Of the proposed solutions of the problem of evil which we have examined, none has stood up to criticism. There may be other solutions which require examination, but this study strongly suggests that there is no valid solution of the problem which does not modify at least one of the constituent propositions in a way which would seriously affect the essential core of the theistic position.

Quite apart from the problem of evil, the paradox of omnipotence has shown that God's omnipotence must in any case be restricted in one way or another, that unqualified omnipotence cannot be ascribed to any being that continues through time. And if God and his actions are not in time, can omnipotence, or power of any sort, be meaningfully ascribed to him?

ALVIN PLANTINGA
The Free Will Defense

1. THE PROBLEM

In this chapter I wish to apply some of the foregoing ideas to one of two traditional topics in the philosophy of religion: the Problem of Evil (which will occupy this chapter) and the Ontological Argument. Perhaps the former constitutes the most formidable objection to theistic belief – or so, at any rate, it has seemed to many. A multitude of philosophers have held that the existence of evil is at the least an embarrassment for those who accept belief in God.[1] And most contemporary philosophers who hold that evil constitutes a difficulty for theistic belief claim to detect *logical inconsistency* in beliefs a theist typically accepts. So, for example, according to H. J. McCloskey:

> Evil is a problem for the theist in that a *contradiction* is involved in the fact of evil, on the one hand, and the belief in the omnipotence and perfection of God on the other.[2]

J. L. Mackie urges the same charge:

> I think, however, that a more telling criticism can be made by way of the traditional problem of evil. Here it can be shown, not that religious beliefs lack rational support, but that they are positively irrational, that the several parts of the essential theological doctrine are *inconsistent* with one another.[3]

And Henry David Aiken substantially repeats this allegation.[4]

Original publication: Pp. 164–93, Alvin Plantinga, *The Nature of Necessity* (Oxford: Oxford University Press, 1971).

Now the alleged contradiction arises, of course, when we consider the fact that evil exists together with the belief that God exists and is omniscient, omnipotent, and wholly good or morally perfect. Obviously these propositions are not *formally* inconsistent; the resources of logic alone do not enable us to deduce an explicit contradiction from their conjunction. But then presumably the atheologian – he who offers arguments against the existence of God – never meant to hold that there was a formal contradiction here; he meant instead that the conjunction of these two propositions is necessarily false, false in every possible world. To show that he is right, therefore, he must produce a proposition that is at least plausibly thought to be necessary and whose conjunction with our original two formally yields a contradiction.

I have argued elsewhere[5] that it is extremely difficult to find any such proposition. I have also argued[6] that the *Free Will Defence* can be used to show that in fact these propositions are not inconsistent. In what follows I wish to look again at the issues involved in the *Free Will Defence* – this time from the vantage point of the foregoing ideas about *possible worlds*.

2.   THE FREE WILL DEFENCE

The Free Will Defence is an effort to show that

(1)   God is omnipotent, omniscient, and wholly good

(which I shall take to entail that God exists) is not inconsistent with

(2)   There is evil in the world.

That is, the Free Will Defender aims to show that there is a possible world in which (1) and (2) are both true. Now one way to show that a proposition p is consistent with a proposition q is to produce a third proposition r whose conjunction with p is consistent and entails q. r, of course, need not be true or known to be true; it need not be so much as plausible. All that is required of it is that it be consistent with p, and in conjunction with the latter entail q. What the Free Will Defender must do, therefore, is find such a proposition.

But first, some preliminary definitions and distinctions. What does the Free Will Defender mean when he says that people are or may be *free*? If a person *S* is free with respect to a given action, then he is free to perform that action and free to refrain; no causal laws and antecedent conditions determine either that he will perform the action, or that he will not. It is within his power, at the time in question, to perform the action, and within his power to refrain. Consider the state *U* of the universe up to the time he takes or decides to take the action in question. If *S* is free with respect to that action, then it is causally or naturally possible both that *U* hold and *S* *take* (or decide to take) the action, and that *U* hold and *S* *refrain* from it.[7] Further, let us say that an action is *morally significant*, for a given person at a given time, if it would be wrong for him to perform the action then but right to refrain, or vice versa. Keeping a promise, for example, would typically be morally significant, as would refusing induction into the army; having an apple for lunch (instead of an orange) would not. And, a person *goes wrong with respect to a morally significant action* if it is wrong for him to perform it and he does, or wrong for him not to and he does not. Still further, suppose we say that a person is *significantly free*, on a given occasion, if he is then free with respect to an action that is morally significant for him. And finally, we must distinguish between *moral* evil and *natural* evil. The former is evil that results from some human being's going wrong with respect to an action that is morally significant for him; any other evil is natural evil.[8] Suffering due to human cruelty – Hitler's treatment of the Jews, for example – would be an example of the former; suffering resulting from an earthquake or tidal wave, an example of the latter. An analogous distinction is made between moral and natural good.

Given these definitions and distinctions, we can make a preliminary statement of the Free Will Defence as follows. A world containing creatures who are sometimes significantly free (and freely perform more good than evil actions) is more valuable, all else being equal, than a world containing no free creatures at all. Now God can create free creatures, but he cannot *cause* or *determine* them to do only what is right. For if he does so, then they are not significantly free after all; they do not do what is right *freely*. To create creatures capable of *moral good*, therefore, he must create creatures capable of moral evil; and he cannot leave these creatures *free* to perform evil and at the same time prevent them from doing so. God did in fact create significantly free creatures; but some of them went wrong in the exercise of their freedom: this is the source of moral evil. The fact that these free creatures sometimes go wrong, however, counts neither against God's omnipotence nor against his goodness; for he could have forestalled the occurrence of moral evil only by excising the possibility of moral good.

I said earlier that the Free Will Defender tries to find a proposition that is consistent with

(1)   God is omniscient, omnipotent, and wholly good

and together with (1) entails that there is evil. According to the Free Will Defence, we must find this proposition somewhere in the above story. The heart of the Free Will Defence is the claim that it is *possible* that God could not have created a universe containing moral good (or as much moral good as this one contains) without creating one containing moral evil.

3.   THE OBJECTION

A formidable objection goes like this. Surely it is logically possible that there be a world containing significantly free creatures who always do what is right. There is certainly no contradiction or inconsistency in this idea. If so, however, there are possible worlds containing moral good but no moral evil. Now the theist says that God is omnipotent – which means, roughly, that there are no non-logical limits to his power. Accordingly, he could have created just any possible world he chose, including those containing moral good but no moral evil. If it is possible that there be a world containing significantly free creatures who never do what is wrong, then it follows that an omnipotent God could have created such a world. If so, however, the Free Will Defence must be mistaken in its insistence upon the possibility that God, though omnipotent, could not have created a world containing moral good without permitting moral evil. As Mackie puts it:

> If God has made men such that in their free choices they sometimes prefer what is good and sometimes what is evil, why could he not have made men such that they always freely choose the good? If there is no logical impossibility in a man's freely choosing the good on one, or on several occasions, there cannot be a logical impossibility in his freely choosing the good on every occasion. God was not, then, faced with a choice between making innocent automata and making beings who, in acting freely, would sometimes go wrong; there was open to him the

obviously better possibility of making beings who would act freely but always go right. Clearly, his failure to avail himself of this possibility is inconsistent with his being both omnipotent and wholly good.[9]

Was it within the power of an omnipotent God to create just any logically possible world? This is the important question for the Free Will Defence, and a subtle question it is. Leibniz, as you recall, insisted that *this* world, the actual world, must be the best of all possible worlds. His reasoning is as follows. Before God created anything at all, he was confronted with an enormous range of choices; he could have created or actualized any of the myriads of different possible worlds. Being perfectly good, he must have chosen to create the best world he could; being omnipotent, he was able to create just any possible world he pleased. He must, therefore, have chosen the best of all possible worlds; and hence *this* world, the one he did create, must be (despite appearances) the best possible. Now Mackie agrees with Leibniz that God, if omnipotent, could have created just any world he pleased and would have created the best world he could. But while Leibniz draws the conclusion that *this* world must be the best possible, Mackie concludes instead that there is no omnipotent, wholly good God. For, he says, it is obvious enough that this actual world is not the best possible.

The Free Will Defender disagrees with both Leibniz and Mackie. First, we have the question whether *there is* such a thing as the best of all possible worlds, or even *a* best. Perhaps for any world you pick, there is a better. But what is really characteristic and central to the Free Will Defence is the claim that God, though omnipotent, could not have created just any possible world he pleased; and this is the claim we must investigate.

4. WHICH WORLDS COULD GOD HAVE CREATED?

We speak of God as *creating* the world; yet if it is α of which we speak, what we say is false. For a thing is created only if there is a time before which it does not exist; and this is patently false of α, as it is of any state of affairs. What God has created are the heavens and the earth and all that they contain; he has not created himself, or numbers, propositions, properties, or states of affairs: these have no beginnings. We can say, however, that God *actualizes* states of affairs; his creative activity results in their being or becoming actual. God has *created* Socrates, but *actualized* the state of affairs consisting in the latter's existence. And God is actualizing but not creating α.

Furthermore, while we may properly say that God actualizes α, it does not follow that he actualizes every state of affairs the latter includes. He does not, as previously mentioned, actualize his own existence; that is to say, he does not create himself. Nor does he create his own properties; hence he does not actualize the state of affairs consisting in the existence of such properties as omniscience, omnipotence, moral excellence, and *being the creator of the heavens and the earth*. But the same is really true of other properties too; God no more creates the property of being red than that of omnipotence. Properties are not creatable: to suppose that they have been created is to suppose that although they exist now, there was a time at which they did not; and this seems clearly false. Again, since God did not create numbers, propositions, pure sets, and the like, he did not actualize the states of affairs consisting in the existence of these things. Nor does he actualize such other necessary states of affairs as *7 + 5's equalling 12*. Necessary states of affairs do not owe their actuality to the creative activity of God. So if we speak of God as actualizing α, we should not think of him as actualizing every state of affairs α includes. But perhaps we may say that he actualizes every *contingent* state of affairs included in α; and perhaps we may say that God *can* actualize a given possible world W only if he can actualize every contingent state of affairs W includes. And now we can put our question: can an omnipotent being actualize just any possible world he pleases – that is, is every possible world such that an omnipotent being can actualize it?

Here more distinctions are needed. Although there are any number of possible worlds in which Abraham never met Melchizedek, God can actualize none of them. That is, he can no longer actualize any of them; for Abraham in fact *did* meet Melchizedek (let us suppose) and not even an omnipotent being can bring it about that Abraham did *not* meet Melchizedek; it is too late for that. Take any time t; at t there will be any number of worlds God cannot actualize; for there will be any number of worlds in which things go differently before t. So God cannot actualize any world in which Abraham did not meet Melchizedek; but perhaps God *could have* actualized such worlds. Perhaps we should say that God could have actualized a world W if and only if for every contingent state of affairs S included by W, there is a time at which it is (timelessly) within his power to actualize S.[10] And now perhaps the atheologian's claim may be put as follows:

(3)   If God is omnipotent, then God could have actualized just any possible world.

But this will not be entirely accurate either – not, at any rate, if God himself is a contingent being. For if he is a contingent being, then there are worlds in which he does not exist; and clearly he could not have actualized any of *these* worlds. Clearly the only worlds within God's power to actualize are those that include his existence. So suppose we restrict our attention to these worlds. Is it true that

(4)   If God is omnipotent, then he could have actualized just any world that includes his existence?

Still more distinctions are needed. In particular, we must look more closely at the idea of *freedom*. According to the Free Will Defender, God thought it good to create free persons. And a person is free with respect to an action A at a time t only if no causal laws and antecedent conditions determine either that he performs A at t or that he refrains from so doing. This is not a comment upon the ordinary use of the word 'free'; that use may or may not coincide with the Free Will Defender's. What God thought good, on this view, was the existence of creatures whose activity is not causally determined – who, like he himself, are centres of creative activity. The freedom of such creatures will no doubt be *limited* by causal laws and antecedent conditions. They will not be free to do just anything; even if I am free, I am not free to run a mile in two minutes. Of course my freedom is also *enhanced* by causal laws; it is only by virtue of such laws that I am free to build a house or walk on the surface of the earth. But if I am free with respect to an action A, then causal laws and antecedent conditions determine neither that I take A nor that I refrain.

More broadly, if I am free with respect to an action A, then God does not *bring it about* or *cause it to be the case* either that I take or that I refrain from this action; he neither causes this to be so through the laws he establishes, nor by direct intervention, nor in any other way. For if he *brings it about* or *causes it to be the case* that I take A, then I am not free to *refrain* from A, in which case I am not free with respect to A. Although of course God may cause it to be the case that I *am* free with respect to A, he cannot cause it to be the case either that I freely take or that I freely refrain from this action – and this though he is omnipotent.[11] But then it follows that there are plenty of contingent states of affairs such that it is not within the power of God to bring about their actuality, or cause them to be actual. He cannot cause it to be the case that I freely refrain from an action A; for if he does so, he causes it to be the case that I refrain from A, in which case I do not do so *freely*.

Now I have been using 'brings it about that' as a rough synonym for 'causes it to be the case that'. Suppose we take the term 'actualize' the same way. Then God can actualize a given state of affairs S only if he can cause it to be the case that S, cause S to be actual. And then there will be many contingent states of affairs S such that there is no time at which God can actualize S. But we said a page back that

> (5) God could have actualized a given possible world W if and only if for every contingent state of affairs S that W includes, there is a time at which God can actualize S.

Given just the possibility that there are created free agents, it follows that there are any number of possible worlds including God's existence and *also* including a contingent state of affairs S such that there is no time at which God can actualize S. Hence (contrary to (4) and to the atheologian's claim) there are any number of possible worlds that God could not have actualized, even though they include his existence: all those containing a state of affairs consisting in some creature's freely taking or refraining from some action. Since a world containing moral good is such a world, it follows that God could not have actualized any world containing moral good; *a fortiori* he could not have actualized a world containing moral good but no moral evil.

The atheologian's proper retort, I think, is as follows. Suppose we concede that not even God can cause it to be the case that I freely refrain from A. Even so, he *can* cause me to be free with respect to A, and to be in some set S of circumstances including appropriate laws and antecedent conditions. He may also know, furthermore, that *if* he creates me and causes me to be free in these circumstances, I will refrain from A. If so, there is a state of affairs he can actualize, cause to be actual, such that if he does so, then I will freely refrain from A. In a broader sense of 'bring about', therefore, he *can* bring it about that I freely refrain from A. In the narrower sense there are many contingent states of affairs he cannot bring about; what is relevant to the Free Will Defence, however, is not this narrow sense, but the broader one. For what is really at issue is whether for each possible world there are some actions God could have taken such that if he *had*, then that morally perfect world (one including moral good but no moral evil) would have been actual.

Perhaps we can sharpen this point. The narrow sense of 'bring about' is such that the sentence

(6) If God brings it about that I refrain from A, then I do not freely refrain from A

expresses a necessary truth. You are free with respect to an action A only if God does not bring it about or cause it to be the case that you refrain from A. But now suppose God knows that if he creates you free with respect to A in some set S of circumstances, you will refrain from A; suppose further that he brings it about (narrow sense) that you *are* free with respect to A in S; and suppose finally that you do in fact freely refrain from A. Then in a broader sense of 'bring about' we could properly say that God has brought it about that you freely refrain from A. We must make a corresponding distinction, then, between a stronger and a weaker sense of 'actualize'. In the strong sense, God can actualize only what he can *cause* to be actual; in that sense he cannot actualize any state of affairs including the existence of creatures who freely take some action or other. But so far we have no reason for supposing that the same holds for *weak* actualization. And what the atheologian requires for his argument, presumably, is not that every possible world (including the existence of God) is one God could have actualized in the *strong* sense; weak actualization is enough for his purposes. What is at issue is not the question whether each world is such that God could have actualized it in the *strong* sense, but (roughly) whether for each world W there is something he could have done – some series of actions he could have taken – such that if he had, W would have been actual. For if God is wholly good and it *was* within his power thus to secure the actuality of a perfect world, then presumably he would have done so. Accordingly the Free Will Defender's claim – that God could not have actualized a world containing moral good without actualizing one containing moral evil – is either irrelevant or unsubstantiated: irrelevant if 'actualize' is taken in the strong sense and unsubstantiated otherwise.

Since it is weak actualization that is relevant, let us henceforth use 'actualize' to mean 'weakly actualize'. And so our question is this:

LEEDS TRINITY UNIVERSITY

could God have actualized just any possible world that includes his existence?

Perhaps we can best proceed by way of an example. Curley Smith, the mayor of Boston, is opposed to the proposed freeway route. From the Highway Department's point of view, his objection is frivolous; he complains that the route would require destruction of the Old North Church along with some other antiquated and structurally unsound buildings. The Director of Highways offers him a bribe of $35,000 to drop his opposition. Unwilling to break with the fine old traditions of Bay State politics, Curley accepts; whereupon the Director spends a sleepless night wondering whether he could have had Curley for $20,000. That is to say, Smedes wonders which of

(7)   If Curley had been offered $20,000, he would have accepted the bribe

or

(8)   If Curley had been offered $20,000, he would have rejected the bribe

is true.

5.   COUNTER FACTUALS

But here an objection arises. (7) and (8), of course, are *counterfactual conditionals*. Subject to all the difficulty and obscurity of that peculiar breed, they contain traps for the unwary. Here, for example, we seem to be assuming that either (7) or (8) must be true. But what is the justification for that? How do we know that at least one of them *is* true? What leads us to suppose that there is an answer to the question what Curley would have done, had he been offered a bribe of $20,000?

This question can be amplified. According to an interesting proposal[12] a counterfactual conditional such as (7) can be explained as follows. Consider those possible worlds that include its antecedent; and then of these consider that one *W* that is *most similar to* the actual world. (7) is true if and only if its consequent – that is,

(9)   Curley took the bribe

is true in W. A counterfactual is true if and only if its antecedent is impossible, or its consequent is true in the world most similar to the actual in which its antecedent is.

This intriguing proposal provokes questions. In the first place, the required notion of similarity is in many respects problematic. What does it mean to say that one possible world is more similar to α than another? In this context, is there such a thing as similarity *uberhaupt*, or should we speak only of similarity in given respects? These are good questions; we have no time to linger over them, but let us pause just long enough to note that we do seem to have an intuitive grasp of this notion – the notion of similarity between states of affairs. Secondly, the proposal presumes that for each contingently false proposition p there is a possible world including p that is uniquely closest (i.e. most similar) to the actual world. So take any such proposition and any proposition q: on the proposal in question, either *if p then q* or *if p then ~q* will be true. This may seem a bit strong: *if I had red hair, Napoleon would not have lost the Battle of Waterloo* is obviously false, but *if I had red hair Napoleon would have won the Battle of Waterloo* does not seem much better. (*Even if*, perhaps, but not *if*.) Indeed, take any such proposition p: on this view there is some entire possible world W such that the counterfactual *if p had been true, W would have obtained* holds. But is it not unduly extravagant to claim that there is some possible world W such that if I had red hair, W would have been actual? Is there a possible world $W*$ such that if α had not been actual, $W*$ would have been? Is there reason to believe that there is a world including the antecedent of (7) and (8) (call it 'A') that is *uniquely closest* to α? Perhaps several worlds include it, each such that none including it is closer.[13] And this leads directly to our question. Perhaps there is a family of closest worlds in which A is true; and perhaps in some of these

(9)   Curley accepted the bribe

is true, while in others it is

(10)   Curley rejected the bribe

that enjoys that distinction. If so, then perhaps we must conclude that neither (7) nor (8) is true; there is then no such thing as *what Curley would have done* under the envisaged circumstances.

Indeed, perhaps the objector need not rest content with the idle suspicion that there may be such a family of worlds; perhaps he can go further. There are possible worlds W and W^* that include A and are *exactly alike* up to 10.00 a.m., 10 November 1973, the time at which Curley makes his response to the bribe offer; in W Curley accepts the bride and in W^* he does not. If $t = 10.00$ a.m., 10 November 1973, let us say that W and W^* *share an initial segment up to t*. We could call the t-initial segment of W 'S_W^{-t}', the subscript 'W' indicating that S is a segment of W, and the superscript '$-t$' indicating that this segment terminates at t. (S_W^{+t} would be the unending segment of W that begins at t.) And of course $S_W^{-t} = S_{W^*}^{-t}$.

It is not entirely easy to give a rigorous characterization of this notion of an initial segment. It is clear that if W and W^* share an initial segment terminating at t, then for any object x and for any time t^* earlier than t, x exists in W^* at t^* if and only if x exists in W^* at t^*. But we cannot say that if a thing x has a property P in W at t^*, then x has P in W^* at t^*. For one property Curley has at t^* in W is that of being such at t he will take the bribe; and of course he does not have *that* property in W^* at t^*. Perhaps there is an intuitive notion of a *non-temporal* property under which we could say that if at t^* x has a non-temporal property P in W then x also has P in W^* at t^*. The problem of course is to say just what this notion of a non-temporal property amounts to; and that is by no means easy. Still the idea of a pair of worlds W and W^* sharing an initial segment is fairly clear; roughly, it amounts to saying that the two worlds are the same up to a certain time t. And if there is no time t^* later than t such that $S_W^{-t^*} = S_{W^*}^{-t^*}$, then at t W and W^* *branch*. Of course there will be a large class of worlds sharing S_W^{-t} with W and W^*; and if e is an event that takes place in W but not in W^*, there will be a class of worlds including S_W^{-t} in which e occurs and another class including it in which e does not.

Suppose we concede (or pretend) that we have this notion of an initial segment well in hand. It may then appear that we can construct a convincing argument for the conclusion that neither (7) nor (8) is true. For each of W and W^* are as similar to α, in the relevant respects, as any world including A. But if they share S_W^{-t}, then are they not *equally* similar, in the appropriate ways, to α? Up to t things are just alike in these two worlds. What happens after t seems scarcely relevant to the question of what Curley would have done if offered the bribe. We should conclude, therefore, that W and W^* are equally similar to α; but these two worlds resemble α as much as any others; hence the closest worlds in which A is true do not speak with a single voice; hence neither (7) nor (8) is true.[14]

What about this argument? In the first place, it proves too much. It gains a specious plausibility from the case we are considering. We do not know, after all, whether Curley would have accepted the bribe – it is a fairly small one and perhaps his pride would have been injured. Let us ask instead whether he would have accepted a bribe of $36,000, everything else being as much as possible like the actual world. Here the answer seems fairly clear: indeed he would have. And this despite the fact that for any possible world W as close as you please to α in which Curley takes the bribe, there is a world W^* that shares the appropriate initial segment with W in which he manfully refuses it.

The argument suffers from another defect, however – one which is more instructive. Suppose we approach it by way of another example. Royal Robbins is climbing the Dihedral Wall of El Capitan. The usual method involving ropes and belays has lost its appeal; he is soloing the Wall unprotected. Just as he reaches Thanksgiving Ledge, some 2500 feet above the Valley floor, one of his hand holds breaks out. He teeters precariously on one foot, regains his balance, and leaps lightly on to the ledge, where he bivouacs; the next day he continues triumphantly to the top. Now suppose we consider

(11) If Robbins had slipped and fallen at Thanksgiving Ledge, he would have been killed.

No doubt we are initially inclined to accept this proposition. But should we? In the actual world Robbins did not fall at Thanksgiving Ledge; instead he nimbly climbed on to it and spent a comfortable night there. Now what happens in the closest worlds in which he falls? Well, there is at least one of these – call it W' – in which he falls at t just as he is reaching the Ledge; at the next moment $t + 1$ (as close as you please to t) he shows up exactly where he is in α at $t + 1$; and everything else goes just as it does in α. Would W' not be more similar to the actual world than any in which he hurtles down to the Valley floor, thus depriving American rockclimbing of its most eloquent spokesman? And if so, should we not rate (11) false?

The answer, of course, is that we are neglecting causal or natural *laws*. Our world α contains a number of these, and they are among its more impressive constituents. In particular, there are some implying (together with the relevant antecedent conditions) that anyone who falls unroped and unprotected from a ledge 2500 feet up a vertical cliff, moves with increasing rapidity towards the centre of the earth, finally arriving with considerable impact at its surface. Evidently not all of these laws are present in W', for the latter shares the relevant initial conditions with α but in it Robbins does not fall to the Valley floor – instead, after a brief feint in that direction, he reappears on the cliff. And once we note that these laws do not hold in W', so the claim goes, we shall no longer be tempted to think it very similar to α, where they do hold.

No doubt there is truth in this reply. But the relationship between causal laws and counterfactuals, like that between Guinevere and Sir Lancelot, is both intimate and notorious. A salient feature of the former, indeed, is that (unlike accidental generalizations) they are said to support or entail counterfactuals. So instead of denigrating W' on the grounds that its laws differ from α's, we might as well have complained, in view of the above connection, that W' lacks some of α's counterfactuals. One measure of similarity between worlds involves the question whether they share their counterfactuals.

We should be unduly hasty, I think, if we drew the conclusion that the possible worlds explanation of counterfactuals is viciously circular or of no theoretical interest or importance. But it does follow that we cannot as a rule *discover* the truth value of a counterfactual by asking whether its consequent holds in those worlds most similar to the actual in which its antecedent holds. For one feature determining the similarity of worlds is whether they share their counterfactuals.

And of course this is relevant to the argument we have been examining. As you recall, it went like this. There are worlds W and W^* that share S_W^{-t}; these worlds, therefore, are equally similar to α in the relevant respects. In W, however, Curley takes the bribe; in W^* he refuses. Accordingly, neither (7) nor (8) is such that its consequent is true in the closest worlds to α in which its antecedent is; hence neither (7) nor (8) is true. But now we see that this argument does not settle the matter. For from the fact that W and W^* share the appropriate initial segment, it does not follow that they are equally similar to α. Suppose that (7) *is* true; then W^* does not share that counterfactual with α, and is to that extent less similar to it than W. Here we have a relevant dissimilarity between the two worlds in virtue of which the one may indeed be more similar to the actual world than the other. Accordingly, the argument fails.

A second argument is sometimes given for the conclusion that we have no right to the assumption that either (7) or (8) is true: perhaps the fact is that

(12)   If Curley had been offered a bribe of $20,000 and had believed that his decision would be headlined in the *Boston Globe*, he would have rejected the bribe.

If so, then (7) is false. But perhaps it is also true that

(13)   If Curley had been offered a bribe of $20,000 and had believed that his venality would remain undetected, he would have accepted the bribe;

in which case (8) would be false. So if (12) and (13) are both true (as they might well be) then neither (7) nor (8) is.

This argument is in error. If we let '$\rightarrow$' represent the counterfactual connective, we see that the crucial inference here is of the form

$$\frac{A \rightarrow C}{\therefore A \ \& \ B \rightarrow C}$$

which is clearly fallacious (and invalid on both the Stalnaker and Lewis semantics for counterfactuals). No doubt it is true that

(14)   If the Pope were a Protestant, he would be a dissembler;

it does not follow that

(15)   If the Pope were a Protestant, had been born in Friesland and been a lifelong member of the Gereformeerde Kerk, he would be a dissembler.

Nor does it follow from (7) that, if Curley had been offered the bribe and had believed his decision would be headlined in the *Globe*, he would have accepted it.

Now of course the failure of these arguments does not guarantee that either (7) or (8) must be true. But suppose we think about a state of affairs that includes Curley's having been offered $20,000, all relevant conditions – Curley's financial situation, his general acquisitive tendencies, his venality – being the same as in fact, in the actual world. Our question is really whether there is something Curley would have done had this state of affairs been actual. Would an omniscient being know what Curley would have done – would he know, that is, either that Curley would have taken the bribe or that he would have rejected it?

The answer, I should think, is obvious and affirmative. There is something Curley would have done, had that state of affairs obtained. But I do not know how to produce a conclusive argument for this supposition, in case you are inclined to dispute it. I do think it is the natural view, the one we take in reflecting on our own moral failures and triumphs. Suppose I have applied for a National Science Foundation Fellowship and have asked you to write me a recommendation. I am eager to get the fellowship, but eminently unqualified to carry out the project I have proposed. Realizing that you know this, I act upon the maxim that every man has his price and offer you $500 to write a glowing, if inaccurate, report. You indignantly refuse, and add moral turpitude to my other disqualifications. Later we reflectively discuss what you would have done had you been offered a bribe of $50,000. One thing we would take for granted, I should think, is that there is a right answer here. We may not know what that answer is; but we would reject out of hand, I should think, the suggestion that there simply is none. Accordingly, I shall temporarily take it for granted, in what follows, that either (7) or (8) is true; as we shall see in section 6 this assumption, harmless as it no doubt is, can be dispensed with.

6.   LEIBNIZ'S LAPSE

Thus armed, let us return to the question that provoked this digression. Was it within God's power, supposing him omnipotent, to actualize just any possible world that includes his existence? No. In a nutshell, the reason is this. There is a possible world W where God strongly actualizes a totality T of states of affairs including Curley's being free with respect to taking the bribe, and where Curley takes the bribe. But there is another possible world $W*$ where God actualizes the very same states of affairs and where Curley *rejects* the bribe. Now suppose it is true as a matter of fact that if God had actualized T, Curley would have accepted the bribe: then God could not have actualized W. And if, on the other hand, Curley would have rejected the bribe, had God actualized T, then God could not have actualized $W*$. So either way there are worlds God could not have actualized.

We can put this argument more fully as follows. Let C be the state of affairs consisting in Curley's being offered a bribe of $20,000 and being free to accept or reject it; let A be Curley's accepting the bribe; and let GC be God's strongly actualizing C. Then by our assumption either

(16) $GC \rightarrow A$

or

(17) $GC \rightarrow \bar{A}$

is true. Suppose, first, that (16) is true. If so, then on the Stalnaker and Lewis semantics there is a possible world W such that GC and A hold in W, and such that A holds in any world as close where GC holds. No doubt in W God strongly actualizes many states of affairs in addition to C; let T be the state of affairs that includes each of these. That is, T is a state of affairs that God strongly actualizes in W; and T includes every state of affairs God strongly actualizes in W. It is evident that if God had strongly actualized T, then Curley would have accepted the bribe, i.e.,

(18) $GT \rightarrow A$.

For GT and A hold in W; by (16), in any world as close as W where GC holds, A holds; but GT includes GC; so, in any world as close as W where GT holds, A holds. Now there is no possible world in which God strongly actualizes A; for A is Curley's *freely* accepting the bribe. But then GT does not include A; for, if it did, any world where God actualizes T would be one where he actualizes A; there are no worlds where he actualizes A; and there are worlds – e.g. W – where he actualizes GT. So there is another possible world W^* where God actualizes the very same states of affairs as he does in W, and in which Curley rejects the bribe. W^* therefore includes GT and $\bar{A}$. That is, in W^* God strongly actualizes T but no state of affairs properly including T; and in W^* $\bar{A}$ holds. And now it is easy to see that God could not have actualized this world W^*.

For suppose he could have. Then there is a state of affairs C^* such that God could have strongly actualized C^* and such that, if he had, W^* would be actual. That is,

(19) $GC^* \rightarrow W^*$.

But W^* includes GT; so

(20) $GC^* \rightarrow GT$.

Now W^* either includes or precludes GC^*; if the latter, GC^* precludes W^*. But in view of (19) GC^* does not preclude W^* unless, contrary to our hypothesis, GC^* is impossible. So W^* includes GC^*. T, furthermore, is the largest state of affairs God actualizes in W^*; T, therefore, includes C^* and GT includes GC^*. Hence the state of affairs GT & GC^* is or is equivalent to GT. By (18), $GT \rightarrow A$; hence

(21) GC^* & $GT \rightarrow A$.

But from (20) and (21) it follows that

(22) $GC^* \rightarrow A$.[15]

But A precludes W^* and hence includes $\bar{W}^*$; so

(23) $GC^* \rightarrow \bar{W}^*$.

(19) and (23), however, are both true only if GC^* is impossible, in which case God could not have actualized C^*. Accordingly, there is no state of affairs C^* such that God could have strongly actualized C^* and such that if he had, W^* would have been actual. If (16) is true, therefore, there are possible worlds including his existence that God could not have actualized: those worlds, namely, where God actualizes T and Curley rejects the bribe. On the other hand, if

(17) $GC \rightarrow \bar{A}$

is true, then by precisely a similar argument there are other possible worlds God could not have actualized. As I have assumed, either (16) or (17) is true; so despite God's omnipotence there are worlds including his existence he could not have actualized.

Now the assumption that either (16) or (17) is true is fairly innocent; but it is also dispensable. For let W be a world where God exists, where Curley is free with respect to the action of taking a \$20,000 bribe, and where he accepts it; and as before, let T be the largest state of affairs God strongly actualizes in W. God's actualizing T (GT) includes neither Curley's accepting the bribe (A) nor his rejecting it ($\bar{A}$); so there is a world W^* where God strongly actualizes T and in which Curley rejects the bribe. Now

(24) $GT \rightarrow A$

is either true or false. If (24) is true, then by the previous argument God could not have actualized W^*.

On the other hand, if (24) is false, then God could not have actualized W. For suppose he could have; then (as before) there would be a state of affairs C such that God could have strongly actualized C and such that, if he had, W would have been actual. That is

(25) $GC \rightarrow W.$

Now if (25) is true, then so is either

(26) $GC \,\&\, GT \rightarrow W$

or

(27) $GC \,\&\, \overline{GT} \rightarrow W.$[16]

Both (26) and (27), however, are false if (24) is. Consider (26): if (25) is true, then W includes GC (unless GC is impossible, in which case, contrary to the assumption, God could not have actualized it); but T is the largest state of affairs God strongly actualizes in W; hence GT includes GC. If so, however, $GC \,\&\, GT$ is equivalent to GT. And, since (24) is false, the same goes for (26).

And now consider (27). Either GC includes GT or it does not. Suppose it does. As we have seen, if GC is possible and (25) is true, then W includes GC; but T includes C; so GT includes GC. So if GC includes GT, then GC and GT are equivalent. But (24) is false; hence so is (25), if GC includes GT. So GC does not include GT; hence $GC \,\&\, \overline{GT}$ is a possible state of affairs. But W includes GT; hence $\overline{GT}$ includes $\overline{W}$; hence $GC \,\&\, \overline{GT}$ includes $\overline{W}$; hence (since $GC \,\&\, \overline{GT}$ is possible) (27) is false.

(24), therefore, is either true or false. And either way there are possible worlds including his existence that God could not have actualized. So there are possible worlds including his existence that God could not have actualized.

If we consider a world in which GT obtains and in which Curley freely rejects the bribe, we see that whether it was within God's power to actualize it depends in part upon what Curley would have done if God had strongly actualized T. Accordingly, there are possible worlds such that it is partly up to Curley whether or not God can actualize them. It is of course up to God whether or not to create Curley, and also up to God whether or not to make him free with respect to the action of taking the bribe at t. But if he creates him, and creates him free with respect to this action, then whether or not he takes it is up to Curley – not God.

Now we can return to the Free Will Defence and the problem of evil. The Free Will Defender, you recall, insists on the possibility that it is not within God's power to create a world containing moral good without creating one containing moral evil. His atheological opponent agrees with Leibniz in claiming that *if* (as the theist holds) God is omnipotent, then *it follows* that he could have created just any possible world (or any such world including his existence) he pleased. We now see that this contention – call it *Leibniz's Lapse* – is a mistake. The atheologian is right in holding that there are many possible worlds containing moral good but no moral evil; his mistake lies in endorsing Leibniz's Lapse. So one of his central contentions – that God, if omnipotent, could have actualized just any world he pleased – is false.

7. TRANSWORLD DEPRAVITY

Now suppose we recapitulate the logic of the situation. The Free Will Defender claims that

(28)   God is omnipotent and it was not within his power to create a world containing moral good but no moral evil

is possible. By way of retort the atheologian insists that there are possible worlds containing moral good but no moral evil. He adds that an omnipotent being could have actualized just any possible world he chose. So if God is omnipotent, it follows that he could have actualized a world containing moral good but no moral evil; hence (28) is not possible. What we have seen so far is that his second premiss – Leibniz's Lapse – is false.

Of course this does not settle the issue in the Free Will Defender's favour. Leibniz's Lapse (appropriately enough for a lapse) is false; but this does not show that (28) is possible. To show this latter, we must demonstrate the possibility that among the worlds God could not have actualized are all the worlds containing moral good but no moral evil. How can we approach this question?

Let us return to Curley and his venality. The latter is unbounded; Curley's bribability is utter and absolute. We could put this more exactly as follows. Take any positive integer n. If (1) at t Curley had been offered n dollars by way of a bribe, and (2) he had been free with respect to the action of taking the bribe, and (3) conditions had otherwise been as much as possible like those that did in fact obtain, Curley would have accepted the bribe. But there is worse to come. Significant freedom, obviously, does not *entail* wrongdoing; so there are possible worlds in which God and Curley both exist and in which the latter is significantly free but never goes wrong. But consider W, any one of these worlds. There is a state of affairs T such that God strongly actualizes T in W and T includes every state of affairs God strongly actualizes in W. Furthermore, since Curley is significantly free in W, there are some actions that are morally significant for him in W and with respect to which he is free in W. The sad truth, however, may be this: among these actions there is one – call it A – such that if God had actualized T, Curley would have gone wrong with respect to A. But then it follows (by the argument of section 6) that God could not have actualized W. Now W was just any of the worlds in which Curley is significantly free but always does only what is right. It therefore follows that it was not within God's power to actualize a world in which Curley produces moral good but no moral evil. Every world God could have actualized is such that if Curley is significantly free in it, he takes at least one wrong action.

The intuitive idea underlying this argument can be put as follows. Of course God can create Curley in various states of affairs that include his being significantly free with respect to some action A. Furthermore, God knows in advance what Curley would do if created and placed in these states of affairs. Now take any one of these states of affairs S. Perhaps what God knows is that if he creates Curley, causes him to be free with respect to A, and brings it about that S is actual, then Curley will go wrong with respect to A. But perhaps the same is true for *any other* state of affairs in which God might create Curley and give him significant freedom; that is, perhaps what God knows in advance is that no matter *what* circumstances he places Curley in, so long as he leaves him significantly free, he will take at least one wrong action. And the present claim is not, of course, that Curley or anyone else is *in fact* like this, but only that this story about Curley is *possibly* true.

If it *is* true, however, Curley suffers from what I shall call *transworld depravity*.[17] By way of explicit definition:

(29)   A person P *suffers from transworld depravity* if and only if for every
world W such that P is significantly free in W and P does only
what is right in W, there is a state of affairs T and an action A such
that
   (1)   God strongly actualizes T in W and W includes every state
         of affairs God strongly actualizes in W,
   (2) A is morally significant for P in W,
and
   (3)   if God had strongly actualized T, P would have gone
         wrong with respect to A.

What is important about the idea of transworld depravity is that if a
person suffers from it, then it was not within God's power to actualize
any world in which that person is significantly free but does no wrong –
that is, a world in which he produces moral good but no moral evil. But
clearly it is possible that everybody suffers from transworld depravity. If
this possibility were actual, then God could not have created any of the
possible worlds that include the existence and significant freedom of
just the persons who do in fact exist, and also contain moral good but
no moral evil. For to do so he would have had to create persons who
were significantly free but suffered from transworld depravity. And the
price for creating a world in which such persons produce moral good is
creating one in which they also produce moral evil.

Now we might think this settles the question in favour of the Free
Will Defender. But the fact is it does not. For suppose all the people that
exist in α suffer from transworld depravity; it does not follow that God
could not have created a world containing moral good without creating
one containing moral evil. God could have created *other people*. Instead
of creating us, he could have created a world containing people all
right, but not containing any of us. And perhaps if he had done that, he
could have created a world containing moral good but no moral evil.

Perhaps. But then again, perhaps not. Return to the notion of *essence*
or *individual concept*: an essence of Curley is a property he has in every
world in which he exists and that is not exemplified in any world by any
object distinct from Curley. An essence *simpliciter* is a property P such
that there is a world W in which there exists an object x that has P
essentially and is such that in no world W^* is there an object that has P
and is distinct from x. More briefly, an essence is an encaptic property
that is essentially exemplified in some world, where an encaptic property entails either P or $\bar{P}$, for every world-indexed property P.

And now recall that Curley suffers from transworld depravity. This fact implies something interesting about Curleyhood, Curley's essence. Take those worlds W such that *is significantly free in W and never does what is wrong in W* is entailed by Curley's essence. Each of these worlds has an important property, if Curley suffers from transworld depravity; each is such that God could not have actualized it. We can see this as follows. Suppose W^* is some world such that Curley's essence entails the property *is significantly free but never does what is wrong in W^**. That is, W^* is a world in which Curley is significantly free but always does what is right. But of course Curley suffers from transworld depravity. This means (as we have already seen) that God could not have actualized W^*. So if Curley suffers from transworld depravity, then Curley's essence has this property: God could not have actualized any world W such that Curleyhood contains the properties *is significantly free in W* and *always does what is right in W*.

We can use this connection between Curley's transworld depravity and his essence as the basis for a definition of transworld depravity as applied to essences rather than persons. We should note first that if E is a person's essence, then he is the instantiation of E; he is the thing that has (or exemplifies) every property in E. To instantiate an essence, God creates a person who has that essence; and in creating a person he instantiates an essence. Now we can say that

(30)   An essence E *suffers from transworld depravity* if and only if for every world W such that E entails the properties *is significantly free in W* and *always does what is right in W*, there is a state of affairs T and an action A such that

    (1) T is the largest state of affairs God strongly actualizes in W,

    (2) A is morally significant for E's instantiation in W,

    and

    (3)   if God had strongly actualized T, E's instantiation would have gone wrong with respect to A.

Note that transworld depravity is an accidental property of those essences and persons it afflicts. For suppose Curley suffers from transworld depravity: then so does his essence. There is a world, however, in which Curley is significantly free but always does what is right. If *that* world had been actual, then of course neither Curley nor his essence would have suffered from transworld depravity. So the latter is essential neither to those persons nor to those essences that exemplify it. But by now it is evident, I take it, that if an essence E *does* suffer from transworld depravity, then it was not within God's power to actualize a possible world W such that E contains the properties *is significantly free in W* and *always does what is right in W*. Hence it was not within God's power to create a world in which E's instantiation is significantly free but always does what is right.

Now the interesting fact here is this: it is possible that every creaturely essence[18] suffers from transworld depravity. But suppose this is true. God can create a world containing moral good only by creating significantly free persons. And, since every person is the instantiation of an essence, he can create significantly free persons only by instantiating some creaturely essences. But if every such essence suffers from transworld depravity, then no matter which essences God instantiated, the resulting persons, if free with respect to morally significant actions, would always perform at least some wrong actions. If every creaturely essence suffers from transworld depravity, then it was beyond the power of God himself to create a world containing moral good but no moral evil. He might have been able to create worlds in which moral evil is very considerably outweighed by moral good; but it was not within the power of omnipotence to create worlds containing moral good but no moral evil. Under these conditions God could have created a world containing no moral evil only by creating one without significantly free persons. But it is possible that every essence suffers from transworld depravity; so it is possible that God could not have created a world containing moral good but no moral evil.

8.   THE FREE WILL DEFENCE TRIUMPHANT

Put formally, you remember, the Free Will Defender's project was to show that

(1)   God is omniscient, omnipotent, and wholly good

is consistent with

(2)   There is evil

by employing the truth that a pair of propositions p and q are jointly consistent if there is a proposition r whose conjunction with p is consistent and entails q. What we have just seen is that

(31)   Every essence suffers from transworld depravity

is consistent with God's omnipotence. But then it is clearly consistent with (1). So we can use it to show that (1) is consistent with (2). For consider the conjunction of (1), (31), and

(32)   God actualizes a world containing moral good.

This conjunction is evidently consistent. But it entails

(2)   There is evil.

Accordingly (1) is consistent with (2); the Free Will Defence is successful.

Of course the conjunction of (31) with (32) is not the only proposition that can play the role of r in the Free Will Defence. Perhaps, for example, it was within the power of God to actualize a world including moral good but no moral evil, but not within his power to actualize one including no moral evil and including as much moral good as the actual world contains. So

(33)   For any world W, if W contains no moral evil and W includes as much moral good as α contains, then God could not have actualized W

(which is weaker than (31)) could be used in conjunction with

(34)   God actualizes a world containing as much moral good as α contains

to show that (1) and (2) are consistent. The essential point of the Free Will Defence is that the creation of a world containing moral good is a co-operative venture; it requires the uncoerced concurrence of significantly free creatures. But then the actualization of a world W containing moral good is not up to God alone; it also depends upon what the significantly free creatures of W would do if God created them and placed them in the situations W contains. Of course it is up to God whether to create free creatures at all; but if he aims to produce moral good, then he must create significantly free creatures upon whose co-operation he must depend. Thus is the power of an omnipotent God limited by the freedom he confers upon his creatures.[19]

9.   GOD'S EXISTENCE AND THE *AMOUNT* OF MORAL EVIL

The world, after all, contains a *great deal* of moral evil; and what we have seen so far is only that God's existence is compatible with *some* evil. Perhaps the atheologian can regroup, arguing that at any rate God's existence is not consistent with the vast amount and variety of evil the universe actually contains. Of course we cannot measure moral evil – that is, we do not have units like volts or pounds or kilowatts so that we could say 'this situation contains about 35 turps of moral evil'. Still we can compare situations in terms of evil; we can see that some contain more moral evil than others. And perhaps the atheologian means to maintain that it is at any rate obvious that God, if omnipotent, could have created a *morally better* world – one containing a better mixture of moral good and evil than α – one, let us say, that contained as much moral good but less moral evil.

But is this really obvious? I do not think so. Possibly this was *not* within God's power, which is all the Free Will Defender needs. We can see this as follows. Of course there are many possible worlds containing as much moral good as α, but less moral evil. Let W^* be any such world. If W^* had been actual, there would have been as much moral good (past, present, and future) as in fact there was, is, and will be; and there would have been less moral evil in all. Now in W^* a certain set of S of essences is instantiated. So to actualize W^*, God would have had to create persons who were the instantiations of these essences. But perhaps one of these essences would have had an unco-operative instantiation. That is, possibly

(35)   There is a member E of S, a state of affairs T, and an action A such that
    (1) E's instantiation freely performs A in W^*,
    (2) T is the largest state of affairs God actualizes in W^*,
and
    (3)   if God had strongly actualized T, E's instantiation would not have performed A.

I say it is possible that (35) is true; but clearly *if* it is, then for reasons by now familiar God could not have actualized W^*. And the fact is it is possible that every morally better world is like W in that God could not have actualized it. For it is possible that for every morally better world there is a member E of S, an action A, and a state of affairs T that meet the conditions laid down in (35). But if so, then (1) is compatible with the existence of as much evil as α does in fact contain.

10.   GOD'S EXISTENCE AND *NATURAL* EVIL

But perhaps the atheologian can regroup once more. What about *natural* evil? Evil that cannot be ascribed to the free actions of human beings? Suffering due to earthquakes, disease, and the like? Is the existence of evil of *this sort* compatible with (1)? Here two lines of thought present themselves. Some people deal creatively with certain kinds of hardship or suffering, so acting that on balance the whole state of affairs is valuable. Perhaps their responses would have been less impressive and the total situations less valuable without the evil. Perhaps some natural evils and some persons are so related that the persons would have produced less moral good if the evils had been absent.[20] But another and more traditional line of thought is pursued by St. Augustine, who attributes much of the evil we find to *Satan*, or to Satan and his cohorts.[21] Satan, so the traditional doctrine goes, is a mighty non-human spirit who, along with many other angels, was created long before God created man. Unlike most of his colleagues, Satan rebelled against God and has since been wreaking whatever havoc he can. The result is natural evil. So the natural evil we find is due to free actions of non-human spirits.

This is a *theodicy*, as opposed to a *defence*.[22] St. Augustine believes that natural evil (except for what can be attributed to God's punishment) is *in fact* to be ascribed to the activity of beings that are free and rational but non-human. The Free Will Defender, on the other hand, need not assert that this is *true*; he says only that it is *possible* (and consistent with (1)). He points to the possibility that natural evil is due to the actions of significantly free but non-human persons. We have noted the possibility that God could not have actualized a world with a better balance of moral good over moral evil than this one displays. Something similar holds here; possibly natural evil is due to the free activity of a set of non-human persons, and perhaps it was not within God's power to create a set of such persons whose free actions produced a greater balance of good over evil. That is to say, it is possible that

(36)   All natural evil is due to the free activity of non-human persons;
       there is a balance of good over evil with respect to the actions of
       these non-human persons; and there is no world God could have
       created which contains a more favourable balance of good over
       evil with respect to the free activity of the non-human persons it
       contains.

Again, it must be emphasized that (36) is not required to be *true*
for the success of the Free Will Defence; it need only be compatible
with (1). And it certainly looks as if it is. If (36) *is* true, furthermore,
then *natural* evil significantly resembles *moral* evil in that, like the latter,
it is the result of the activity of significantly free persons. In fact
both moral and natural evil would then be special cases of what we
might call *broadly moral evil* – evil resulting from the free actions
of personal beings, whether human or not. (Of course there is a
correlative notion of broadly moral good.) To facilitate discussion,
furthermore, let us stipulate that the *turp* is the basic unit of evil
and that there are 10^{13} turps of evil in the actual world; the total
amount of evil (past, present, and future) contained by α is 10^{13}
turps. Given these ideas, we can combine (35) and (36) into one
compendious statement:

(37)   All the evil in the actual world is broadly moral evil; and every
       world that God could have actualized, and that contains as much
       broadly moral good as the actual world displays, contains at least
       10^{13} turps of evil.

Now (37) appears to be consistent with (1) and

(38)   God actualizes a world containing as much broadly moral good as
       the actual world contains.

But (1), (37), and (38) together entail that there is as much evil as α
contains; so (1) is consistent with the proposition that there is as
much evil as α contains. I therefore conclude that the Free Will
Defence successfully rebuts the charge of inconsistency brought against
the theist. If evil is a problem for the believer, it is not that the existence of evil – moral or natural – is inconsistent with the existence of
God.

NOTES

1   Epicurus, for example, as well as David Hume, some of the French
    Encyclopedists, F. H. Bradley, J. McTaggart, J. S. Mill, and many others.
2   'God and Evil', *Philosophical Quarterly*, 10 (1960), 97.
3   'Evil and Omnipotence', *Mind*, 64 (1955), 200.
4   'God and Evil', *Ethics*, 68 (1957–8), 79.
5   *God and Other Minds*, chapter 5.
6   Ibid., chapter 6.
7   Of course it does not follow that if S is free with respect to some of his
    actions, then what he will do is in principle unpredicable or unknowable.
8   This distinction is not very precise (how, exactly, are we to construe
    'results from'?); but perhaps it will serve our present purposes.
9   'Evil And Omnipotence,' p. 209.
10 To say that God could have actualized W suggests that there is some time
    – some past time – such that God could have performed the action of
    actualizing W at that time. Thus it suggests that actualizing a possible
    world requires but a moment or at any rate a limited stretch of time. This
    suggestion must be resisted; perhaps God's actualizing a possible world
    requires an unlimited span of time; perhaps it requires his action at *every*
    time, past, present, and future.
11 Just to simplify matters I shall henceforth take it for granted that *if God
    exists, he is omnipotent* is a necessary truth.
12 See Robert Stalnaker, 'A Theory of Conditionals', in N. Rescher, *Studies
    in Logical Theory* (*American Philosophical Quarterly*, supplementary mono-
    graph, 1968), p. 98.
13 More radically, perhaps there are no such closest worlds at all; perhaps
    for any world including A, there is a closer that also includes it. See David
    Lewis, *Counterfactuals* (Blackwell, 1973), chapter 1, section 1.3. According
    to Lewis, a counterfactual $A \rightarrow B$ is true if and only if either A is
    impossible or some world W in which A and C hold is more similar to
    the actual world than any world in which A and $\bar{C}$ hold. In writing this
    section I have benefited from Lewis's analysis; I am grateful to him for a
    criticism that triggered substantial improvement in the argument of this
    chapter.
14 This argument surfaced in discussion with David Kaplan.
15 The argument form involved here is

$$\frac{\begin{array}{l} A \rightarrow B \\ A\ \&\ B \rightarrow C \end{array}}{\therefore A \rightarrow C}.$$

This form is intuitively valid and valid on both Stalnaker and Lewis semantics.

16 The form of argument involved here, namely

$$\frac{A \rightarrow B}{\therefore (A \mathbin{\&} C \rightarrow B) \, v \, (A \mathbin{\&} \bar{C} \rightarrow B);}$$

is intuitively valid and valid on both Stalnaker and Lewis semantics.

17 I leave as homework the problem of comparing transworld depravity with what Calvinists call 'total depravity'.

18 I.e. every essence entailing *is created by God*.

19 See William Wainwright, 'Freedom and Omnipotence', *Noûs*, 2 (1968), 293–301.

20 As in John Hick's *Soul-making* theodicy; see his *Evil and the God of Love* (London: Macmillan), 1966.

21 See 'The Problem of Free Choice', in *Ancient Christian Writers*, vol. 22 (New York: Paulist/Newman Press), pp. 71ff.; and *Confessions and Enchiridion*, tr. and ed. by Albert C. Outler (Philadelphia: Westminster Press), pp. 341–6.

22 I am indebted to Henry Schuurman for this use of these terms.

PART III

THE EVIDENTIAL PROBLEM OF EVIL

It is one thing for p to be logically consistent with q and another thing entirely for p to make it likely that q is false. That Jones swore he would kill Smith and was seen running away from Smith's house about the time that Smith was murdered is logically consistent with Jones's being entirely innocent of Smith's murder. But it is, of course, evidence against the claim that Jones was entirely innocent of Smith's murder. So too, showing that the existence of all the terrible evils in our world is logically consistent with God's existence does not mean that the existence of all the terrible evils in our world doesn't make it unlikely that God exists. The evidential argument from evil maintains that the evils in our world do make the existence of God unlikely, or makes some hypothesis that precludes the existence of God more likely than the hypothesis that God exists. In a written exchange Rowe argues in support of an evidential argument from evil, while Howard-Snyder and Bergmann argue that the evidential argument from evil fails to establish that it is unlikely that God exists. Rowe's essay is followed by a brief response from Howard-Snyder and Bergmann; and their essay is followed by a brief response from Rowe. In his main essay Rowe asks us to focus on particular instances of horrendous evils and consider the goods we have some conception of, including (according to theism) the greatest possible good a human being can enjoy – eternal life in the loving presence of God. He then argues that an all-powerful, infinitely wise being could easily achieve these goods without having to permit those horrendous evils, and concludes that we are rationally justified in believing that many of the horrendous evils in the world are such that no good at all justifies God in permitting them. But since God exists only if some good or other does justify him in permitting each of these horrendous evils, it is therefore unlikely that God exists.

Howard-Snyder and Bergmann argue in response that Rowe's argument involves an assumption that he has no good reason to accept: that the goods we know of are representative of the goods there are. For clearly an all-knowing being may well know of goods beyond our wildest dreams. Since we don't know of these goods and the conditions of their realization, Howard-Snyder and Bergmann reason that we are in no position to judge how likely it is that there are no goods that justify such a being in permitting all the horrendous evils that we know to exist in our world. They suggest that the only way we would be justified in making that judgment is if we knew that the goods we know of are a representative sample of the goods there are. Since we don't know that, Howard-Snyder and Bergmann conclude that Rowe's argument is inadequate. The replies by Rowe on the one side and Howard-Snyder and Bergmann on the other focus on the issues raised in their original essays.

In his essay, "Statement and Strategy: Rethinking the Evidential Argument from Evil," Schellenberg notes the controversy created by Rowe's premise: "If God exists, then E (the evil of horrific suffering) does not exist, unless there is a good reason for God to permit E." Rowe argues that horrendous evils exist that God would have no good reason to permit. But theists respond that given the paucity of our knowledge in relation to God's, if there is a good reason for God to permit these horrendous evils we have no reason to think we would know it. Thus the burden seems to fall on Rowe to show that if God exists we would likely know the goods that require him to permit all this evil. Schellenberg suggests that the way forward for the evidential argument from evil is to simplify Rowe's original argument by deleting the controversial "unless there is a good reason for God to permit E." By arguing directly from both the awfulness of horrific suffering and the goodness of God for the revised premise, "If God exists, then E (the evil of horrific suffering) does not exist," Schellenberg seeks to place the theist in the role of having to suggest goods that would justify an all-powerful being in permitting horrific suffering. He then critically discusses whether these suggested goods can reasonably be thought to justify God in permitting the evil of horrific suffering.

In his essay on pain and pleasure, Draper argues that what we know about pains and pleasures in our world is a good deal more likely on what he calls "the hypothesis of indifference" (neither the nature nor the condition of sentient beings on earth is the result of benevolent or malevolent actions performed by nonhuman persons) than it is on theism. For, since God would need to have a morally good reason for permitting pain that is biologically useless, we expect that if theism were true there would be a close connection between certain moral goods and biologically useless pains. But no such expectation accompanies the hypothesis of indifference. Similarly, if theism is true we would expect that God would have good reasons for producing pleasure for his creatures even if it is not biologically useful. Whereas, on the hypothesis of indifference we would not expect this. He then argues that our observations concerning the way pains and pleasures are distributed among sentient creatures better confirms the hypothesis of indifference than theism, making it more reasonable (barring a stronger argument for theism than for the hypothesis of indifference, or a plausible theodicy explaining why God might well permit the distribution of pleasure and pain to be as it is) to believe the hypothesis of indifference than to believe theism. In a wide-ranging response Peter van Inwagen endeavors to counter Draper's argument by arguing that the assumption of theism doesn't provide *prima facie* grounds for expecting the distribution of pain and pleasure to be different than it is. Instead, van Inwagen argues that we are in no position to make any judgment as to how likely, or unlikely, it is that our observations about pains and pleasures would be the same, or different, if theism is true. And if that should be so, we cannot conclude that theism is less likely than Draper's hypothesis of indifference. For our not being able to judge how likely, or unlikely, what we know about the distribution of biologically useless pleasure and pain would be if theism is true leaves open the possibility that it is very likely indeed.

Draper's argument, like Rowe's, has generated considerable discussion in the literature on the problem of evil. They, along with the critical responses, serve as a good introduction to the evidential argument from evil.

7

DANIEL HOWARD-SNYDER, MICHAEL BERGMANN, AND WILLIAM L. ROWE

An Exchange on the Problem of Evil

Grounds for Belief Aside, Does Evil Make Atheism More Reasonable than Theism

THE ISSUE

The question assigned to us for discussion is this: "Grounds for belief in God aside, do the evils in our world make atheistic belief more reasonable than theistic belief?" The initial clause in this question is important. For it is one thing to argue that the evils in our world provide such compelling reasons for atheism that the reasons for the existence of God are insufficient to swing the pendulum back in favor of the existence of God, and another thing to argue that, *putting aside* whatever reasons there may be for believing that God exists, the evils that occur in our world make belief in atheism more reasonable than belief in theism. If we put aside grounds for belief in the existence of God, the likelihood that God exists cannot reasonably be assigned any probability beyond .5 – where 1 represents God's existence as certain, and 0 represents certainty that God does not exist. So, if we start from an initial point of God's existence having a likelihood of .5 or less, and *restrict* ourselves to the evidence generated by the enormous amount of horrendous evil that occurs daily in our world, it should strike anyone that the likelihood of God's existence can only go downward from .5.[1] To reach such a judgment is perfectly consistent with holding that once the reasons supportive of the existence of God are brought into the equation the likelihood of God's existence is in fact positive, somewhere between .5 and 1. So, we should not confuse arguing that the negative evidence of evil shows God's existence to be unlikely, *even taking into account* the positive reasons there are to think that God exists, with arguing that *putting aside* the positive reasons there are to think that God exists, the evils that occur in our world make atheistic belief more reasonable than theistic belief. The issue in this discussion is only the latter: Apart from taking into account the positive reasons there are to think that God exists, do the evils that occur in our world make atheistic belief more reasonable than theistic belief? I shall argue that they do.

Before proceeding to argue that point, however, it is important to be clear on what theism is. Theism is the view that there exists an all-powerful, all-knowing, perfectly good being (God). We can call this view *restricted theism*. It is *restricted* in that it does not include any claim that is not entailed by it.[2] So, theism itself does not include any of the following claims: God delivered the ten commandments to Moses, Jesus was the incarnation of God, Muhammad ascended into heaven. These are claims made in specific theistic religions; thus they are a part of an *expanded* form of theism: Judaic theism, Christian theism, or Islamic theism. The importance of not taking theism to include the claims held by only one particular religion among the three major theistic religions of the West is that the inclusion would make theism less likely; for if we identify theism with a particular one among the great theistic religions, then the truth of theism itself is made to depend on all the essential beliefs of that particular theistic religion. The other side of this coin is that philosophers who wish to defend theism ought not to suppose that the assumption of theism entitles them to assume any of the special claims associated with their own particular theistic religion. Since most of the philosophers in the Anglo-American tradition who defend theism are adherents of some version of Christian theism, they should beware of confusing the assumption that theism is true with the altogether different, and less likely assumption, that Christian theism is true.

THE ARGUMENT

Do the evils that occur in our world significantly lower the likelihood of God's existence?[3] Let's begin thinking about this problem by considering a simple argument from the existence of some of the evils in our world to the nonexistence of God.

(1) There exist horrendous evils that an all-powerful, all-knowing, perfectly good being would have no justifying reason to permit.

(2) An all-powerful, all-knowing, perfectly good being would not permit an evil unless he had a justifying reason to permit it.
therefore,

(3) God does not exist.

If theists reject this argument for the nonexistence of God, they must either reject the first premise or the second premise. Most theists accept the second premise, as do nontheists. So, most theists must reject the first premise, holding instead that God has a justifying reason for permitting each and every horrendous evil that occurs. But what would be a justifying reason for God to permit some terrible evil he could prevent? Since an evil is something that by its very nature is bad, God's justifying reason for permitting it would have to include something else – either some outweighing good that, all things considered, he wishes to realize and cannot realize without permitting that evil,[4] or some equal or worse evil that, all things considered, he wishes to prevent and cannot prevent without permitting that evil. And the question we must ask ourselves is whether it is rational for us to believe that all the terrible evils that occur daily in our world are like that? Is it rational to believe that each evil is such that were an all-powerful, all-knowing being to prevent it, he would have to forfeit some outweighing good?[5]

Perhaps it will make the issue before us a bit more concrete if we focus on some examples of terrible evils, rather than just terrible evils in the abstract. Here are two examples:

> A fawn is horribly burned in a forest fire caused by lightning. It lies on the forest floor suffering terribly for five days before death relieves its suffering.

> A five-year-old girl is brutally beaten, raped and strangled in Flint, Michigan on New Year's eve a few years ago.

The theist must believe that for each of these evils there is some greater good to which it leads, a good that an all-powerful being simply could not realize without permitting that evil. But is what the theist believes about these two evils really so? Is there really some great good that an all-powerful being could bring about only by permitting that fawn to be badly burned and to suffer intensely for five long days before death relieves its torment? And is there really some great good that an all-powerful being could bring about only if he permits that little five-year-old girl in Flint, Michigan to be savagely beaten, raped, and strangled? And even if it should somehow be so in these two cases, is it true that *all* the instances of intense human and animal suffering occurring daily in our world lead to greater goods in such a way that even an *all-powerful, all-knowing* being could not have achieved *any* of those goods without permitting the instances of suffering that supposedly lead to them? In light of our knowledge of the scale of human and animal suffering occurring daily in our world, the idea that none of those instances of suffering could have been prevented by an all-powerful being without the loss of a greater good must strike us as an extraordinary idea, quite beyond our belief. And if it does strike us in this way, the first premise of the argument we are considering – There exist evils that an all-powerful, all-knowing perfectly good being would have no justifying reason to permit – is bound to strike us as plausible, something quite likely to be true. But since the second premise is generally agreed to be true, we should then conclude that it is likely that our conclusion is true, that God does not exist.

It is important here to understand two points about the argument just presented. First, the argument is not, nor is it meant to be, a *proof* that God does not exist. To be a *proof* of its conclusion an argument must be such that its conclusion logically follows from its premises and its premises are known with certainty to be true. The argument we are considering meets the first condition, but not the second. The conclusion deductively follows from the two premises, but its first premise is not known with certainty to be true. The claim is only that the first premise is one we are rationally justified in believing to be true. And since our confidence in the truth of the conclusion should not exceed our confidence in the premises from which it follows, the claim is only that the premises provide sufficient rational support for that conclusion. Second, the truth of the first premise does not logically depend on any claim about the two examples of the fawn and the five-year-old girl. The examples are meant to *illustrate* the profound difficulty in really believing that an all-powerful, all-knowing being is incapable of achieving his noble ends without having to permit such horrendous, undeserved suffering. But if there were only a few such examples as these, perhaps it would not be unreasonable to believe that somehow even an infinitely intelligent, all powerful being could not achieve his good ends without permitting them. But, of course, our world is not like that. It is the *enormous amount* of apparently pointless, horrendous suffering occurring daily in our world that grounds the claim in the first premise that there are pointless evils in our world, evils that an all-powerful being could have prevented without forfeiting some outweighing good. But, again, it is not being asserted that the existence of pointless evils is known with certainty, only that it is quite likely that pointless evils occur.

EVALUATING TWO RESPONSES

I

Having looked at a particular argument from evil against theistic belief, we can now consider and critically evaluate two theistic responses to this argument. The first response the theist may put forth goes something like this.

"The first point I want to make is that thus far we have been given no reason at all to think that premise (1) is true. For all you have pointed out is that we don't know what the good is that justifies God in permitting any of these horrendous evils, like the fawn's suffering or the little girl's suffering. But to argue from the fact that we don't know what the good is that justifies God in permitting a certain evil to the conclusion that there is no such good is to engage in a fallacious argument from ignorance: we don't know of any justifying good, therefore there isn't any. So, you haven't really given any good reason at all to think that there are terrible evils for which there are no God-justifying goods. All that you have shown, if you have shown anything, is that if these evils do serve some God-justifying goods, we don't know what they are. And the interesting question to ask about our ignorance of these justifying goods is this: Given that God's mind *infinitely transcends* ours, is it really at all likely that the goods for the sake of which he permits much horrendous suffering will be goods we comprehend? After all, isn't God in relation to us like good, loving parents in relation to their small child? Such parents may permit their very young child to suffer a painful surgical procedure for a good the child simply cannot comprehend. So too, we should expect that if God exists he may permit many instances of human or animal suffering so as to realize goods our minds simply cannot comprehend. And if that is so, the fact that we don't know the goods that justify God in permitting much horrendous suffering cannot really be a reason for thinking he doesn't exist. For it is just what we should expect to be true if he does exist."[6]

What are we to make of this response by the theist? Are we really just arguing from ignorance? Perhaps we can come to see that we are not by first distinguishing between goods we know about (goods within our ken) and goods beyond our ken. Consider the suffering of the five-year-old girl as she was brutally beaten, raped, and strangled on New Year's Eve a few years ago in Flint, Michigan. I believe that no good we know about justifies God in permitting that suffering. By "goods we know about" I *mean* goods that we have some cognitive grasp of, even though we may have no knowledge at all that they have occurred or ever will occur. For example, consider the good of the little girl experiencing complete felicity in the everlasting presence of God. Theists consider this an enormous personal good, perhaps the greatest personal good possible for the little girl. So, even though we don't have a very clear grasp of what this great good involves, and even though we don't know that such a good will ever be actualized, I include the good of her experiencing complete felicity in the everlasting presence of God among *the goods we know about.* Of course, if some good we know about does justify God in permitting her suffering, that good must have already been actualized or be actualized at some point in the future. But the notion of a good we know about extends to many future goods and to goods that never have and never will occur. And what we have good reason to believe is that none of the goods we know about justifies God in permitting the horrendous suffering of that little girl. For with respect to each such good we consider, we have reason to believe either that it isn't good enough to justify God in permitting that evil, or that it could likely be actualized by God without his having to permit the horrendous suffering of that little girl, or that some equal or better good could likely be actualized by God without his having to permit the horrendous suffering of that little girl.

Of course, even granting that we know of many great goods and have reason to think that none of these goods justifies God in permitting the little girl's suffering, there still remains the possibility that some good we cannot even conceive does so. And it is here that the theist may appeal to the analogy between the good parent and God. For we cannot deny that some good the child's mind cannot even conceive may justify the parents in permitting the child to suffer. And by analogy won't the same be true of God in relation to us as his children? Indeed, since the disparity between his mind and ours may greatly exceed that of the good parents' minds to the mind of their child, isn't it likely that the goods that justify him in permitting us to suffer will often be beyond our comprehension? But against this argument from analogy, two points need to be made.

First, although arguments from analogy are rather weak, the analogy in question has some merit if drawn between a good parent and a good deity of considerable but nevertheless *finite* power and knowledge. For, like the good parent, a deity with great but *finite* powers may reasonably believe that he cannot realize some important future good for some of his creatures without permitting a present evil to befall them. And there may be occasions when, like the good parent, the finite deity is simply unable to prevent a dreadful evil befalling his creatures even though there is no good at all served by it. But the theistic God has unlimited power and knowledge. A good parent may be unable to prevent some suffering her child undergoes, or even the child's death from some painful disease. Can we seriously think that an *infinitely* powerful, all-knowing deity was powerless to prevent the horror of Auschwitz? A good parent may see that she cannot realize some important future good for her child without permitting some present evil to befall the child. Can we seriously think that there is some far off future good for the victims of Auschwitz, a good that a deity of *infinite* power and knowledge judged to be worth the horror of Auschwitz, and was powerless to achieve without permitting that horror? Perhaps we can if we turn from reason to faith. But the infinite distance between the God of traditional theism and the good mother with the sick child doesn't, in my judgment, provide human reason with good grounds for thinking that such a being would be powerless to prevent many of the countless, seemingly pointless horrors in our world without losing some goods so distant from us that even the mere conception of them must elude our grasp.

But suppose we do reason from the good-parent analogy to the behavior of an all-powerful, all-knowing, infinitely good deity. I think we shall see that the good-parent analogy leads in a different direction from what its proposers desire. We know that when a good, loving parent permits her child to suffer severely in the present for some outweighing good the child *cannot comprehend*, the loving parent then makes every effort to be consciously present to the child during its period of suffering, giving special assurances of her love, concern, and care. For the child may believe that the parent could prevent her present suffering. So, of course, the parent will be particularly careful to give her child special assurances of her love and concern during this period of permitted suffering for a distant good the child does not understand. And indeed, what we know about good, loving parents, especially when they permit their children to suffer intensely for goods the children cannot comprehend, is that the parents are almost always consciously present to their children during the period of their suffering, giving special assurances of their love and care. So, on the basis of the good-parent analogy, we should infer that it is likely that God too will almost always be consciously present to humans, if not other animals, when he permits them to suffer for goods they cannot comprehend, giving special assurances of his love for them. But since countless numbers of human beings undergo prolonged, horrendous suffering without being consciously aware of God's presence or any special assurances of his love and comfort, we can reasonably infer either that God does not exist or that the good parent analogy is unable to help us understand why God permits all the horrendous suffering that occurs daily in our world.

Our conclusion about the theist's first response is this. The argument in support of premise (1) is not an argument from ignorance. It is an argument from our knowledge of many goods and our reasonable judgment that none of them justifies God in permitting instances of horrendous evil. It is also an argument from our knowledge of what a being of infinite power, intelligence, and goodness would be disposed to do and would be capable of doing. Of course, there remains the logical possibility both that some goods incomprehensible to us justify God in permitting all these horrendous evils that occur daily in our world and that some further goods incomprehensible to us justify God in not being consciously present to so many who endure these horrendous evils. So, we cannot *prove* that premise (1) is true. Nevertheless, the first response of the theist should, I believe, be judged insufficient to defeat our reasons for thinking that premise (1) is probably true.

Before turning to the theist's second response, we should note that some theists will protest the conclusion we've come to about the first response. Here is what such a theist may say:

"Your distinction between goods we know about and goods beyond our ken is well-taken. Moreover, you are right to insist that your argument is not a flagrant example of an argument from ignorance. But there is one quite important point you have failed to establish. It is crucial to your argument that we should expect to know the goods for the sake of which God permits much terrible suffering or, failing such knowledge, be particularly aware of God's presence and his love for us during the period of intense suffering for goods we cannot comprehend. For if we have no good reason to expect to know these goods, or to experience God's presence and love during our suffering, then the fact that we don't know them and don't experience God's presence and love won't really count against the existence of God. And my point is that God may have good reasons (unknown to us) for not revealing these goods to us. And he also may have good reasons (unknown to us) for not disclosing himself and his love during the period when many suffer terribly for goods they cannot comprehend. How are you able to show that this point of mine is just a mere *logical possibility* and not the way things really are? I think you need to treat more seriously than you do the distinct possibility that God's reasons for permitting so much horrendous suffering, and his reasons for not being consciously present to us during our suffering, involve goods that are presently incomprehensible to us."

The theist here raises an important point. Using the theist's own good-parent analogy, I argued that there is reason to think that when we don't know the goods for the sake of which God permits some horrendous suffering, it is probable that, like the good parent, he would provide us, his children, with special assurances of his love and concern. Since many endure horrendous suffering without any such special assurances, I suggested that we have further reason to doubt God's existence. And the theist's only reply can be that there are still further unknown goods that justify God in not being consciously present to us when we endure terrible suffering for goods beyond our ken. And I've allowed that we cannot *prove* that this isn't so. It remains a logical possibility. I've said, however, that we can conclude that premise (1) is probably true. But the theist says that I'm not justified in concluding that premise (1) is probably true unless I give a reason to think it likely that there are no unknown goods that justify God in permitting much horrendous suffering or no unknown goods that justify God in not being present to us when we endure suffering for unknown goods. The theist may grant me that no goods we know of play this justifying role. But before allowing me to conclude that it is probable that premise (1) is true and, therefore, probable that God does not exist, the theist says I must also provide some grounds for thinking that no unknown goods play that justifying role.

Suppose we are unsure whether Smith will be in town this evening. It is just as likely, say, that he will be out of town this evening as that he will be in town. Suppose, however, that we do know that *if* Smith is in town it is just as likely that he will be at the concert this evening as that he won't be. Later we discover that he is not at the concert. I conclude that given this further information (that he is not at the concert) it is now less likely that he's in town than that he's out of town, that given our information that he is not at the concert, it is more likely that he is out of town than that he is in town. I do admit, however, that I haven't done anything to show that he is not actually somewhere else in town. All I've established is that he is not at the concert. I acknowledge that it is logically possible that he's somewhere else in town. Nor do I know for certain that he is not somewhere else in town. All I claim is that it is *probable* that he is not in town, that it is *more likely* that he is not in town than that he is in town. Those who want to believe that Smith is in town may say that I'm not justified in concluding that it is *probable* that he's out of town *unless* I give some reason to think that he is not somewhere else in town. For, they may say, all I've done is exclude one of the places he will be if he is in town. Similarly, the theist says that if God exists then either all the horrendous evils we consider serve unknown goods or some of them serve goods we know of. We might even agree that if God exists it is equally likely that some of the justifying goods will be known to us as that all of the justifying goods will be beyond our ken. After all, when we understand why God may be permitting some terrible evils to occur, those evils will be easier to bear than if we haven't a clue as to why God is permitting them to occur. Suppose we then consider the goods we know of and reasonably conclude that none of them justifies God in permitting any of these horrendous evils that abound in our world. The theist may even agree that this is true. I then say that it is *probable* God does not exist. The theist says I'm not justified in drawing this conclusion *unless* I give some reason to think that no unknown goods justify God in permitting all these terrible evils. For, he says, all I've done is exclude one sort of good (goods known by us) as God's justification for permitting any of these terrible evils. Who is right here?

Let's go back to the claim that it is *probable* that Smith is not in town this evening. How can we be justified in making that claim if we've learned only that he is not at the concert? The reason is this. We originally knew that it was equally likely that he would be out of town as in town. We also agreed that *if* he is in town it is equally likely that he will be at the concert as that he won't be. Once we learn he is not at the concert, the likelihood that he is out of town must increase, as does the likelihood that he is somewhere else in town. But since it was equally likely that he is out of town as in town, if the likelihood that he is out of town goes up it then becomes greater than .5, with the result that it is *probable* that he is not in town.

Turn now to the existence of God and the occurrence of horrendous evils. Either God exists or he does not. Suppose for the moment that like the case of Smith being or not being in town, each of these (God exists, God does not exist) is equally likely on the information we have prior to considering the problem of evil.[7] Consider again the many horrendous evils that we know to occur in our world. Before we examine these evils and consider what sort of goods (known or unknown) justifies God (if he exists) in permitting them, suppose it is as likely that the justifying goods for *some* of these evils are known to us as that the justifying goods for *all* of these evils are unknown to us. We then examine the known goods and those horrendous evils and come to the conclusion that no known good justifies God in permitting *any* of those horrendous evils. That discovery parallels our discovery that Smith is not at the concert. And the result is just the same: it is then more probable than not that God does not exist.

II

The second response the theist can give to the challenge of the problem of evil is the following:

> "It is a mistake to think that the goods for which God permits these horrendous evils are totally beyond our ken. For religious thinkers have developed very plausible *theodicies* that suggest a variety of goods that may well constitute God's reasons for permitting many of the horrendous evils that affect human and animal existence. When we seriously consider these theodicies we can see that we have good reason to think that premise (1) is false. For these theodicies provide us with plausible accounts of what may be God's justifying reasons for permitting the evils that occur in our world."

The theist's first response was to argue both that we have given no reason at all for thinking that premise (1) is true and that our ignorance of many goods that God's mind can comprehend prevents us from being able to establish that premise (1) is probably true. In the second response, the theist proposes to give a good reason for thinking that premise (1) is false. And, of course, to the extent that theodicies do provide a good reason for rejecting premise (1), to that extent the theist will have pointed the way to reconciling the existence of God with the fact that our world contains the horrendous evils that it does. But do these theodicies really succeed in providing a good reason for rejecting premise (1)? I believe they do not. But to demonstrate this we would have to show that these theodicies, taken together, are really unsuccessful in providing what could be God's reasons for permitting the horrendous evils in the world. Although I believe this can be done, I propose here to take just one of these theodicies, the one most commonly appealed to, and show how it fails to provide a good reason for rejecting premise (1). I refer to the *free will theodicy*, a theodicy that has played a central role in defense of theism in the theistic religions of the West.

Developed extensively by St. Augustine (AD 354–430), the free will theodicy proposes to explain all the evils in the world as either directly due to evil acts of human free will or to divine punishment for evil acts of human free will. The basic idea is that rather than create humans so that they behave like automatons, acting rightly of necessity, God created beings who have the power to act well or ill, free either to pursue the good and thereby enjoy God's eternal blessing or to pursue the bad and thereby experience God's punishment. As things turned out, many humans used their free will to turn away from God, freely choosing to do ill rather than good, rejecting God's purpose for their lives. Thus, the evils in the world that are not bad acts of human free will, or their causal effects, are due to God's own acts of punishment for wrongful exercises of human free will.

The cornerstone of this theodicy is that human free will is a good of such enormous value that God is justified in creating humans with free will even if, as Augustine held, God knew in advance of creating them that certain human beings would use their freedom to do ill rather than good, while knowing that others would use their freedom to do only (or mostly) what is good. So, all the horrendous evils occurring daily in our world are either evil acts of free human beings and their causal effects or divine punishments for those acts. And the implication of this theodicy is that the good of human free will justifies God in permitting all these horrendous acts of evil and their causal effects, as well as the other evils resulting from plagues, floods, hurricanes, etc., that are God's ways of punishing us for our evil acts.

While this theodicy may explain some of the evil in our world, it cannot account for the massive amount of human suffering that is not due to human acts of free will. Natural disasters (floods, earthquakes, hurricanes, etc.) bring about enormous amounts of human and animal suffering. But it is obvious that such suffering is not proportionate to the abuses of free will by humans. So, we cannot reasonably think that such disasters are God's way of punishing human free choices to do evil. Second, while being free to do evil may be essential to genuine freedom, no responsible person thinks that the good of human freedom is so great as to require that no steps be taken to prevent some of the more flagrant abuses of free choice that result in massive, undeserved suffering by humans and animals. Any moral person who had power to do so would have intervened to prevent the evil free choices that resulted in the torture and death of six million Jews in the Holocaust. We commonly act to restrict egregious abuses of human freedom that result in massive, undeserved human and animal suffering. Any moral being, including God, if he exists, would likely do the same. And since the free will theodicy is representative of the other attempts to justify God's permission of the horrendous evils in our world, it is reasonably clear that these evils cannot be explained away by appeal to theodicies.

In this essay I have argued that, putting aside whatever reasons there may be to think that the theistic God exists, the facts about evil in our world provide good reason to think that God does not exist. While the argument is only one of probability, it provides a sound basis for an affirmative answer to the question that is the focus of this exchange.

William L. Rowe

NOTES TO "GROUNDS FOR BELIEF ASIDE"

1 At best it can but remain the same. For no reasonable person would argue that all the horrendous evils that occur daily in our world are to be counted as *evidence for* the existence of God.

2 Theism itself does not include the claim that God created a world. For theists hold that God was free not to create a world. They hold that there is a possible world in which God exists but creates nothing at all. What theism may be taken to include is the claim that any contingent things that exist depend for their existence on God's creative act.

3   Portions of the following are drawn from my essay "God and Evil," *The Annual Proceedings of the Center for Philosophic Exchange*, No. 28, 1997–8, 4–15.
4   It could be that the outweighing good cannot be realized by God without his permitting *that* evil or *some other* evil just as bad. But for ease of understanding the fundamental issue I will ignore this complication.
5   To avoid needless complexity, I'll not mention the other possibility; that God permits the evil in question so as to prevent some equal or greater evil.
6   This response has been elegantly developed by Stephen Wykstra in "The Human Obstacle to Evidential Arguments from Suffering: On Avoiding the Evils of 'Appearance,'" *International Journal for Philosophy of Religion* 16 (1984): 73–93. Also see "Evil and the Theistic Hypothesis: A response to Wykstra," *International Journal for Philosophy of Religion* 16 (1984): 95–100.
7   As we noted earlier, given that we are putting aside reasons for the existence of God, the existence of God is, at best, no more likely than is the nonexistence of God.

Reply to Rowe

We will limit our replies to Rowe's chapter to the following three points:[1]

1   Throughout Rowe's chapter, one finds "the theist" rejecting his argument, *and nobody else*. No atheist objects; no agnostic. Just "the theist." This gives the misleading impression that you have to be a theist to reject it, or that only theists reject it, or that nontheists can't reject it, or mustn't, or in fact don't. None of this is true, however. Many intelligent nontheists do not find Rowe's argument persuasive. For example, many agnostics – those who neither believe there is a God nor believe there isn't – reject it for the kinds of reasons we laid out in our chapter. In fact, everything we said there could be said by an agnostic or an atheist.

2   Rowe insists that his atheistic arguments from evil are not arguments from ignorance. Thus, he denies that his arguments depend on noseeum assumptions. We beg to differ. Here are two examples of his depending on a noseeum assumption.

First, he says: "the idea that none of those instances of suffering could have been prevented by an all-powerful being without loss of a greater good must strike us as an extraordinary idea, quite beyond belief."

But if we are in the dark about what goods there are and what omnipotence-constraining connections there are between such goods and the permissions of such evils, how could that idea seem "extra-ordinary…quite beyond belief"? Only if we assume that there probably aren't any such goods or omnipotence-constraining connections if we don't detect any.

Second, Rowe says that each good we know of is such that "we have reason to believe either that it isn't good enough to justify God in permitting that evil, or that it could likely be actualized by God without his having to permit the horrendous suffering [in question]." But how could we have a reason to believe "God could obtain the goods we know of without permitting the evils we see" if we are in the dark about what omnipotence-constraining connections there are between such goods and the permission of such evils? Here too Rowe seems to be assuming that there probably are no such connections if we don't detect any.

3   Rowe considers one last attempt to defend what he calls "the first response" to his argument from evil. In his reply to this last attempt, he uses the example of Smith and the concert. Let T signify "Smith is in town this evening" and let C signify "Smith is at the concert this evening." We can then state Rowe's example as follows:

- $Pr(T/k) = 0.5$
- $Pr(\text{not-}T/k) = 0.5$
- $Pr(C/T\&k) = 0.5$
- $Pr(\text{not-}C/T\&k) = 0.5.$[2]

He sensibly concludes that if we know these things and then learn that not-C, we may conclude that T is less likely than not-T. So far, so good.[3] Next, Rowe tries to draw the parallel with the case of theism and evil. Let G signify "God exists" and let A signify "Some good we know of justifies God in permitting all the horrendous evils we see." We can, says Rowe, state the parallel case like this:

- $Pr(G/k) = 0.5$
- $Pr(\text{not-}G/k) = 0.5$
- $Pr(A/G\&k) = 0.5$
- $Pr(\text{not-}A/G\&k) = 0.5$

Again, he sensibly concludes that if we know these things and then learn that not-A we may conclude that G is less likely than not-G.[4]

What we've been given here is an easily digestible version of Rowe's new Bayesian argument from evil, the one we discussed in section 4 of our chapter. Our response is essentially the same as the response we gave there.

The first thing to notice is that Rowe's argument about Smith's whereabouts could not get off the ground unless Pr(not-C/T&k) is not high. For if it is extremely high, then not-C will not significantly lower the likelihood of T. (If Pr(not-C/T&k) is as high as 1, not-C won't lower the likelihood of T at all!) In other words, if not-C is just what you would expect if T were true, then learning not-C won't make T less likely than it would otherwise be.

For similar reasons, Rowe's parallel argument about God and evil doesn't have a chance unless Pr(not-A/G&k) is not high. Rowe tries to avoid this problem by simply *asserting* that this latter probability is equal to 0.5. But why think that? In fact, why think Pr(not-A/G&k) isn't extremely high, perhaps as high as 1? These questions will be familiar to those who have read our chapter. For not-A (i.e., no good we know of justifies God in permitting all the horrendous evils we see) is a lot like P from our paper (i.e., no good we know of justifies God in permitting E1 and E2). And just as we are in no position to tell that Pr(P/G&k) is high or that it is low or that it is middling, so also we are in no position to tell that Pr(not-A/G&k) is high or that it is low or that it is middling. Rowe's argument simply takes for granted that we are in a position to assign a value of 0.5 here when in fact we are in the dark about what probability to assign.

Michael Bergmann and Daniel Howard-Snyder

NOTES TO "REPLY TO ROWE"

1   An additional point that we haven't the space to develop is this. Rowe makes it clear, in the paragraph following his introduction of premise 2, that that premise should be understood as follows:

- An all-powerful, all-knowing, perfectly good being would prevent the occurrence of any terrible evil he could, unless he could not do so without thereby losing some greater good or permitting some evil equally bad or worse.

But this implies that there is a minimum amount of terrible evil that God must permit in order for the greater goods involved in his purposes to be secured. For a persuasive objection to that implication, see Peter van Inwagen's "The Problem of Evil, the Problem of Air, and the Problem of Silence," *Philosophical Perspectives* 5 (1991), esp. 64, n. 11, and his "The Magnitude, Duration, and Distribution of Evil: A Theodicy," *Philosophical Topics* (1988), 67–8.

2   On p. 150 of our chapter we explain our use of the symbol "k" and the notation "Pr(x/y)".

3   The idea here seems to be that since not-T entails not-C, we know that Pr(not-C/not-T&k) = 1 and that Pr(C/not-T&k) = 0. So we know that Pr(not-C/not-T&k) > Pr(not-C/T&k). This, I take it, is why Rowe concludes that learning not-C makes T less likely than not-T.

4   Rowe is assuming that just as not-T entails not-C, so also not-G entails not-A.

Grounds for Belief in God Aside, Does Evil Make Atheism More Reasonable than Theism?

Many people deny that evil makes belief in atheism more reasonable for us than belief in theism. After all, they say, the grounds for belief in God are much better than the evidence for atheism, including the evidence provided by evil. We will not join their ranks on this occasion. Rather, we wish to consider the proposition that, setting aside grounds for belief in God and relying only on the background knowledge shared in common by nontheists and theists, evil makes belief in atheism more reasonable for us than belief in theism. Our aim is to argue against this proposition. We recognize that in doing so, we face a formidable challenge. It's one thing to say that evil presents a reason for atheism that is, ultimately, overridden by arguments for theism. It's another to say that it doesn't so much as provide us with a reason for atheism in the first place. In order to make this latter claim seem initially more plausible, consider the apparent design of the mammalian eye or the apparent fine-tuning of the universe to support life. These are often proposed as reasons to believe in theism. Critics commonly argue *not* merely that these supposed reasons for theism are overridden by arguments for atheism but *rather* that they aren't good reasons for theism in the first place. Our parallel proposal with respect to evil and atheism is, initially at least, no less plausible than this proposal with respect to apparent design and theism.

We begin by laying out what we will refer to as "the basic argument" for the conclusion that *grounds for belief in God aside, evil does not make belief in atheism more reasonable for us than belief in theism*:

I.   Grounds for belief in God aside, evil makes belief in atheism more reasonable for us than belief in theism only if somebody has a good argument that displays how evil makes atheism more likely than theism.

II.   Nobody has a good argument that displays how evil makes atheism more likely than theism.

III.   So, grounds for belief in God aside, evil does not make belief in atheism more reasonable for us than belief in theism. (from I & II)

Before we get down to work, we need to address several preliminary questions.

1   PRELIMINARY QUESTIONS

What do we mean by "a good argument" here? We have nothing out of the ordinary in mind. A good argument conforms to the rules of logic, none of its premise is obviously false, and there are other standards as well. But for our purposes, it is important to single out one more *minimal standard*, namely:

- Every premise, inference, and assumption on which the argument depends must be more reasonable for us to affirm than to refrain from affirming.

The proponent of the basic argument says that nobody has a good argument that displays how evil makes atheism more likely than theism because this minimal standard has not been satisfied.

Now, how can we tell that nobody has a good argument of the sort in question? While some have argued that there *couldn't* be such an argument, we think that a more promising strategy is to consider one by one each argument from evil, laboriously checking whether every premise, assumption, and inference is more reasonable to affirm than to refrain from affirming. If every argument written by recognized authorities on the topic were to have a premise, inference, or assumption that failed to pass the test, then we'd have pretty good reason to think that nobody has an argument of the sort in question. Unfortunately, to complete the work this strategy requires would take a book. So we must rest content in this chapter with only a start at undertaking it.

But which arguments should we focus on here? It would be uncharitable to focus on lousy arguments. We will focus on two, both of which are recognizably identified with our friend and esteemed colleague – who also happens to be the most frequently anthologized proponent of an affirmative answer to our title question – William Rowe.

2   NOSEEUM ARGUMENTS

We begin with an analogy introduced to show how our minimal standard for a good argument works and to develop an important principle for assessing a certain popular kind of argument from evil.

Suppose we asked a friend who claimed that there is no extraterrestrial life why he thought that, and he responded like this: "I don't have any way to *prove* that there is none. I am in no position to do that. But it is reasonable to think there is none. After all, so far as we can tell, there isn't any. We've never detected any other life-forms, nor have we received any signals or codes from distant galaxies – and we've been searching pretty hard. While this doesn't add up to proof, surely it makes it *more* likely that there is no extraterrestrial life than that there is, even *significantly* more likely." What should we make of our friend's reasoning?

2.1   *Noseeum arguments in general*

Well, notice first of all that he argued for his claim like this:

(a)   So far as we can tell (detect), there is no extraterrestrial life.
        So, it is more likely than not (perhaps significantly so) that
(b)   There is no extraterrestrial life.

This argument follows a general pattern:

So far as we can tell (detect), there is no x.
        So, it is more likely than not (perhaps significantly so) that
There is no x.

Let's call this general pattern a *no-see-um* argument: we don't see um, so they ain't there![1]

Notice that our friend did not claim that (a) *guarantees* the truth of (b). He merely claimed that it makes it *more likely than its denial*, perhaps quite a bit more. So we can't just retort that there *could be* extraterrestrial life even if we don't detect any. That's true, but it's irrelevant. What is relevant, however, is that his noseeum argument relies on a certain assumption. To see it, consider some other noseeum arguments.

Suppose that, after rummaging around carefully in your fridge, you can't find a carton of milk. Naturally enough, you infer that there isn't one there. Or suppose that, on viewing a chess match between two novices, Kasparov says to himself, "So far as I can tell, there is no way for John to get out of check," and then infers that there is no way. These are clear cases in which the noseeum premise makes the conclusion more likely than its denial – significantly more likely.[2] On the other hand, suppose that, looking at a distant garden, so far as we can see, there are no slugs there. Should we infer that it is more likely that there are no slugs in the garden than that there are? Or imagine listening to the best physicists in the world discussing the mathematics used to describe quantum phenomena; so far as we can tell, they don't make any sense at all. Should we infer from this that it is more likely that they don't make any sense than that they do? Clearly not. So what accounts for the difference between these two pairs of cases?

Notice that it is more likely than not that you would see a milk jug in the fridge if one were there, and it is more likely than not that Kasparov would see a way out of check if there were one. That's because you and Kasparov have what it takes to discern the sorts of things in question. On the other hand, it is not more likely than not that we would see a slug in a distant garden if there were one there; and it is not more likely than not that we'd be able to understand quantum mathematics if it were understandable. That's because we don't have what it takes to discern the sorts of things in question, in those circumstances with the cognitive equipment we possess. A general principle about noseeum arguments is lurking here, namely:

- A noseeum premise makes its conclusion more likely than not only if *more likely than not we'd detect (see, discern) the item in question if it existed.*

Call the italicized portion *The Noseeum Assumption*. Anybody who uses a noseeum argument makes a noseeum assumption of this form. Let's return to our friend, the antiextraterrestrialist.

2.2 *The antiextraterrestrialist's noseeum assumption*

He gave a noseeum argument and thereby made a noseeum assumption, namely this one:

● More likely than not we'd detect extraterrestrial life-forms if there were any.

Our minimal standard for a good argument implies that his noseeum argument is a good argument only if it is more reasonable to *affirm* his noseeum assumption than to *refrain* from affirming it. Is it more reasonable to do that?

Clearly not. After all, if there were extraterrestrial life forms, how likely is it that some of them would be intelligent enough to attempt contact? And of those who are intelligent enough, how likely is it that any would care about it? And of those who are intelligent enough and care about it, how likely is it that they would have the means at their disposal to try? And of those with the intelligence, the desire, and the means, how likely is it that they would succeed? Nobody has a very good idea how to answer these questions. We can't begin to say with even the most minimal degree of confidence that the probabilities are low, or that they are middling, or that they are high. We just don't have enough to go on. For this reason we should be *in doubt* about whether *more likely than not we'd detect extraterrestrial life-forms if there were any*. So it is *not* more reasonable to affirm our friend's noseeum assumption than to refrain from affirming it.

It is important to see that we are not saying that it is highly likely that we would *not* discern any extraterrestrial life-forms; nor are we saying that it is more likely that we would not detect extraterrestrial life-forms than that we would. Rather, our point is that it is not reasonable for us to make any judgment about the probability of our detecting extraterrestrial life-forms if there were any. That's all it takes for it *not* to be more reasonable for us to affirm than to refrain from affirming this noseeum assumption.

3 NOSEEUM ARGUMENTS FROM EVIL

In this section, we will apply the main points of section 2 to some popular noseeum arguments from evil.

3.1 Standard noseeum arguments from evil

Here's a standard argument from evil:

(1) There is no reason that would justify God in permitting certain instances of intense suffering.
(2) If God exists, then there is a reason that would justify God in permitting every instance of intense suffering.
(3) So, God does not exist.

From the vantage of the title question, our main concern is whether noseeum arguments in defense of premise 1 make it more reasonable for us to believe it than to refrain from believing it. Let's look into the matter closely.[3]

Consider the case of a fawn, trapped in a forest fire occasioned by lightning, who suffers for several days before dying (call this case "E1"). Or consider the case of the five-year-old girl from Flint, Michigan who, on January 1, 1986, was raped, severely beaten, and strangled to death by her mother's boyfriend (call this case "E2"). How could a God who loved this fawn and this child and who had the power to prevent their suffering permit them to suffer so horribly? Of course, God might permit E1 and E2 if doing so is necessary to achieve for the fawn and the child (or, perhaps, someone else) some benefit whose goodness outweighs the badness of their suffering. But what could the benefit be? When we try to answer that question, we draw a blank. We just can't think of a benefit that is both sufficiently great to outweigh the badness of their suffering and such that God can't obtain it without permitting E1 and E2. So far as we can tell, there isn't one. While this doesn't *prove* that there is no reason, surely, says the atheistic objector, it makes it more likely than not that there is none, perhaps even a good deal more likely.

In short, the noseeum argument here goes like this:

(1a)   So far as we can tell, there is no reason that would justify God in permitting E1 and E2.
        So it is more likely than not that
(1b)   There is no reason that would justify God in permitting E1 and E2.
        So it is more likely than not that
(1)   There is no reason that would justify God in permitting certain instances of intense suffering.

Other noseeum arguments from evil are just like this except that they focus on the *amount* of suffering rather than on particular instances of intense suffering or horrific evil. What should we make of these noseeum arguments? Many people think that we *do* see how God would be justified in permitting E1 and E2, that we *do* see how God would be justified in permitting so much rather than a lot less intense suffering. While this strategy is not wholly without merit, we will not pursue it here.[4] Rather, we begin by noting that each of these noseeum arguments from evil makes a noseeum assumption, specifically:

• More likely than not we'd detect a reason that would justify God in permitting ... if there were one,

where the ellipsis is filled in with either "E1 and E2" or "so much intense suffering rather than a lot less" or "so much intense suffering rather than just a little less." Nothing we have to say hangs on the difference, so we'll focus on the first. Call it the *Atheist's Noseeum Assumption*. Is it more reasonable to affirm it than to refrain from affirming it?

3.2   Considerations against the atheist's noseeum assumption

Several considerations suggest that it is *not* more reasonable to affirm than to refrain from affirming the Atheist's Noseeum Assumption.[5]

1   Two aspects of the atheist's noseeum inference should make us wary. First, they take "the insights attainable by finite, fallible human beings as an adequate indication of what is available in the way of reasons to an omniscient, omnipotent being." But this is like supposing that when you are confronted with the activity or productions of a master in a field in which you have little expertise, it is reasonable for you to draw inferences about the quality of her work just because you "don't get it." You've taken a year of high-school physics. You're faced with some theory about quantum phenomena and you can't make heads or tails of it. Certainly it is unreasonable for you to assume that more likely than not you'd be able to make sense of it. Similarly for other areas of expertise: painting, architectural design, chess, music, and so on. Second, the atheist's noseeum inference "involves trying to determine whether there is a so-and-so in a territory the extent and composition of which is largely unknown to us." It is like someone who is culturally and geographically isolated supposing that if there were something on earth beyond her forest, more likely than not she'd discern it. It is like a physicist supposing that if there were something beyond the temporal bounds of the universe, more likely than not she'd know about it (where those bounds are the big bang and the final crunch).

All these analogies and others like them point in the same direction: we should be of two minds about affirming the claim that more likely than not we'd be aware of some reason that would justify God in permitting E1 and E2, if there were one.

2 Knowledge has progressed in a variety of fields of enquiry, especially the physical sciences. The periodic discovery of previously unknown aspects of reality strongly suggests that there will be further progress of a similar sort. Since future progress implies present ignorance, it wouldn't be surprising if there is much we are currently ignorant of. Now, what we have to go on in charting the progress of the discovery of fundamental goods (like freedom, love, and justice) by our ancestors is meager to say the least. Indeed, given the scant archeological evidence we have, and given paleontological evidence regarding the evolutionary development of the human brain, it would not be surprising at all that humans discovered various fundamental goods over tens of thousands of years dotted by several millennia-long gaps in which nothing was discovered. Hence, given what we have to go on, it would not be surprising if there has been the sort of periodic progress that strongly suggests that there remain goods to be discovered. Thus it would not be surprising if there are goods of which we are ignorant, goods of which God – in His omniscience – would not be ignorant.

3.3   Considerations in favor of the Atheist's Noseeum Assumption

So there is good reason to be in doubt about the Atheist's Noseeum Assumption. In addition, there are good reasons to reject the considerations that have been offered in its favor.

Consider, for example, the supposed fact that for thousands of years we have not discovered any new fundamental goods in addition to the old standbys – friendship, pleasure, freedom, knowledge, etc. One might think that the best explanation of this fact is that there are no new fundamental goods to be discovered. Hence, the argument goes, our inability to think of a reason that would justify God in permitting E1 and E2 makes it likely that there is no such reason.[6] But this ignores the live possibility that, due to our cognitive limitations, we are (permanently or at least currently) unable to discover certain of the fundamental goods there are. And we have no reason to think this "cognitive limitation" hypothesis is a worse explanation of our lack of discovery than the hypothesis that there are no new goods to be discovered.

Others claim that if we confess skepticism about the Atheist's Noseeum Assumption, then we'll have to do the same thing in other areas as well, resulting in excessive and unpalatable skepticism in those other areas. They ask us to consider claims like these:

(1)   The earth is more than 100 years old.
(2)   You are not constantly dreaming.
(3)   There is no reason that justified Hitler in conducting the Holocaust.

They say that since doubts about (1)–(3) are unreasonable, excessive, and unpalatable, so is doubt about the Atheist's Noseeum Assumption.[7] What should we make of this argument?

It seems eminently sensible insofar as it recommends that we be consistent in our skepticism rather than apply it only when doing so serves our agenda. And we agree that doubts about (1)–(3) are unreasonable. But our main concern is whether the comparison is apt. Most of us think that doubts about (1)–(3) are unreasonable because we're pretty sure that we have what it takes to believe these things reasonably even if we can't say exactly how and even though we don't have a knockdown argument for them. Do any of us, however, have even a modicum of assurance that we've got what it takes to believe reasonably that there is no reason outside our ken that would justify God in permitting E1 and E2? Think of it like this: To be in doubt about the Atheist's Noseeum Assumption involves being in doubt about whether there is a reason outside our ken that would justify God in permitting E1 and E2. Is being in doubt about whether there is such a reason like being in doubt about (1)–(3) – unreasonable, excessive, unpalatable, a bit wacky, over the top? Or is it more like being in doubt about these three claims, claims none of us is in a position to make reasonably?

(4) There is no extraterrestrial life.
(5) There will be no further developments in science as radical as quantum mechanics.
(6) There is no atheistic explanation outside our ken for the apparent fine-tuning of the universe to support life.

In light of the considerations mentioned in section 3.2 (and others like them), we submit that doubts about whether there is a God-justifying reason outside our ken are more like doubts about (4)–(6) than like doubts about (1)–(3). We suggest, therefore, that since doubts about (4)–(6) are sensible, sane, fitting, reasonable, and otherwise in accordance with good mental hygiene, so are doubts about the Atheist's Noseeum Assumption.

It might seem that if we're going to be skeptical about the Atheist's Noseeum Assumption, then we're going to have to be skeptical about reasoning about God altogether. By our lights, that would be an unhappy consequence of our argument. Fortunately, however, we don't need to go that far. Our arguments support agnosticism only about what reasons there are that would justify God in permitting E1 and E2, or more generally the horrific, undeserved suffering in our world. Such limited skepticism need not extend to every argument for theism or to all reflection on the nature of God.

3.4   Summing up

The Atheist's Noseeum Assumption says that more likely than not we'd see a God-justifying reason if there were one. We have argued that it is not reasonable to accept it. We aren't saying that it is highly likely that we would *not* see a reason; nor are we saying that our not seeing a reason is more likely than our seeing a reason. Rather, given the considerations mentioned in sections 3.2 and 3.3, we're saying that it is not more reasonable to affirm than to refrain from affirming the Atheist's Noseeum Assumption. In light of the minimal standard for a good argument mentioned in section 1, this is enough to show that arguments from evil depending on the Atheist's Noseeum Assumption are not good arguments.

4   ROWE'S NEW BAYESIAN ARGUMENT

Rowe has come to recognize that noseeum arguments have some of the weaknesses discussed above. And, presumably because of this recognition, he has recently abandoned them in favor of another argument relying on Bayes' Theorem, a fundamental principle used in probabilistic reasoning.[8] In this new Bayesian argument, he aims to show that

P.   No good we know of justifies God in permitting E1 and E2

provides us with a good reason for atheism – i.e., for not-G (where "G" is theism). We will note some flaws in this argument which, despite Rowe's efforts, include its dependence on noseeum assumptions.

The argument goes like this. Let "k" be the background knowledge shared in common by nontheists and theists alike and let "Pr(x/y)" refer to the probability of x given the assumption that y is true (this probability will be a number greater than or equal to 0 and less than or equal to 1). According to Bayes' Theorem:

$$\frac{Pr(G/P\&k)}{Pr(G/k)} = \frac{Pr(P/G\&k)}{Pr(P/k)}.$$

(The rough idea is that P makes G less likely than it would otherwise be – i.e., $Pr(G/P\&k) < Pr(G/k)$ – only if G makes P less likely than it would otherwise be.) A quick perusal of this equation shows us that if $Pr(P/G\&k) < Pr(P/k)$, then $Pr(G/P\&k) < Pr(G/k)$. And if $Pr(G/P\&k) < Pr(G/k)$, then, as I said, P makes G less likely than it would otherwise be, i.e., P gives us a reason for atheism. Thus, if Rowe can show that $Pr(P/G\&k) < Pr(P/k)$, it looks like he will have established his conclusion.

Rowe thinks he can show that $Pr(P/G\&k) < Pr(P/k)$. We don't have the space to lay out his argument in any detail. But, as he acknowledges, his argument assumes that $Pr(P/G\&k)$ is less than 1. For if $Pr(P/G\&k)$ were equal to 1, it would be impossible for $Pr(P/G\&k)$ to be less than $Pr(P/k)$ (since 1 is as high as probabilities go). Furthermore, if $Pr(P/G\&k)$ were only very slightly less than 1, then the right-hand side of the above equation would be equal to some number very slightly less than 1, such as 0.95. And of course the left side will be equal to exactly the same number, which means that $Pr(G/P\&k)$ could be only slightly less than Pr(G/k). But that would mean that P provides us with only a very negligible reason for atheism instead of a moderate or good reason for atheism. So an important question arises: why should we suppose that Pr(P/G&k) is not extremely high, perhaps even as high as 1?

As it turns out, Rowe doesn't answer this question. Instead, he argues that we have no good reason for thinking that Pr(P/G&k) is high.[9] But this isn't enough. Even if we have no good reason for thinking it *is* high, that doesn't mean we have good reason for thinking that it is *not* extremely high. So our question remains.

The truth is that our question is enormously difficult to answer. In fact, by our lights, we presently have no good reason to think that Pr(P/G&k) is not extremely high, perhaps even as high as 1. We just aren't in a good position to judge that Pr(P/G&k) is low, or that it is middling or that it is high. We should shrug our shoulders and admit that we don't have enough to go on here. So Rowe's new Bayesian argument is (at best) incomplete because he hasn't given us a reason for thinking that Pr(P/G&k) isn't high.

There are two *further* troubles with his argument. The first additional trouble is that in order to give us a reason for thinking that Pr(P/G&k) isn't high, Rowe must explain why it isn't highly *un*likely, given G and k, that we would be aware of the goods that justify the permission of E1 and E2. Unfortunately, many of the candidate reasons that come to mind here depend on illegitimate noseeum assumptions. For example, Rowe argues that if we were *not* aware of the goods that justify the permission of E1 and E2, it is likely that we would be given comforting words from God telling us that he has reasons for such permission – reasons that are beyond our ken. But k includes the knowledge that very often we lack such comforting communication – that we experience divine silence instead. Thus, given G and k, Rowe thinks it is likely that we *would* know of the goods justifying permission of E1 and E2.[10]

But notice that this argument depends on the assumption that:

- If God exists and the goods that justify permission of E1 and E2 are beyond our ken, then it is unlikely that we would experience divine silence.

The problem with this assumption is that it takes for granted that it is unlikely that there is a good that justifies divine silence in the face of evils like E1 and E2. But what reason do we have for thinking *that* unlikely? We can't rely on our inability to discern such a good. To do so would be to depend on a noseeum assumption – one that is illegitimate in ways analogous to those described in sections 3.2 and 3.3.

The second additional problem with Rowe's new Bayesian argument is that he presumes (as he does in his noseeum argument) that we reasonably believe that

>   P.   No good we know of justifies God in permitting E1 and E2.

But is that right? Let's focus on E2. Consider the good of both the little girl and her murderer living together completely reconciled (which involves genuine and deep repentance on the part of the murderer and genuine and deep forgiveness on the part of the little girl) and enjoying eternal felicity in the presence of God. That is a possible good we know of (which isn't to say we know it will obtain). Is it reasonable for us to affirm that *that* good doesn't justify God in permitting E2? No. We aren't in a position to judge that its goodness doesn't outweigh the evil of E2. Nor are we in a position to determine that it (or something like it) doesn't require the permission of E2 (or something as bad or worse). For it is not only our knowledge of what possible goods there are that may be limited. Our knowledge of the logical (i.e., omnipotence-constraining) connections between the obtaining of certain goods and the permission of evils like E2 might also be limited (it wouldn't be the least bit surprising if it were). Just as we are in the dark about whether known goods are representative of the goods there are, so also we are in the dark about whether the omnipotence-constraining connections we know of are representative of the omnipotence- constraining connections there are. Consequently, our inability to discern such a connection doesn't give us a good reason to think there is none. Likewise, the fact that we can't intelligently compare the magnitude of the good mentioned above with the magnitude of E2 doesn't give us a good reason for thinking the former does not outweigh the latter. Thus, even the acceptance of P seems to depend on our making certain questionable noseeum assumptions.[11]

5   CONCLUSION

We've raised some serious questions about explicit noseeum arguments from evil. And we've pointed out that Rowe's new Bayesian argument is incomplete, and that certain obvious attempts to complete it (as well as the acceptance of P itself) seem to depend, implicitly, on questionable noseeum assumptions. But we haven't shown that nobody has a good argument from evil. To show that we would have to consider other arguments in the literature and other ways to complete Rowe's Bayesian argument or to support P. In closing, we'll mention briefly two arguments that seem to refrain from depending on noseeum assumptions and which deserve serious reflection.

First, Paul Draper argues that atheism explains the actual pattern of pain and pleasure in the world better than theism does. The focus here is not on our inability to see a justifying reason but on our supposed ability to see that an atheistic explanation is superior to a theistic one.[12] Second, Michael Tooley argues that since

1 Permission of suffering is justified only if it is, in some way, for the sake of the sufferer

and

2 Animal suffering in cases like E1 cannot benefit the sufferer

there is suffering whose permission is unjustified and, hence, there is no God.[13] Notice that this argument does not depend on an inference from known goods to unknown goods. Instead, it takes for granted that we know a general moral principle (i.e., premise 1) which, together with certain information we supposedly have about animal capacities, enables us to make a generalization about *all* the goods there are (i.e., that none of them − even the ones we don't know of − could justify the permission of E1).

Draper's argument has received considerable discussion in the literature (much of which suggests that it doesn't satisfy the minimal standard for a good argument identified in section 1).[14] Tooley's has received virtually none. So let's ask ourselves, briefly: Are there any considerations that would lead us to think *Tooley's* argument fails to satisfy our minimal standard? That's hard to say. But here are some pertinent questions. First, regarding premise 1: Is this a true general moral principle?[15] Can the state be justified in confiscating the land and home of one its citizens against her will in order to construct an irrigation canal required for the survival of many of its other citizens *provided it supplies compensation?* For that matter, is compensation even necessary? What if the state lacks the resources to supply compensation? Are these considerations about a state and its citizens relevant to our present worries about God and his suffering creatures? I.e., could *God* be constrained (by the limits of logical possibility) in achieving his purposes in ways analogous to those in which the state is constrained? Regarding premise 2 (according to which dying fawns *can't* benefit from their final moments of suffering): Must the sufferer be able to appreciate fully (or even partially) the sense in which he or she benefits from the suffering?[16] People take seriously the idea that humans (even the severely mentally handicapped) can experience post-mortem goods – are we right not to take this possibility seriously with respect to animals?

Other arguments from evil deserve serious consideration before anyone can claim that the strategy recommended at the outset of this chapter is successful. We have only pointed the way toward a more extensive defense of it.[17]

Daniel Howard-Snyder and Michael Bergmann

NOTES TO "GROUNDS FOR BELIEF IN GOD ASIDE"

1   The "noseeum" lingo is Stephen Wykstra's. See his "Rowe's Noseeum Arguments from Evil," in Daniel Howard-Snyder (ed.), *The Evidential Argument from Evil* (Bloomington, Indiana: Indiana University Press, 1996).

2   Another case of legitimate reliance on a noseeum premise is in the strategy recommended in the second to last paragraph of section 1.

3   The noseeum arguments we mention in this section are simplified versions of arguments in Rowe's work, especially his classic essay, "The Problem of Evil and Some Varieties of Atheism," collected in *The Evidential Argument from Evil*.

4   This strategy, often called "giving a *theodicy*," has a venerable history. For literature on the topic, as well as other relevant issues, see Barry Whitney, *Theodicy: An Annotated Bibliography, 1960–1991* (Bowling Green, Ohio: Philosophy Documentation Center, 1998), second edition, as well as the bibliographies in Michael Peterson (editor), *The Problem of Evil* (Notre Dame, Indiana: University of Notre Dame Press, 1992) and *The Evidential Argument from Evil*.

5   The considerations we mention here are developed by William Alston. The first is in his "Some (Temporarily) Final Thoughts on Evidential Arguments from Evil," in *The Evidential Argument from Evil*, pp. 316–19. The second is in his "The Inductive Argument Evil and the Human Cognitive Condition," in *The Evidential Argument from Evil*, p. 109.

6   See Michael Tooley, "The Argument from Evil," *Philosophical Perspectives* (1991): 111–16.
7   Richard Gale, "Some Difficulties in Theistic Treatments of Evil," in *The Evidential Argument from Evil*, pp. 208–9; Bruce Russell, "Defenseless," in *The Evidential Argument from Evil*, pp. 196–98; Theodore Drange, *Nonbelief and Evil* (Amherst, New York: Prometheus, 1998), p. 207.
8   "The Evidential Argument from Evil: A Second Look," in *The Evidential Argument from Evil*.
9   "The Evidential Argument from Evil: A Second Look," pp. 274–6.
10 See Rowe's "Evidential Argument from Evil: A Second Look," p. 276. Rowe himself does *not* try to use this argument to show that Pr(P/G&k) is not high.
11 For more on the points of this section, see Michael Bergmann, "Skeptical Theism and Rowe's New Evidential Argument from Evil" (forthcoming in *Noûs*).
12 See Draper, "Pain and Pleasure: An Evidential Problem for Theists," collected in *The Evidential Argument from Evil*.
13 See "The Argument from Evil," pp. 110–11.
14 See both essays by Peter van Inwagen, both essays by Draper, the second contribution by Alvin Plantinga and Alston's concluding paper in *The Evidential Argument from Evil*. See also Howard-Snyder, "Theism, the Hypothesis of Indifference, and the Biological Role of Pain and Pleasure," *Faith and Philosophy* (1994).
15 For more on this question, see van Inwagen, "The Magnitude, Duration, and Distribution of Evil: A Theodicy," in *God, Knowledge, and Mystery* (Ithaca, New York: Cornell University Press, 1995), pp. 121–2, and Alston, "The Inductive Argument from Evil," pp. 111–12.
16 See Alston, "The Inductive Argument from Evil," p. 108.
17 Thanks to William Alston, Andrew Cortens, Del Kiernan-Lewis, Michael Murray and Timothy O'Connor for comments on an earlier draft of this essay.

Reply to Howard-Snyder and Bergmann

My friends, Dan Howard-Snyder and Mike Bergmann, think that the enormous amount of seemingly pointless, horrendous evil occurring daily in our world gives us no good reason at all to think it unlikely that God exists. For, on the assumption that God exists, they believe we have no good reason to think it probable either that there would be any less horrendous evil or that God would help us understand what some of the justifying goods are that he is powerless to bring about without permitting all this horrendous evil. In support of their view they liken my argument for the probable nonexistence of God to the reasoning of someone who concludes that there is probably no extraterrestrial life because we don't detect any communications from extraterrestrials. I believe they are right to reject the inference to the likely nonexistence of extraterrestrials from our failure to detect communications from them. For, as they point out, we have no good reason to think that extraterrestrials would know that we exist, or would care about us enough to want to communicate with us, or would have anything like sufficient power and knowledge to devise a way to communicate with us. So, given these considerations, we cannot reasonably infer the nonexistence of extraterrestials from our not having detected any communications from them. As opposed to what we don't know about extraterrestrials, however, we do know that God, if he exists, most certainly knows that we exist, most certainly loves us and cares for us, and, being infinitely powerful, is able to prevent any of the horrendous evils that befall us. Furthermore, given his infinite knowledge, God would know how to achieve the very best lives possible for us with the minimum of horrible suffering. My friends, however, believe that we have no sufficient reason at all to think it *even likely* that God could achieve the very best for us (humans and animals) were he to have prevented the Holocaust, the terrible suffering of the fawn, the horrible suffering of the little girl, or any of the other countless evils that abound in this world. Why on earth do they believe this? The basic reason is this: *God's knowledge of goods and the conditions of their realization extends far beyond our own.* Because God's knowledge extends far beyond our own they think it just may be that God would know that even he, with his infinite power, cannot achieve the best for us without permitting all the horrendous evils that occur daily in our world. And they also think it just may be that God can achieve the best for us only if he keeps us in the dark as to what the good is that justifies him in permitting any of these horrendous evils. But what their view comes to is this. Because we cannot rule out God's knowing goods we do not know, we cannot rule out their being goods that justify God in permitting *any amount of evil whatever* that might occur in our world. If human and animal life on earth were *nothing more than a series of agonizing moments from birth to death,* the position of my friends would still require them to say that we cannot reasonably infer that it is even likely that God does not exist. For, since we don't know that the goods we know of are representative of the goods there are, we can't know that it is likely that there are no goods that justify God in permitting human and animal life on earth to be nothing more than a series of agonizing moments from birth to death. But surely such a view is unreasonable, if not absurd. Surely there must be some point at which the appalling agony of human and animal existence on earth would render it unlikely that God exists. And this must be so even though we all agree that God's knowledge would far exceed our own. I believe my theistic friends have gone considerably beyond that point when in light of the enormous proliferation of horrendous evil in this world they continue to insist that we are unjustified in concluding that it is unlikely that God exists.

They characterize my argument as a "noseeum" argument. But this is not quite correct. There are lots of things we can conceive of occurring in our world which we don't *see* occurring. My argument is basically a "noconceiveum" argument, not a "noseeum" argument. We cannot even *conceive* of goods that may occur and would justify God in permitting the terrible evils that afflict our world. Of course, being finite beings we can't expect to know all the goods God would know, any more than an amateur at chess should expect to know all the reasons for a particular move that Kasparov makes in a game. But, unlike Kasparov who in a chess match has a good reason not to tell us how a particular move fits into his plan to win the game, God, if he exists, isn't playing chess with our lives. In fact, since understanding the goods for the sake of which he permits terrible evils to befall us would itself enable us to better bear our suffering, God has a strong reason to help us understand those goods and how they require his permission of the terrible evils that befall us. My friends, however, do seem to think we can conceive of goods that may require God to permit at least some of these awful evils. They suggest that for all we know the following complex good may occur: the little five-year-old girl meets up with her rapist-killer somewhere in the next life, and he then repents and begs her forgiveness for savagely beating, raping, and strangling her, and she then forgives him with the result that both of them live happily ever after in the presence of God. What are we to make of this suggestion as to why God permitted the little girl to be brutally beaten, raped, and strangled? Well, they are right in holding that even God cannot bring about this complex good without permitting that individual to brutally beat, rape, and strangle the little girl. But that alone won't justify God in permitting that to happen to her. For it is eminently reasonable to believe that God could win the soul of the little girl's rapist-killer without having to permit him to do what he did to her. And even if he can't, is it right for any being to permit the little girl to be robbed of her life in that way just so her killer could have something bad enough on his conscience to ultimately seek forgiveness? It is one thing to knowingly and freely give up one's life for the sake of another and quite another thing to have it ripped away, against one's will, just so someone else can later be led to repentance. If this is the best that can be done to find a good we know of that may justify God in permitting the little girl to be brutally beaten, raped, and strangled, the evidential argument from evil will surely remain a thorn in the side of theism for some time to come.

William L. Rowe

8

J. L. SCHELLENBERG

Stalemate and Strategy: Rethinking the Evidential Argument from Evil

A ROAD FROM (AND TO) ROWE

To justify your atheism by means of William Rowe's evidential argument from evil, just put forward the inoffensive

(1) If God exists, then E (the evil of horrific suffering) does not exist, unless there is a good reason for God to permit E,[1]

offer the lack of any sign of a good reason for E as strong evidence for

(2) There is no good reason for God to permit E,

and then, pointing to the obvious existence of E and the absence (in your case at least) of strong independent evidence for theism, infer that

(3) God does not exist.[2]

Short and sweet – or so this recipe for justified atheism has seemed to many. But the sentiment is not universally shared. Over and over in the literature we are told that Rowe's evidence for (2) is no good: critics rival the zeal of W. K. Clifford himself in their claim that it is wrong always, everywhere, and for anyone to accept (2) on its basis.

Original publication: J. L. Schellenberg, "Stalemate and Strategy: Rethinking the Evidential Argument from Evil," *American Philosophical Quarterly*, 37(4) (Pittsburgh: North American Philosophical Association Publications Inc.).

I am grateful to Paul Draper, Daniel Howard-Snyder, and William Rowe for their comments on earlier drafts of this chapter.

Indeed, an increasingly influential view is that *any* evidence put forward to support a negative existential claim in respect of God's reasons for evil can be undercut through appropriate reflection on the Divine nature or our own. Thus William Alston: "The point is that the [defender of the evidential argument] is attempting to support a particularly difficult claim, a claim that there isn't something in a certain territory, while having a very sketchy idea of what is in that territory, and having no sufficient basis for an estimate of how much of that territory falls outside our knowledge."[3] If Alston and his many likeminded colleagues are right, then arguments from evil relying on (2) fail to provide any thinking person with justification for atheism.

A lot of time has been devoted to (2) in the last 20 years. Rowe and others have defended it. A legion of theistic warriors has attacked it. One would think evidential arguments from evil can't get along without it. But this is far from true: we can develop an evidential argument that avoids the terrible (2) and circumvents the skeptical theist's critique. Now evidential arguments absent (2) have been offered once or twice already.[4] But skeptical theists (on a bit of a roll here) have extended their critique so as to apply as well to such alternative formulations of the argument.[5] And the debate, thus enlarged, has only become more complicated and difficult to adjudicate. Indeed, we seem to have arrived at something of a stalemate. This essay seeks to provide a way out of the stalemate – an approach at once plausible and simple which bypasses (2) and also furnishes us with a clear and persuasive answer to the skeptical maneuvers of theists like Alston. My arguments will show that, utilizing this approach, individuals aware of horrific suffering who lack both an explicit theodicy and the theodicy afforded by strong countervailing evidence for theism (call the latter an *implicit* theodicy)[6] can provide for themselves rational justification for atheism. That is to say, we will leave individuals of the sub-class in question exactly where Rowe sought to position them in the 1979 essay that got us all thinking about these matters.

A New Direction: The Approach Outlined and Defended

Let's begin by following the winding path of discussion back a bit and asking why the evidential arguer consented to start with (1) in the first place. Why start with (1) instead of, say,

(1′)   If God exists, then E does not exist?

(1′), while resembling (1), is stripped of the latter's "unless" clause. Startling in its nakedness, it rouses us to consider our alternatives more carefully. Clearly, if we put forward a premise including the "unless" clause and seek to argue to atheism from *there*, we will need to defend (2). But why should we do this? Perhaps our arguer can defend the stronger and simpler claim of (1′) instead. If "God" names a being unsurpassably great and "E" names horrific suffering, surely much can be said in favor of (1′). But if so, and if (utilizing modus tollens) we seek to reason from *here* to atheism, then we can also get along without (2).

Now it may be objected that this move was already tried – unsuccessfully – by J. L. Mackie, who put forward as a necessary truth in his famous logical argument from evil that if God exists, evil does not. But an assimilation of my approach to Mackie's would be overhasty. For one thing, my arguer refers not to evil in general but only to horrific suffering. For another, she need not claim that (1′) is a necessary truth.[7] (Of course she need not deny it either.) She may content herself with supporting the claim that it is *true*, suggesting reasons sufficient in certain relevant circumstances to justify someone in believing that God would prevent E.[8]

But what reasons? How can the evidential arguer proceed here? Well, naturally she will begin by urging us to attend to exactly how appalling the evil in question is: imagine a few days spent contemplating what slow death was like for the little girl suffocating underground as a result of an earthquake, or how it felt for that woman in the news to be repeatedly raped and tortured before being killed. Some significant expenditure of time – as opposed to the perfunctory few seconds most of us devote to this – is surely required to fully appreciate the extreme intrinsic badness of this evil, and the strength of the reason for (1′) that badness represents.

She will, secondly, point to the fact that persons we would regard as emotionally and morally sensitive, individuals capable of entering deeply and sympathetically into the experience of another and given to compassion (call this bundle of qualities *empathy*), are deeply opposed to things of this nature: they recoil in anger and disgust and sadness at even second-hand reports of such terrible events, and do whatever they can to prevent their occurrence (or to ameliorate the situation if prevention is impossible). And this point can be developed. For the *greater* one's empathy and the *closer* one's proximity to horrific suffering, the stronger one's determination and effort to alleviate this suffering, as well as to prevent it from occurring again. (Imagine yourself given a shot of empathy and transferred from that comfortable spot in front of your television to the side of a famine-sufferer in Mozambique.) It follows that we should expect someone with *maximal* empathy and *maximal* proximity to horrific suffering to have a negative, oppositional, reaction that is *maximally* strong. But then *God* would have such a reaction to horrific suffering. It follows that if ever God encountered horrific suffering, God would seek to eliminate it, and to prevent it from occurring again. Hence, given Divine omnipotence, horrific suffering has long since been done away with, if God exists. But an even stronger conclusion is warranted. For a being disposed to react to horrific suffering in the manner indicated who was antecedently apprised of its nature, and could do it, would clearly prevent such suffering from ever coming into existence in the first place. Now God obviously satisfies this description as well: a being unsurpassably great would have little trouble carrying out such a task, and would not need maximal proximity to actual horrific suffering to be maximally aware of all it could show. Hence if God exists, *there is no horrific suffering and never has been.* This reasoning, the evidential arguer may say, is sufficient to form the belief that $(1')$ is true in many a rational inquirer, and sufficient to justify that belief in the absence of defeaters.

Of course it doesn't take long to think of defeaters that might be suggested. Our argument, it may be said, gains its seeming plausibility only by neglecting some important differences between the Divine consciousness and our own. Specifically, it is because our finite minds are limited in what they can hold and – especially given an empathetic disposition – likely to be *overwhelmed* by contact with horrific suffering that such contact tends to generate a strong negative response. But then, since God's mind would be *un*limited, we are not justified in extrapolating from what we have discovered about ourselves to the Divine case.[9] Besides, the objector may say, God would look at things from the perspective of eternity and have more than one short slice of time in view: God would have to consider the place of horrific suffering within a person's whole life and the place of that person within the *universe* as a whole. We are not in the same position when we respond to such suffering, and we do not know that we would respond in the same way if we were.

These objections are unconvincing. That horrific suffering has the effects it does have in the empathetic is a function not of our limited capacities but of its recognized *importance*: those who are empathetic have indeed the more *developed* capacities required to achieve such a recognition and convey it to the rest of us (who are often a little slow in this department), as well as to work unstintingly to remove or to prevent horrific suffering in light of it, which would perhaps be difficult if such suffering simply "overwhelmed" them. Hence the fact that God's mind, unlike our own, is unlimited is irrelevant here. (Notice how difficult it is to resist or qualify the judgment of importance. It is logically embedded in the empathetic response; thus in valuing the latter – as we all do – we implicitly approve of the former.)

As for the suggestion concerning God and eternity: this simply rides roughshod over a central point here, namely that a Creator, if indeed unsurpassably great, would be more intimately acquainted and concerned with each creature than anything else could be. It produces an image of a God aloof from creaturely affairs, a God who observes us, as from above, from the great *distance* required to see everything, in which perspective things that seem important to us just don't seem as important. We should resist travelling down this road. If God empathizes with created beings as no one else can, then God must take on *their* perspective and be appropriately affected by it. Then we do not have a God who says: "Oh, if you could only see things from my vantage point, you would realize that those years of suffering and torture are no more significant than a slight bruise." Then the cries of the mother for her child are the cries of God, too.

It may seem, however, that the full force of the point about eternity has not yet been felt. The objector may concede that a God *would* empathize with creatures during the time of their suffering, while adding and stressing that this might well be a limited time, to be followed by heaven, in which they experience the goods God knew about all along, for the sake of which God was willing to have them endure (and to endure with them) the horrors of their lives. Surely with our puny intelligence we cannot rule out the notion that our lives are unfolding within some such scenario.

To deal with this we need only develop our argument a little further, in a direction already suggested. Think of a caring mother, that paragon of empathy. The horrific suffering of her child demands and determines her response in the face of everything else she knows. When confronted with such evil she does not concern herself with the question of what distant goods it may serve: the only good she then seeks is *the end of this suffering*. Analogy suggests that her attitude of unqualified opposition to horrific suffering would be shared by God – or at any rate, it does so if our understanding of God is not so impoverished as to refer only to masculine attributes.

But the persistent objector will now propose that even the nature of *creaturely* good may elude us, and stress once again the farther reach of omniscience. The mother of our example, she may say, only allows the horror of her child's suffering to determine her response "in the face of everything else she knows" because her knowledge does not include awareness of any great good for her child, or for other intelligent or sentient beings, that depends on his suffering in this way. If things were *different* – if, for example, she saw that the overall good of her child or of other beings could not be secured without going along with an evil villain's intention to cause such suffering – her response might not be the same. And we are in no position to deny that things are different in the case of God and E. No matter how bad things are, we lack the cognitive wherewithal to render the judgment needed here about what God is aware of.

Well, let's grant the objector's point about the mother, controversial though it is, and focus on whether the good, or deepest good, of creatures brought into being by God might really be seen by God to depend on the permission of horrific suffering.[10] We can even incorporate the objector's point into our original claim, so that it now reads as follows: the greater one's empathy and the closer one's proximity to horrific suffering *and the firmer one's assurance that no creature will thereby be prevented from realizing the good appropriate to it*, the stronger one's determination and effort to alleviate this suffering, as well as to prevent it from occurring again. Does this make it any more difficult to reach the conclusion we are seeking to justify with respect to God? The answer is pretty clearly no. For while God would see that horrific suffering might be the consequence of creating certain goods or might carry good things in its train, it seems absurd, given the resources of Divinity, to suppose that valuable lives could not be secured by God in the absence of such goods. And so it seems absurd to suppose that God is in a position like that of the mother described by the objector, who must simply put up with the horrific suffering of her child to realize his good or the good of other beings. Surely God can provide for the needs of creatures without horrific suffering!

But might there not be, unknown to us, greater goods than these, which profoundly enhance the lives of creatures and *do* depend on horrific suffering? In particular, might not the good of *personal* beings, beings who share in the mysterious nature of God, in some fashion be bound up with such suffering? Well, let's cut to the heart of the matter and consider the greatest and deepest good any personal being can experience given the existence of God. If theists are right, we are not in the dark about what this is: it is a positive, ongoing (indeed, unending) and growing *relationship* with God. Suppose, as seems plausible, that they are right. Now notice this important point: while as many writers have undertaken to show, horrific suffering need not prevent the realization of such a good in a person's life, *its absence need not prevent it either.* By appealing to Divine resourcefulness we might seek to establish that lives horribly marred by suffering may nonetheless participate in relationship with God, or even be redemptively related to the lives of others, but the very same point surely justifies the claim that the permission of horrific suffering is not *required* for there to be persons who experience this greatest of all goods. (Notice that this is quite compatible with the claim that the permission of various other sorts of suffering *is* required.) Indeed, if God is infinitely deep and unsurpassably rich, then even if horrors are by some metaphysical mechanism or by the nature of the world God chooses to create excluded from personal life from the beginning, there must remain an *infinite number* of ways of growing into wholeness and fulfilment in God – an infinite number of possible journeys into self, the world and God that realize the ultimate in meaning and goodness for finite created persons, which omnipotence and omniscience could facilitate.[11] (Here the *objector* fails to ruminate long enough on the content of theism.) If now we add to the objector's point – as surely we must – that it is *only* if a caring mother sees that the good of her child or of other creatures depends on his horrific suffering that she could fail to prevent it, given the opportunity to do so, we can see that it yields a conclusion quite contrary to what was intended: God, a reality infinitely abundant and vast, inexhaustibly resourceful and empathetic, would both recognize and cherish the possibility of excluding creaturely horror *without* endangering the creaturely good, and so might be expected to exhibit, in creation, the attitude of the mother *originally* described.

What this simple point reveals is the error of supposing that the horrific suffering of creatures might well be countenanced by God for the sake of some "greater good" so long as the permission of that suffering did not stand in the way of their deepest good. In the place of this common but (as we can now see) far too lax assumption we must nail the thesis that the horrific suffering of creatures would *not* be countenanced by God, even for the sake of a "greater good," so long as the *prevention* of that suffering did not stand in the way of their deepest good. To put this in a slightly different way: given what we know of empathetic parents, not just any "greater good" would do in the circumstances in question; only one constituted (or entailed) by the creation of beings able to experience the good appropriate to them *at all*. The permission of horrific suffering might well be required for some creaturely good whose total goodness, on some utilitarian scale, outweighs the evil, or even for some good representing *one way* of experiencing the good appropriate to creaturely life. But if there can be persons and other exalted beings capable of experiencing the good appropriate to them even where there is no horrific suffering, who could be justified in permitting such suffering? Who, while perfectly empathetic, *would* permit it?

It seems, then, that the argument from empathy is able to survive critical scrutiny. But there is yet a third reason for supposing that such a proposition as (1′) is true to which our evidential arguer may appeal in response to suspicions about that claim, namely that the nonexistence of the evil to which it refers is required by some *good* God would seek to produce. (Where a heavenly parent would surely provide bread, we receive a stone instead.) When we say, for example, that cancer of the throat is an evil God might wish to prevent, we may have in mind not only that it is intrinsically extremely bad or that it repels the empathetic, but also that there is a good state of affairs God might be expected to wish to produce, whose existence that evil precludes. At the most obvious level this good will be a certain minimum of well-being for all God's creatures, but we may also refer more specifically to such things as the opportunity for created beings to fulfill good intentions or realize laudable life goals. Evils, in short, may be instrumentally *as well as* intrinsically bad. (And so we need another reversal: a move away from the current emphasis on the goods horrific suffering may facilitate toward a recognition of the important goods it *prevents*.) Now it is not hard to think of relevant goods that all instances of horrific suffering preclude. And for certain particular cases, there may be yet more impressive or meaningful or theologically significant goods to consider (the completion of important phases of spiritual development, say), which suggests a way of making the evidential argument even more powerful than it would otherwise be: narrow the range of "E" to the particular horror in question. Responding to this awareness, the evidential arguer may select some relevant good g and proceed by analogy with the analogy/disanalogy argument outlined above, arguing that if God exists, so does g (and from there, by hypothetical syllogism, to (1')), grounding her argument in various observations concerning human parents, to be sure, but also in such *differences* between God and ourselves as that a God would be even *more* focused on procuring for creatures the goods it is in their interest to possess. ("If you, then, though you are evil, know how to give good gifts to your children, how much more will your Father in heaven give good gifts to those who ask him!" (Matt. 7: 11))

Despite the proof-texts supporting such reasoning, there will again be objections. A critic may say that we have reason to be in doubt about whether God would want creatures to experience g (maybe it is not happiness, but some higher-order good like virtue or usefulness that God wants us to enjoy), or, assuming it is g, whether it is at just any stage of creaturely development that God would wish it to be experienced (perhaps we should only expect to be happy in heaven); or she may say that we have reason to be in doubt about what goods it is in the best interest of creatures to possess. But some of the candidate replacements for g are, as indicated, necessary for the most basic well-being or meaningful existence at any time. Thus a perfectly good God would surely want us to experience them. Notice also that the goods excluded by horrific evil are not restricted to such things as happy or pleasurable states, which many writers are inclined to say might well be qualified or postponed by God in favor of higher-order goods, but include as well those very higher-order goods! Take, for example, virtue. Serious and unrelenting abuse in childhood may in many (e.g. in some sociopaths) remove the conditions of its development. Or usefulness. While, as Richard Swinburne argues, we may be benefited by being useful in the production of good for others without knowing it, there is surely (as he recognizes) greater goodness in usefulness that is voluntarily chosen, and whose consequences one can appreciate as they unfold.[12] Think, then, of those individuals whose opportunity for usefulness in this or that respect and experience thereof (e.g. through the development of great musical gifts or the application in good works of a natural compassion) is thwarted by the torment of horrific suffering.

As for whether we know what is in the best interest of creatures: surely certain necessary conditions are obvious – such things as nourishment and basic comfort and liberty of movement and activity for nonpersonal sentient beings, and for their personal counterparts, education and meaningful activity and loving relationships and access to any God there may be, not to mention virtue and usefulness. Where, then, such things are thwarted and absent on account of horrific suffering, we have reason to conclude that something God would love and seek has been lost. If we notice, further, that God would be only so much more than we the seeker of those things that nourish the lives of created beings, then we are in a position to argue that where the filling for "g" refers to one of *these* things, if God exists, so does g. And the argument will of course be reinforced if, as seems highly plausible, we can show that God can have personal and other creatures who achieve their deepest good without permitting g's absence. For – and here we have a variation on earlier reasoning – each of the goods we have discussed appears to have a place in the lives of creatures such that its absence would not be countenanced by a Divine Parent so long as its presence did not stand in the way of their deepest good.

We have, then, a surprisingly large supply of evidence on which the evidential arguer may draw in supporting that audacious-seeming proposition (1′). And this evidence looks forceful indeed: given that attempts to undercut it have proven unsuccessful, it does seem that someone could be justified by it in believing such a proposition as (1′). To make this more precise, we can formulate a sufficient condition for the epistemic justification of belief on evidence:

> An individual S is epistemically justified in believing that p in response to evidence e if (i) S does to some degree believe that p on e, (ii) has considered all available epistemic reasons for not believing that p on e, (iii) finds none to be a good reason, and (iv) has fulfilled all relevant epistemic duties in the course of her investigation.[13]

With this in place, we may put our claim as follows: the conjunctive condition referred to here can be satisfied by individuals belonging to the sub-class mentioned at the beginning of this essay who form the belief that (1′) is true in response to such evidence as we have cited. And for the benefit of those enamored of the reasoning of Alston et al. in response to Rowe, it may be emphasized that an argument for this belief can rely on the *positive* claim that such evidence exists. *The negative existential claim (2) need not appear or be independently defended anywhere.*

INTO THE WIND: REPLIES TO FURTHER OBJECTIONS

Now of course, if there are additional defeaters one must overlook in order to form the belief that $(1')$ is true in response to such evidence, then the aforementioned justification does not obtain, for the evidential arguer or anyone else. We have already dealt with specific objections to each of our arguments, but further reflection on behalf of the critic suggests the possibility of resistance to any approach of the sort developed here. So let us turn our attention to these more general objections.

It may be tempting, first of all, to think that the evidential arguer cannot get along without a defense of (2). (And so she faces the under-cutting defeaters Rowe faces.) Surely our arguer *must* make – and so defend – (2)'s negative claim. For if that claim is false, so is hers. More precisely:

(4)   If there is a good reason for God to permit E, then it is not the case that, if God exists, E does not exist.

But by contraposition we obtain

(5)   If it is the case that, if God exists, E does not exist, then there is no good reason for God to permit E.[14]

This is a conditional our arguer has to accept and – given her acceptance of $(1')$ – she is clearly committed to its antecedent. Therefore, the objector may say, she is committed to its consequent as well, that is, to (2).

So far so good. But it does not follow that the proponent of our approach has to argue on independent grounds for the consequent at any point. She may point out that if her positive claim is correct and there are powerful considerations supporting the antecedent of (5), *this itself* provides grounds to affirm its consequent, and justifies her in believing both antecedent and consequent if a relevant defeater cannot be found. So although the objection is right in pointing out the evidential arguer's commitment to the negative existential claim in question, its suggestion that she must defend it on an independent basis seems misguided and question-begging.

The objector may now wish to know whether this does not open the floodgates to all sorts of implausible maneuvering. Wouldn't Rowe himself, if this reasoning is accepted, be in a position to accuse his accusers of begging the question? "I claim to have good evidence," he might say, "for my view that (2) is true. But if (2) is true, then there are no unknown good reasons for God to permit evil. Hence if my evidence *is* good, it is evidence as well for the latter claim. But then in requiring me to produce some additional argument in reply to your suggestion that there might be unknown reasons, you beg the question against me."

Well, such a move would indeed be implausible. But this is because the evidence Rowe explicitly advances in support of (2) – that we can think of no good reason for God to permit E – is only part of the evidence he *uses*: implicit in his argument is the assumption that human research would likely reveal a good reason for God to permit E if such a reason existed, and it is this assumption that his critics attack. And so in suggesting that Rowe lacks adequate support for his claim they do not beg the question against him; they are directly addressing his evidence instead of assuming without argument that it is inadequate. But the objector who in the present context claims that (2) must be shown to be true on independent grounds is *not* directly addressing the evidence that has been put forward, and *is* assuming without argument that this evidence is inadequate in the course of defending a claim we have no reason to accept if it is adequate. Hence this objector, unlike those who object to Rowe, *is* begging the question.

Those who continue to find our answer to the objection presently under consideration dubious may be offered the following additional observations. (1) is equivalent to

(6)   If there is no good reason for God to permit E, then, if God exists, E does not exist.

But by contraposition we obtain

(7)   If it is not the case that, if God exists, E does not exist, then there is a good reason for God to permit E.

Now, because of the inoffensiveness of (1), this is a conditional everyone party to the debate will accept. And theists who recognize the existence of E, in addition to accepting (7), are committed to accepting its antecedent. So they are committed to its consequent as well – a proposition claiming, in effect, that there is a theodicy for E. But notoriously, theists aware of what's going on here don't want to give independent arguments for the consequent of (7). They *believe* it, but don't want to defend it directly for the very good reason that the evil named by E *resists* attempts at explicit theodicy; indeed, it was selected by the evidential arguer precisely because of this feature. How then do they support it, when support is needed? Well, by reference to their reasons for believing "God exists and E exists," which conjunction provides a basis for believing the antecedent of (7) and, as we have seen, *entails* that there is a theodicy for E. If this strategy can be applied in the case of (7) (and everyone involved in the debate – not only theists – seems to regard it as acceptable in principle), perhaps we will be forgiven for applying it to (5).

It may now be said, in an attempt to discriminate between the two projects, that while the strategy described is in principle acceptable, it is inapplicable here. Having restricted ourselves to the claim that (1′) is true, the only possible basis for affirming it has indeed been put out of reach. Why? Well, quite simply because reasons for affirming (1′) as true must be reasons supporting its necessity. (If, for example, God is by nature unsurpassably empathetic, then this is necessarily the case.) Hence if we allow that we have no good reasons of the latter sort, we can hardly add that we nonetheless have some of the *former* sort.[15]

This is not convincing. Though reasons of the sort in question commonly refer to properties (such as unsurpassable empathy) that a God would necessarily possess, their application will depend, in part, on properties of the world in question. They can be *differentially applicable* – forceful and undefeated in some worlds though not in others. Suppose, for example, that our arguer restricts the range of "E" in (1′) to the relevant experiences of a certain newborn and its parents, whose lives were shattered when a chunk of ice freed itself and fell from a hospital roof, killing the child, just as his parents proudly carried him out the hospital door. And suppose that in a moment of epistemic abandon she puts forward as her sole reason for (1′)'s *necessity* the necessary truth that God loves parents and children. Now it might seem possible to show that (1′), so construed, is not necessarily true. One might argue, for example, that there is a possible world W containing these parents and this child in which the death of the child coincides with the end of earthly existence and the beginning of a new heavenly existence for everyone. In such a world, it would be said, the existence of God is not a sufficient condition for the prevention of this evil. But suppose the evidential arguer now adopts what may seem a more becoming modesty and changes her tack, claiming only that (1′) is *true*, not that it is necessarily true. It is important to note that the argument just mentioned, even if successful in relation to the original claim, would have no tendency at all to defeat the aforementioned reason as a reason for believing the *revised* claim *unless W is the actual world*. And of course it is not. That reason may therefore continue to support (1′) as true even if it no longer supports it as necessarily true, which is to say that it need not do the latter job to do the former.

"All right," says the objector, "perhaps a focus on truth rather than on necessity wouldn't undermine your case by putting out of reach the only real reasons you can appeal to here. But it might still be harmful in other ways. Consider Alvin Plantinga's free will defense, so widely regarded as successful. Some reasons cited in possibility arguments (such as the crass eschatological defense you cited earlier) may indeed be such that we can clearly see they do not apply in the actual world, but others – like those cited in *his* defense – may be different. How, given our very limited understanding of the matters involved here, can we be justified in making the fine discrimination involved in saying that the conditions to which he refers are possible *but not actual*?"[16]

Well, it may be that the evidential arguer judges *all* the relevant and apparently possible claims to be, like the eschatological claim, clearly inapplicable in the actual world. And, of course, she may not find herself discriminating between possibility and actuality claims in the manner indicated in the first place: perhaps, less than sanguine even about the former, she affirms neither. (Maybe even the apparent obviousness of the eschatological claim's possibility disappears upon reflection.) It might well be, for example, that she wishes to question certain of the intuitions underlying Plantinga's free will defense, such as his apparent view that, possibly, all of the suffering humans actually experience is part of the price of the type of personal freedom God would prefer, or his view that, possibly, God would prefer paying that price to letting that freedom go and realizing some other form of goodness. This is not to say that she is now inclined to argue that the conjunction of claims Plantinga regards as possible here (or their disjunction) is *im*possible. Given her purposes, that is neither here nor there. What she must say is that there are reasons of various kinds supporting (1′) as true, some or all or the conjunction of which she finds more compelling than the free will defense – or any similar defence – as applied in this context. (Having had her reasons for (1′) returned to her by the objector and recognized as applicable in this discussion, she may proceed once more to *use* them in dealing with defeaters.)

At this stage the objector may turn to arguing in a more general way for the epistemic possibility of reasons for God to permit E. What we need to see here, she may say, is just that it would *not be at all surprising* if there were reasons actually providing a justification for God to permit E, that nothing we know or justifiedly believe rules this out. Perhaps all of the reasons for God to permit evil we can actually get our hands on are inadequate, but for all we know or justifiedly believe, there may be unarticulated, perhaps nonarticulable, unknown reasons that justify God in permitting E.[17]

Such claims are question-begging, however. One of the merits of the approach defended here is that it focuses on providing sufficient justification for the belief that (1′) is true. If that justification has been provided, then, for those who have it, it *would* be surprising if there were reasons (known or unknown) impelling God to permit E; then, also, there *is* something they justifiedly believe that rules out such reasons, namely (1′). Now if the points raised by skeptical theists attacked that justification directly, we'd have something to think about (and indeed, we have already considered and rejected such objections, especially in the previous section). But as here presented they do not. Instead, they *assume* that that justification is inadequate. Hence they are question-begging.

Perhaps it will now be said that the objector can avoid begging the question by providing an argument for her claim. She may have evidence of her own which supports that claim, and which does not depend for its force on denying force to ours. So, what evidence? Well, it might be suggested that we tell a story that is internally consistent and according to which God permits E. Perhaps the story says that, because of the need for constant miraculous intervention, the cost of preventing E would be massive irregularity in a physical universe such as ours, and that God would value the avoidance of this metaphysical defect highly enough to allow E to occur.[18] We might then go on to point out that, given our ignorance concerning matters metaphysical and moral we would need to understand in order to assess the story, we *cannot* do so and must instead concede that we have no good reason to deny its truth. But then, given that its truth entails the falsity of our claim, we have no good reason to deny that that claim is false, and so a defeater for our evidence.

But, again, what if the evidential arguer finds herself lacking the ignorance referred to here? Maybe even after considerable reflection she cannot lose her sense that the good mentioned by the story is just not great enough (the apparent irregularity caused by miracles seeming inelegant and distasteful from one perspective, resourceful and sensitive from another; whereas horrific suffering is plainly awful beyond words), or that the story's abstract, comparative approach to value is here beside the point (a God of empathy being unlikely to approach horrific suffering that way), or – a related idea – that the good in question is of a completely irrelevant kind (the ultimate good of sentient creatures being a good of the relevant kind). And of course, it may seem clear to her that avoiding massive irregularity in the created world would not require the permission of E in the first place. (It is, after all, only a *subset* of suffering we are talking about here. And would not their prevention by a Divine being simply instantiate an elegant metaphysical regularity of another kind? Besides, why should anyone – especially a theist willing to countenance talk of heaven and hell and purgatory – suppose that God is restricted to *physical* worlds when seeking a suitable environment for the free personal development of creatures in relation to the creator?) The availability of such information – which, notice, includes information from premises of the evidential arguer's defense of (1') – means that the evidential arguer is not at all ignorant as to the likelihood of truth in the story. Indeed, if observant, she will recognize that she has good reason to reject it as *false*.

At this stage the objector may make an attempt to put forward only evidence clearly *not* presupposing the failure of our arguments – evidence, this time, suggesting the existence of *unknown* reasons for E, which when taken in conjunction with the evidence put forward by the evidential arguer, leaves her without sufficient justification for her claim. What might belong to this evidence? Well, perhaps such claims as that, given our cognitive limitations and evolutionary heritage, we have reason to suppose that our grasp of the nature of goodness is quite limited. There may indeed be values we cannot so much as conceive of. If any such value were to figure in a reason for God to permit E (on which God would be inclined to act), we certainly wouldn't know it. And it seems quite likely that such a value would figure in any reason for horrific evil God might have. For a good great enough to justify such suffering would have to be very great indeed, and we have some reason from experience to expect degree of value to be correlated with degree of complexity.[19]

Such claims can be made without contradicting the evidential arguer at any point. Suppose also that they cannot be shown to be false. They are for all of that inadequate to their assigned task. Notice that the objector says there may be unknown values, full stop, not that there may be unknown values *providing a reason for God to permit E*. She could not make the latter, more specific, claim without begging the question. Neither does she say that the former claim provides undefeated *support* for the latter. This too would assume that our arguments are unsuccessful and beg the question. But then it is hard to see how anything relevant to the objector's aim has been put forward! There may be much about goodness that we do not and cannot know, but the evidential arguer can happily admit this while continuing to affirm, on the basis of what we *do* know, that God would not permit E. She may also happily concede the objector's further point that *if* there is a reason sufficient to move God to permit E, we might not know it. This conditional claim is harmless; what we require is reason to believe its *antecedent*, and none has been provided. The conclusion of all this is that general skeptical theistic arguments of the sort we have been considering are likely to be either question-begging, as above, or just irrelevant, as in this case.

One final argument may be offered to skeptics unconvinced by what has come before. Consider the following proposition:

(8)   If God exists, then (for at any rate some of us) physical death is not the end.

Many thinkers – and not just theists – would upon reflection judge this proposition to be probable, in the normative sense of "such as a fully reasonable individual would, given the evidence available, believe to some degree." For if God exists, disembodied personal existence is not impossible (since God, by definition, is personal and lacks a body); and one might expect as well that a perfectly loving God would seek to keep in existence those who have entered into a loving relationship with God, so that the relationship might be more fully consummated. (Within the bounds of earthly existence, the sort of unrestricted communion perfect love would seek is just not possible.) Such considerations are available to theist and non-theist alike, and may (and do) lead to the belief that (8) is true in many reasonable individuals who reflect upon them. Notice how easily such a belief is reached. No talk *here* of reasons a God might have for *not* seeing to it that at any rate some of us survive death. Yet surely there are as many areas of human ignorance relevant to the exclusion on independent grounds of *such* reasons as there are in the case of (1'). How could we show, on independent grounds, that there is no great good God might seek to realize that is essential to the execution of God's design plan and requires that death be the end for us all? But such problems do not exercise us. No skeptical tradition has arisen seeking to undermine (8). Why? Well, one may hope it is not because (8), unlike (1'), does not threaten theism. (In any case, not all of us are theists.) Is it, perhaps, because our reasons *for* believing that (8) is true seem to us sufficiently powerful to render unnecessary such probing into God's reasons? Notice that even theists who say they believe (8) partly on the basis of revelation would rule out the idea of overriding reasons for God to make death the end on the basis of their positive case *for* (8) (it's just a different case). And surely this is, in principle, an acceptable approach. But then what is to prevent us from applying it in the case of (1')? Surely not skeptical theism.[20]

It would seem, therefore, that our approach in this essay can be defended against the skeptical theistic attack. By focusing – as strangely, many philosophers fail to do – on what makes certain evils so bad (and so likely to be opposed by God) in the first place, we can render question-begging or otherwise impotent the claim (and apparent support for the claim) that there might, for all we know or justified believe, be reasons to permit those evils moving God to do so. By focusing on what we *know*, we can turn aside arguments seeking sustenance from what we *don't* know. And other defeaters we have considered seem equally powerless. Since all available avenues of defeat apart from the rebutting defeater constituted by a powerful explicit or implicit theodicy appear thus to be dead ends, we may conclude that those who recognize the existence of horrific evil and *lack* a rebutting defeater of the sort in question can be justified by our evidence in believing that God does not exist. And that is what was to be shown.

NOTES

1   Most of those who read this chapter will have no trouble finding intuitive access to the class of sufferings labelled "horrific" and identifying (and distinguishing from non-horrific sufferings) evils belonging to it. Anyone who does have trouble with these tasks should see Marilyn McCord

Adams, *Horrendous Evils and the Goodness of God* (Ithaca, NY: Cornell University Press, 1999), pp. 26–29.

2 The classic statement of Rowe's argument appears in his "The Problem of Evil and Some Varieties of Atheism," *American Philosophical Quarterly* 16 (1979): 335–41. Though Rowe seems at times to be arguing from the apparent pointlessness of particular instances of horrific suffering, a careful reading reveals that his argument takes in *all* horrific suffering, and uses particular instances to *illustrate* the horror of such suffering.

3 "The Inductive Argument from Evil and the Human Cognitive Condition," in Daniel Howard-Snyder, *The Evidential Argument from Evil* (Bloomington and Indianapolis: Indiana University Press, 1996), p. 120. Alston's piece is one of *eight* in the Howard-Snyder collection (hereafter, HS) that defend one version or another of the skeptical thesis.

4 For examples, see the essays by Paul Draper and Rowe's second essay in HS.

5 See, for example, the two essays by Peter van Inwagen and the second essay by Alston in HS.

6 An *explicit* theodicy makes it possible for us to justifiedly believe that a good reason for God to permit E exists by telling us what that reason is. (Of course, what we want here is an *adequate* theodicy. This is left tacit in the text: "explicit theodicy" should be understood as "adequate explicit theodicy.") Use of the word "implicit" here draws attention to the fact that the existence of God (in conjunction with the existence of E) *entails* the existence of a theodicy for E, and so sufficient evidence of the former is at the same time evidence of the latter and can justify us in believing that the latter exists even if we are unable to say what it is.

7 One qualification: the arguer may wish to suggest that what distinguishes the evidential argument from Mackie's is a clear restriction of discussion to the actual world, and rephrase her claims (including (1')) to reflect this fact. As I have argued elsewhere (see my "α-claims and the Problem of Evil," *Sophia* (Australia) 32 (1993): 56–61), when we observe such a restriction by converting claims like (1') into claims about the actual world, assertions of possibility, actuality and necessity coincide. (Then, indeed, all of the reconstructions of Mackie's argument and animadversions surrounding it can seem to constitute a gigantic red herring.)

8 This suggests that the primary evidence to be considered here is not E, but *our evidence for (1')*. Confusion may result from a failure to see this.

9 Cf. Adams, *Horrendous Evils and the Goodness of God*: "[T]he Divine mind is at once too vast and too stable to experience our participation in horrors in anything like the way we do" (p. 174). Adams adds to this some "compensating" points concerning the Christian doctrine of the Incarnation, namely that God identifies with those who suffer in and through the

crucifixion of Christ, and that this "Divine identification makes the victim's experience of horrors so meaningful that one would not retrospectively wish it away" (pp. 166–7). But "Divine identification" would not (or, at any rate, should not) suffice to render horrific suffering meaningful in retrospect to the sufferer if there were no reason to view it positively *other than* that allegedly provided by the identification. (I might be moved by my mother's willingness to identify with my suffering in the dentist's chair by sitting there herself and letting the dentist drill into her teeth, but suppose I discover that our teeth would have been just fine without the dental work and that my mother knew this. What then?) And Adams suggests no such reason. Indeed, she seems to support the view of this essay when she admits that "[a] horror-free life that ended in beatific intimacy with God would also be one in which the individual enjoyed incommensurate good" (p. 167).

10   As it happens, we do not need to consider possible explicit theodicies to do so: we can make a general point that favors a negative answer to this question and requires a theodicy to be *defeated*, thus allowing us to continue to work within the parameters set out at the beginning of this essay.

11   Note that there is no reason to suppose that a world created by God must be a *physical* world. And no doubt there are not just many physical worlds but also many non-physical worlds from which an omnipotent creator might choose. More on this later.

12   Richard Swinburne, *Providence and the Problem of Evil* (Oxford: Clarendon Press, 1998), pp. 103–4.

13   The applicability of a deontological understanding of justification is here assumed without argument. Something like it is apparently assumed and applied by Rowe, and quite prevalent in recent discussion.

14   Perhaps it will be suggested that even though E does not in fact come into being, there may still be a good reason for God to permit E. God may *permit* something that nonetheless does not come to pass. And it may be said that in that case (5) (and also (4)) is not necessarily true, contrary to what is here being claimed. But this seems to rest on a misunderstanding. (4) and (5) do not claim or imply that if E does not occur, there is no good reason for God to permit E – that E's nonoccurrence is a sufficient condition for the absence of such a reason. Neither do these propositions claim or imply that the nonoccurrence of E *in conjunction with God's existence* is such a sufficient condition. Rather, what they claim is that the truth of a certain *conditional* – "If God exists, E does not exist" – is a sufficient condition for the absence of a good reason for God to permit E. And this claim, unlike the previous two, is true. (For if there were such a reason, God might freely choose to act on it, and so the unequivocal claim of the conditional would be false.)

15 Michael Tooley seems to take this line. See his "The Argument from Evil," in James E. Tomberlin (ed.), *Philosophical Perspectives, 5 Philosophy of Religion, 1991* (Atascadero, CA: Ridgeview Pub. Co., 1991), p. 97.

16 Plantinga suggests such an argument. See section 1 of his "Epistemic Probability and Evil", essay 5 in HS.

17 For such skeptical moves, couched in the language of what would "not be surprising" or what is "true for all we know or justifiedly believe," see especially the essays by Peter van Inwagen and Daniel Howard-Snyder in HS.

18 Both this approach and the example are adapted from the work of Peter van Inwagen. See his essays in HS.

19 These points are taken from the essay by Daniel Howard-Snyder and Alston's second essay in HS.

20 If we deny this, a reductio argument looms – an argument, that is, suggesting that many of the claims we (rightly) consider ourselves justified in believing are in fact unjustified. For some interesting related remarks, see the end of Paul Draper's second essay in HS.

9

PAUL DRAPER

Pain and Pleasure: An Evidential Problem For Theists

I THE NATURE OF THE PROBLEM

I will argue in this essay that our knowledge about pain and pleasure creates an epistemic problem for theists. The problem is not that some proposition about pain and pleasure can be shown to be both true and logically inconsistent with theism. Rather, the problem is evidential. A statement reporting the observations and testimony upon which our knowledge about pain and pleasure is based bears a certain significant negative evidential relation to theism.[1] And because of this, we have a *prima facie* good epistemic reason to reject theism – that is, a reason that is sufficient for rejecting theism unless overridden by other reasons for not rejecting theism.

By "theism" I mean the following statement:

There exists an omnipotent, omniscient, and morally perfect person who created the Universe.

I will use the word "God" as a title rather than as a proper name, and I will stipulate that necessary and sufficient conditions for bearing this title are that one be an omnipotent, omniscient, and morally perfect person who created the Universe. Given this (probably technical) use of the term "God," theism is the statement that God exists.

Some philosophers believe that the evils we find in the world create an evidential problem for theists because theism fails to explain these evils (or most of what we know about them). (See, for example, (Hare 1968).) This

Original publication: Paul Draper, "Pain and Pleasure: An Evidential Problem for Theists," *Noûs* 23 (1989): 331–50.

position is attractive. It seems to reflect the intuitions of a great many people who have regarded evil as an epistemic problem for theists. After all, the most common way of stating the problem of evil is to ask a why-question like "if God exists, then why is there so much evil in the world?" And such questions are either genuine or rhetorical requests for explanation. Moreover, the relevance of theodicies to this alleged problem of evil is quite clear, since a theodicy can very naturally be understood as an attempt to explain certain evils or facts about evil in terms of theism.

But other philosophers who agree that theism fails to explain most of the evils we find in the world deny that this creates an epistemic problem for theists – that is, they deny that this explanatory failure is a *prima facie* good reason to reject theism. This disagreement has led to a debate over how much evil, if any, theism needs to explain to avoid disconfirmation. (See, for example, (Yandell 1969a and 1969b), (Kane 1970), (Mavrodes 1970, pp. 90–111), (Ahern 1971), (Hare 1972), and (Yandell 1972).) What the members of both sides of this debate have failed to recognize is that one cannot determine what facts about evil theism needs to explain or how well it needs to explain them without considering alternatives to theism. The important question, a question that David Hume asked (1980, Part XI, pp. 74–75) but that most contemporary philosophers of religion have ignored, is whether or not any serious hypothesis that is logically inconsistent with theism explains some significant set of facts about evil or about good and evil much better than theism does.

I will argue for an affirmative answer to this question. Specifically, I will compare theism to the following alternative, which I will call "the Hypothesis of Indifference" ("HI" for short):

HI: neither the nature nor the condition of sentient beings on earth is the result of benevolent or malevolent actions performed by non-human persons.

Unlike theism, HI does not entail that supernatural beings exist and so is consistent with naturalism. But HI is also consistent with the existence of supernatural beings. What makes HI inconsistent with theism is that it entails that, if supernatural beings do exist, then no action performed by them is motivated by a direct concern for our well-being. Now let "O" stand for a statement reporting both the observations one has made of humans and animals experiencing pain or pleasure and the testimony one has encountered concerning the observations others have made of sentient beings experiencing pain or pleasure. By "pain" I mean physical or mental suffering of any sort. I will argue that the pain and pleasure in our world create an epistemic problem for theists by arguing that:

C: HI explains the facts O reports much better than theism does.

One problem with this formulation of C is that the verb "to explain" has a number of distinct but easily confused meanings. For my purposes here, it will suffice to point out that in some instances the claim that one hypothesis explains some observation report much better than another is equivalent in meaning, or at least bears a close conceptual connection, to the claim that the truth of that observation report is much less surprising on the first hypothesis than it is on the second. Since I suspect that it is only in these instances that comparisons of explanatory power support comparisons of probability. I will reformulate C as the claim that the facts O reports are much more surprising on theism than they are on HI, or, more precisely, that the antecedent probability of O is much greater on the assumption that HI is true than on the assumption that theism is true. By the "antecedent" probability of O, I mean O's probability, independent of (rather than temporally prior to) the observations and testimony it reports. So my reformulation of C is best expressed as follows:

C: Independent of the observations and testimony O reports, O is
      much more probable on the assumption that HI is true than on the
      assumption that theism is true.

For the sake of brevity, I will use $P(x/y)$ to represent the probability of the statement x, *independent of the observations and testimony O reports*, on the assumption that the statement y is true. Using this notation, I can abbreviate C in the following way:

C: $P(O/HI)$ is much greater than $P(O/theism)$.

One last elucidatory remark about C. The probabilities employed in C are epistemic ones rather than, for example, statistical, physical, or logical probabilities.[2] Thus, they can vary from person to person and from time to time, since different persons can be in different epistemic situations at the same time and the same person can be in different epistemic situations at different times. For example, suppose that six hands of poker are dealt. Then the epistemic probability that one hand includes four aces will be different for those players who inspect their hands and find no aces and those players who inspect their hands and discover one or more aces. And the epistemic probability for any of the six players that one hand includes four aces will be different before inspecting his or her hand than after inspecting it.

Now suppose that I succeed in showing that C is true (relative to my own and my readers' epistemic situations). Then the truth of C is (for us) a *prima facie* good (epistemic) reason to believe that theism is less probable than HI. Thus, since the denial of theism is obviously entailed by HI and so is at least as probable as HI, the truth of C is a *prima facie* good reason to believe that theism is less probable than not. And since it is epistemically irrational to believe both that theism is true and that it is less probable than not, the truth of C is also a *prima facie* good reason to reject (i.e., to cease or refrain from believing) theism.

In section II, I will argue that C is true. However, my argument will depend on the assumption that theodicies do not significantly raise P(O/theism). In section III, I will defend this assumption. And in section IV, I will discuss the significance of C's truth.

II THE BIOLOGICAL UTILITY OF PAIN AND PLEASURE

The claim that P(O/HI) is much greater than P(O/theism) is by no means obviously true. The fact that O reports observations and testimony about pleasure as well as pain should make this clear. So an argument for this claim is needed. I will argue that it is the biological role played by both pain and pleasure in goal-directed organic systems that renders this claim true. In order to explain precisely why this is so, I will need to introduce a concept of "biological usefulness."

Though no one doubts that organic systems are goal-directed in some objective sense, it is by no means easy to provide a precise analysis of this kind of goal-directedness. As a first approximation, we may say that a system S is "goal-directed" just in case for some property G that S has exhibited or will exhibit, a broad range of potential environmental changes are such that: (i) if they occurred at a time when S is exhibiting G and no compensating changes took place in the parts of S, then S would cease to exhibit G and never exhibit G again, and (ii) if they occurred at a time when S is exhibiting G, then compensating changes would take place in the parts of S, resulting in either S's continuing to exhibit G or in S's exhibiting G once again. (Cf. (Boorse 1976) and (Ruse 1973).) Notice that to be goal-directed in this sense does not entail direction to the conscious end of some intelligent being. Notice also that the organic world is made up of complex and interdependent goal-directed systems, including ecosystems, populations of organisms, organisms, parts of organisms, parts of parts of organisms, and so on.

I will call the goals to which organic systems are directed in this sense their "biological goals." And I will say that a part of some goal-directed organic system S is "biologically useful" just in case (i) it causally contributes to one of S's biological goals (or to one of the biological goals of some other goal-directed organic system of which it is a part), and (ii) its doing so is not biologically accidental. (It is in virtue of clause (ii) that, for example, a non-fatal heart attack that prevents a person from committing suicide cannot be called biologically useful.) Notice that much of the pain and pleasure in the world is biologically useful in this sense. Consider, for example, the pain my cat Hector felt when he jumped on top of a hot oven door. Hector's quick response to this pain enabled him to avoid serious injury, and he now flees whenever an oven door is opened. Hector's pain in this case, like much of the pain reported by O, was biologically useful. For it causally contributed to two central biological goals of individual organisms, namely, survival and reproduction, and its doing so was plainly not accidental from a biological point of view. Of course, there is also much pain and pleasure in our world that is not biologically useful: for instance, masochistic pleasure and pain resulting from burns that ultimately prove fatal. (I will sometimes call this kind of pain and pleasure "biologically gratuitous.")

This notion of biological utility enables me to introduce a statement logically equivalent to O that will help me show that C is true. Let "O1," "O2," and "O3" stand for statements respectively reporting the facts O reports about:

(1)   moral agents experiencing pain or pleasure that we know to be biologically useful,

(2)   sentient beings that are not moral agents experiencing pain or pleasure that we know to be biologically useful, and

(3)   sentient beings experiencing pain or pleasure that we do not know to be biologically useful.

Since O is obviously logically equivalent to the conjunction of O1, O2, and O3, it follows that, for any hypothesis h:

$P(O/h) = P(O1 \& O2 \& O3/h)$.

But the following theorem of the mathematical calculus of probability holds for epistemic probability:

$P(O1 \& O2 \& O3/h) = P(O1/h) \times P(O2/h \& O1) \times P(O3/h \& O1 \& O2)$.[3]

Thus, C is true – P(O/HI) is much greater than P(O/theism) – just in case:

A: $P(O1/HI) \times P(O2/HI \& O1) \times P(O3/HI \& O1 \& O2)$

is much greater than

B: $P(O1/theism) \times P(O2/theism \& O1) \times P(O3/theism \& O1 \& O2)$.

I will argue that A is much greater than B by arguing that each of the multiplicands of A is either greater or much greater than the corresponding multiplicand of B. As I will explain in section III, my arguments will assume that theodicies do not significantly raise P(O/theism).

Let us begin with O1, which reports those facts reported by O about humans (who are moral agents) experiencing pain or pleasure that we know to be biologically useful. We know antecedently – that is, we know independent of the observations and testimony O reports – that humans are goal-directed organic systems, composed of parts that systematically contribute to the biological goals of these systems. This seems to give us reason to expect that human pain and pleasure, if they exist, will also systematically contribute to these goals. (And this is, of course, precisely what O1 reports.) But notice that pain and pleasure are in one respect strikingly dissimilar to other parts of organic systems: they have intrinsic moral value. Pain is intrinsically bad, and pleasure is intrinsically good. Does this difference substantially decrease the amount of support that our antecedent knowledge about humans gives to the "prediction" that pain and pleasure, if they exist, will systematically contribute to biological goals? I submit that it does if we assume that theism is true, but does not if we assume that HI is true. It is this difference between HI and theism that makes P(O1/HI) much greater than (P(O1/theism).

Allow me to explain. HI entails that, if pain and pleasure exist, then they are not the result of malevolent or benevolent actions performed by nonhuman persons. So on HI, the moral difference between pain and pleasure and other parts of organic systems gives us no antecedent reason to believe that pain and pleasure will not play the same biological role that other parts of organic systems play. Indeed, a biological explanation of pain and pleasure is just the sort of explanation that one would expect on HI. But theism entails that God is responsible for the existence of any pain and pleasure in the world. Since God is morally perfect, He would have good moral reasons for producing pleasure even if it is never biologically useful, and He would not permit pain unless He had, not just a biological reason, but also a morally sufficient reason to do so. And since God is omnipotent and omniscient, He could create goal-directed organic systems (including humans) without biologically useful pain and pleasure. So theism entails both that God does not need biologically useful pain and pleasure to produce human goal-directed organic systems and that, if human pain and pleasure exist, then God had good moral reasons for producing them, reasons that, for all we know antecedently, might very well be inconsistent with pain and pleasure systematically contributing to the biological goals of human organisms. Therefore, we would have much less reason on theism than on HI to be surprised if it turned out that human pain and pleasure differed from other parts of organic systems by not systematically contributing to the biological goals of those systems. Hence, since O1 reports that the pain and pleasure experienced by humans (who are moral agents) do contribute in this way, P(O1/HI) is much greater than P(O1/theism).

One might object that from theism and our antecedent knowledge that goal-directed organic systems exist we can infer that the biological functions of the parts of those systems are themselves morally worthwhile, which gives us reason on theism that we do not have on HI to expect pain and pleasure to have biological functions. It might be thought that this counterbalances the reasons offered above for concluding that O1 is antecedently much more likely given HI than it is given theism.[4] Now we obviously cannot infer from theism and our antecedent knowledge that, the greater the number of functioning parts in an organic system, the more valuable the system. We might be able to infer that organic systems are valuable and that the parts of these systems that have biological functions are valuable because the systems could not exist without functioning parts. But this does not imply that we have as much or even close to as much reason on theism as on HI to expect pain and pleasure to have biological functions. For an omnipotent and omniscient being could produce such systems without biologically useful pain and pleasure. Thus, since a morally perfect being would try to accomplish its goals with as little pain as possible, the value of organic systems gives us no reason on theism to expect pain to have biological functions. And since pleasure has intrinsic value and so is worth producing whether or not it furthers some other goal, the value of organic systems gives us very little reason on theism to expect pleasure to have biological functions.

O2 reports the observations and testimony reported by O about sentient beings that are not moral agents (e.g., young human children and nonhuman animals) experiencing pain or pleasure that we know to be biologically useful. Independent of the observations and testimony O reports, we know that some sentient beings that are not moral agents are biologically very similar to moral agents. Since O1 implies that moral agents experience biologically useful pain and pleasure, this knowledge makes it antecedently likely on HI & O1 that some sentient beings that are not moral agents will also experience biologically useful pain and pleasure. Now at first glance, one might think that this knowledge makes the existence of such pain and pleasure just as likely on theism & O1. After all, from the assumption that theism and O1 are both true it follows that God has good moral reasons for permitting biologically useful pain. But there is an important difference between the biologically useful pain that O1 reports and the biologically useful pain that O2 reports. Given theism & O1, we have reason to believe that God permits the pain O1 reports because it plays some sort of (presently indiscernible) moral role in the lives of the humans that experience it. But the pain O2 reports cannot play such a role, since the subjects of it are not moral agents. This difference is plainly not relevant on HI & O1, but it gives us some reason on theism & O1 to expect that the good moral reasons God has for permitting moral agents to experience pain do not apply to animals that are not moral agents, and hence some reason to believe that God will not permit such beings to experience pain. So $P(O2/HI \& O1)$ is somewhat greater than $P(O2/theism \& O1)$.

O3 reports facts about sentient beings experiencing pain or pleasure that we do not know to be biologically useful. This includes much pain and pleasure that we know to be biologically gratuitous, as well as some that is not known to be useful and is also not known to be gratuitous. I will give a two-part argument for the conclusion that P(O3/HI & O1 & O2) is much greater than P(O3/theism & O1 & O2).

First, we obviously have much more reason on theism & O1 & O2 than we have on HI & O1 & O2 to expect sentient beings (especially nonhuman animals) to be happy – in any case much more happy than they would be if their pleasure were limited to that reported by O1 and O2. Instead, when the facts O3 reports are added to those reported by O1 and O2, we find that many humans and animals experience prolonged and intense suffering and a much greater number are far from happy. In addition, we have more reason on theism & O1 & O2 than on HI & O1 & O2 to expect to discover a close connection between certain moral goods (e.g., justice and virtue) and biologically gratuitous pain and pleasure, but we discover no such connection.

Second, we have, antecedently, much more reason on HI & O1 & O2 than on theism & O1 & O2 to believe that the fundamental role of pain and pleasure in our world is a biological one and that the presence of biologically gratuitous pain and pleasure is epiphenomenal, a biological accident resulting from nature's or an indifferent creator's failure to "fine tune" organic systems. And this is undeniably supported (though not entailed) by what O3 reports. To demonstrate this, a couple definitions are needed. First, by "pathological" pain or pleasure. I mean pain or pleasure that results from the failure of some organic system to function properly. For example, pain caused by terminal cancer and sadistic pleasure are pathological in this sense. And second, by "biologically appropriate" pain or pleasure, I mean pain or pleasure that occurs in a situation which is such that, it is biologically useful that pain or pleasure is felt in situations of this sort. For instance, the pain felt by a person killed in a fire is not biologically useful, but it is biologically appropriate because it is biologically useful that humans feel pain when they come in contact with fire. Clearly much of the pain and pleasure reported by O3 is either pathological or biologically appropriate, and very little is known to be both non-pathological and biologically inappropriate.[5] And this is exactly what one would expect if pain and pleasure are fundamentally biological rather than moral phenomena, and so is much more to be expected on HI & O1 & O2 than on theism & O1 & O2.

Therefore, assuming that theodicies do not significantly raise P(O/theism), the first and third multiplicands of A are much greater than the first and third multiplicands of B, and the second multiplicand of A is greater than the second multiplicand of B. And this implies that P(O/HI) is much greater than P(O/theism).

III   THE MORAL VALUE OF PAIN AND PLEASURE

In addition to their biological roles, pain and pleasure also play various moral roles in our world. By appealing to these roles, the theist might hope to explain some of the facts O reports in terms of theism, and thereby render O less surprising on theism than it is initially. This would seem to be the theist's most promising strategy for undermining the argument for C given above. Theodicies can be treated as attempts to carry out such a strategy.[6] While few would deny that most theodicies are rather obvious failures, it is widely thought that plausible theistic explanations of suffering can be constructed by appealing to the intrinsic or instrumental moral value of free will. So it is necessary to determine what effect such theodicies have on P(O/theism). Additionally, it is important to evaluate the increasingly popular position that evidential arguments from evil against theism fail because the disproportion between omniscience and human knowledge makes it quite likely, on the assumption that God exists, that humans would not understand why God permits evil. (For a defense of this position, see (Wykstra 1984).)

A.   Evaluating theodicies

Explaining some phenomenon in terms of a statement usually involves adding other statements to that statement. This is certainly true in the case of theodicies, which typically add to the claim that God exists the claims that God has a certain goal, that even God must produce or permit certain evils in order to accomplish that goal, and that accomplishing the goal is, from a moral point of view, worth the evils. I will say that a statement h* is an "expansion" of a statement h just in case h* is known to entail h. (Notice that h* can be an expansion of h even if it is logically equivalent to h.) The effect of a theodicy on P(O/theism) can be assessed by identifying an appropriate expansion T_n of theism that the theodicy employs and then using the following principle to evaluate P(O/theism) (cf. (Adams 1985, appendix, p. 252)):

$$P(O/\text{theism}) = (P(T_n/\text{theism}) \times P(O/T_n)) + (P(\sim T_n/\text{theism}) \times P(O/\text{theism} \& \sim T_n)).[7]$$

I will call this principle the "Weighted Average Principle" ("WAP" for short) because it identifies one probability with a probability weighted average of two others. Roughly, WAP tells us that P(O/theism) is the average of $P(O/T_n)$ and P(O/theism & $\sim T_n$). This average, however, is a probability weighted average, the weights of which are $P(T_n/\text{theism})$ and P($\sim T_n$/theism). The higher $P(T_n/\text{theism})$, the closer P(O/theism) will be to $P(O/T_n)$. And the lower $P(T_n/\text{theism})$, the closer P(O/theism) will be to P(O/theism & $\sim T_n$).

WAP clarifies the relationship between theodicies and the argument for C I gave in section II. For example, suppose that, for some expansion T_n of theism that a certain theodicy employs, $P(T_n/\text{theism})$ is high. My argument for C in section II ignores this theodicy and so in effect equates P(O/theism) with P(O/theism & $\sim T_n$). Since $P(T_n/\text{theism})$ is high, WAP tells us that P(O/theism) is actually closer to $P(O/T_n)$ than to P(O/theism & $\sim T_n$) (assuming that these are not the same). To successfully defend my assumption in section II that this theodicy does not significantly raise P(O/theism), I would need to show that $P(O/T_n)$ is not significantly greater than P(O/theism & $\sim T_n$). In other words, I would need to show that, independent of the observations and testimony O reports, we have little or no more reason on T_n than we have on theism & $\sim T_n$ to believe that O is true.

B. Free will and the advancement of morality

Most free will theodicies appeal to a certain sort of moral freedom, which I will call "freedom*." An action is free* only if (i) it is free in an incompatibilist sense – that is, in a sense incompatible with its being determined by antecedent conditions outside the agent's control – and (ii) if it is morally right, then at least one alternative action that is open in an incompatibilist sense to the agent is such that it would be morally wrong for the agent to perform that alternative action. This concept of freedom is used to give the following theistic explanation of immorality.

Freedom* has great value (either because morally right actions that are freely* performed are more valuable than right actions that are not freely* performed or because, following Hick (1966), moral virtue that is acquired by freely* performing right actions is more valuable than moral virtue that is not freely* acquired). For this reason, God endows humans with freedom*. However, since it is logically impossible to force a person to freely* perform a right action instead of a wrong one, God cannot give humans freedom* and ensure that humans will never perform morally wrong actions. Unfortunately, humans sometimes abuse their freedom* by performing wrong actions. Nevertheless, God is justified in giving humans freedom* because a world in which humans freely* perform both right and wrong actions is (provided that the balance of right over wrong actions or of morally good humans over morally bad humans is sufficiently favorable) better than a world in which immorality is prevented by withholding freedom* from humans.

Notice that, so far, we have no explanation of the existence of pain. For there are morally right actions and morally wrong actions that do not entail the existence of pain. Wrong actions of this sort include some instances of breaking promises, killing, attempting to cause pain, and depriving someone of pleasure. So God could have given humans freedom* without permitting pain. The first version of the free will theodicy that I will evaluate adds to the above explanation of immorality the proposal that God permits pain in order to advance morality. This proposal can be spelled out in the following way. God wants humans to freely* perform right actions instead of wrong ones. Of course, as mentioned above, He cannot force humans to freely* perform only morally right actions, but He would have some control over the balance of right over wrong actions because even free* choices can be influenced and because God would know what free* choices humans would make (or would be likely to make[8]) in various situations. In particular, God might use pain to influence humans to freely* perform right actions instead of wrong ones. Also, some right actions entail the existence of pain, and God might know prior to creating humans that some or all humans would perform (or would be likely to perform) these right actions if given the chance. Therefore, God might use pain to obtain a more favorable balance of freely* performed right actions over wrong actions.

This version of the free will theodicy employs the following expansion of theism:

T_1:   God exists, and one of His final ends is a favorable balance of freely* performed right actions over wrong actions.[9]

I doubt that a consensus could ever be reached about $P(T_1/\text{theism})$. For T_1 presupposes several very controversial metaphysical and ethical positions. For example, it presupposes that the concept of "freedom*" is coherent, that humans have freedom*, and that freedom* is of great value. Since I obviously do not have the space here to discuss how plausible these claims are, I will assume for the sake of argument that $P(T_1/\text{theism})$ is high.

I will argue, however, that $P(O/T_1)$ is not significantly higher than $P(O/\text{theism} \ \& \sim T_1)$. This implies that, even if $P(T_1/\text{theism})$ is high, our first version of the free will theodicy does not significantly increase $P(O/\text{theism})$. If, as I will assume, it is morally permissible for God to use pain to advance morality, then we have reason on T_1 that we do not have on theism $\& \sim T_1$ to expect that the world will contain both pain that influences humans to perform morally right actions and pain that is logically necessary for some of the right actions humans perform. Since O reports the existence of pain of both these sorts, we have a predictive success for the theodicy. But O also reports both that pain often influences humans to perform morally wrong actions and that pain is logically necessary for many of the wrong actions humans perform. And we have reason on T_1 that we do not have on theism $\& \sim T_1$ to be *surprised* by these facts. Furthermore, the observations and testimony O reports provide strong evidence that the world does not presently contain a very impressive balance of right over wrong actions performed by humans and that this is due in part both to a variety of demoralizing conditions like illness, poverty and ignorance, and to the absence of conditions that tend to promote morality. All of this is even more surprising on T_1 than on theism $\& \sim T_1$. (Cf. (Adams 1985, pp. 250–251).) So T_1's "predictive" advantages are counterbalanced by several serious "predictive" disadvantages, and for this reason $P(O/T_1)$ is not significantly greater than $P(O/\text{theism} \ \& \sim T_1)$.

C.   Free will and responsibility

Some free will theodicists claim that God gives humans the freedom* to bring about suffering (either by producing it or by failing to prevent it) in order to increase the responsibility humans have for their own well-being and the well-being of others and thereby increase the importance of the moral decisions humans make. By an "important" moral decision, these theodicists mean a decision upon which the presence or absence of something of great positive or negative value depends. The key value judgement here is that, all else held equal, the more important the moral decisions we are free* to make, the more valuable our freedom* is. By not preventing us from freely* bringing about evils, including serious ones, God increases our control over how valuable the world is and thereby increases the value of our freedom*. This theodicy employs the following expansion of theism:

T_2:   God exists, and one of His final ends is for humans to have the freedom* to make very important moral decisions.

I will assume, once again, that $P(T_2/\text{theism})$ is high, and I will argue that this second version of the free will theodicy does not significantly raise $P(O/\text{theism})$ by arguing that $P(O/T_2)$ is not significantly greater than $P(O/\text{theism} \& \sim T_2)$.

I will begin by arguing that Richard Swinburne (1979, Ch. 11) fails in his attempt to extend this theodicy so that it accounts for pain for which humans are not morally responsible. (I will call this sort of pain "amoral pain.") Swinburne believes that free will theodicies that employ T_2 can account for such pain because (i) they explain why God gives humans the freedom* to bring about suffering and (ii) amoral pain is necessary if humans are to have genuine freedom* to bring about suffering. Swinburne defends (ii) in the following way. Freedom* to bring about suffering requires the knowledge of how to bring about suffering. And humans can obtain such knowledge in only one of two ways: either by God telling them how to bring about suffering or by experiencing how this is done. Unfortunately, if God told humans how to bring about suffering, then humans would know that God exists, and hence would have little temptation to do evil and so no genuine freedom* to bring about suffering. So for humans to have such freedom, they must learn by experience how to bring about suffering, and hence must learn this either by observing suffering for which no human is morally responsible or by observing suffering brought about by other humans. But for any particular kind of suffering, there must have been a first time that a human brought it about, and so a time when a human knew how to bring it about despite never having observed suffering of that kind brought about by a human. Hence, if humans are to learn by experience how to bring about suffering, then amoral pain must exist. Therefore, such suffering is necessary for humans to have the freedom* to bring about suffering.

I will make three comments about this argument for (ii). First, even if it is sound, it obviously does not provide an adequate theistic account of amoral pain from which humans gain no new knowledge about how to produce or prevent suffering. Second, even if it is sound, it does not provide an adequate theistic explanation of most of the amoral pain that does give humans new knowledge of this sort. For an omnipotent and omniscient being could have greatly decreased the variety of ways in which humans know how to harm others, and so greatly decreased the amount of amoral pain needed for this knowledge, without decreasing the amount of harm humans can do to others and so without decreasing the amount of control that humans have over the well-being of others. Third, and most importantly, the argument is not sound. As Stump (1983) and Moser (1984) have observed, God could, without permitting amoral pain, give humans the knowledge of how to bring about suffering without revealing His existence and so without undermining human freedom*. For example, as Stump (pp. 52–53) has pointed out, humans might regularly have vivid, message-laden dreams and learn of their reliability, and yet not be compelled to believe in God.

So if this second version of the free will theodicy raises $P(O/\text{theism})$ at all, it is because we have reason on T_2 that we do not have on theism & $\sim T_2$ to expect the existence of pain for which humans are morally responsible. Now giving humans the freedom* to bring about intense suffering is certainly one way (though not the only way) of giving humans the freedom* to make important moral decisions. So assuming that there is no better way,[10] we have some reason on T_2 to expect humans to have such freedom, and so reason on T_2 to expect the existence of pain for which humans are morally responsible. But even granting all this, it can be shown that $P(O/T_2)$ is not significantly greater than $P(O/\text{theism} \& \sim T_2)$ by showing that other facts O reports are even more surprising on T_2 than they are on theism & $\sim T_2$.

An analogy between God and a good parent will be useful here. Ironically, such an analogy is often used to defend this sort of theodicy. For example, Swinburne (1979) responds to the objection that God should not give humans the freedom* to seriously harm others by asserting that the objector is asking that God "make a toy-world, a world where [our choices] matter, but not very much" (p. 219). Such a God "would be like the over-protective parent who will not let his child out of sight for a moment" (p. 220). But Swinburne neglects to ask whether or not humans are worthy of the freedom* to seriously harm others. A good parent gradually increases a child's responsibility as the child becomes capable of handling greater responsibility. Children who are unworthy of a certain responsibility are not benefitted by parents who give them that responsibility. On the assumption that T_2 is true, one would expect that God would behave like a good parent, giving humans great responsibility only when we are worthy of it. I am not claiming that on T_2 one would expect God to impose a good moral character on humans before He gives them serious responsibilities. Nor am I claiming that creatures who are worthy of great responsibility would never abuse that responsibility. Rather, I am claiming that on T_2 one would expect God to give all or some humans less responsibility – and in particular no ability to do serious evils – until they freely* developed the strength of character that would make them worthy of greater responsibility. And if at some point humans become worthy of and are given great responsibility, but nevertheless abuse this responsibility to such an extent that they are no longer worthy of it, then one would on T_2 expect God, like a good parent, to decrease the amount of responsibility humans have until they are worthy of a second chance.

But O conflicts with all of these expectations. Many humans are plainly not worthy of the freedom* to do serious evils. Nor is the human race making any significant amount of moral progress. If God exists, then for centuries He has been allowing his children to torment, torture, and kill each other. Thus, even if they were once worthy of great responsibility, they no longer are, and hence are not benefitted by having such responsibility. So like T_1, T_2's predictive advantages are counterbalanced by several serious predictive disadvantages. Therefore, $P(O/T_2)$ is not significantly greater than $P(O/\text{theism } \& \sim T_2)$, and hence this second version of the free will theodicy fails to significantly raise $P(O/\text{theism})$.

D.   The "infinite intellect defense"

Some philosophers think that "evidential arguments from evil" can be refuted by pointing out that, since God's knowledge about good and evil is limitless, it is not all that surprising that He produces or permits evils for reasons that are unknown to humans. The expansion of theism suggested here is the following:

> T_3: God exists and has a vast amount of knowledge about good and evil and how they are related that humans do not have.

Since $P(T_3/\text{theism}) = $ one, $P(O/\text{theism}) = P(O/T_3)$. But this does not reveal any defect in my argument for C. For antecedently – that is, independent of the observations and testimony O reports – we have no reason to think that God's additional knowledge concerning good and evil is such that He would permit any of the facts O reports to obtain. Of course, an omnipotent and omniscient being might, for all we know antecedently, have moral reasons unknown to us to permit the evil reported by O. But it is also the case that such a being might, for all we know antecedently, have moral reasons unknown to us to prevent this evil. Indeed, we have no more reason antecedently to believe that such a being would know of some great good unknown to us whose existence entails the existence of the pain O reports than we have reason to believe that such a being would know of some great good unknown to us whose existence entails the nonexistence of the pain or the pleasure that O reports. And an omnipotent and omniscient being might very well know of means, far too complicated for humans to understand, by which He could obtain certain goods without the evil O reports. Of course, *given the facts O reports*, we have some reason on T_3 to expect that humans will be unable to produce a plausible theistic explanation of those facts. But HI gives us even more reason to expect this. So human ignorance does not solve the theist's evidential problems.

Hence, none of the theodicies we have considered significantly raises $P(O/\text{theism})$. Therefore, relative to the epistemic situations of those of us who are unable to think of some other much more successful theodicy (i.e., all of us, I suspect), C is true: $P(O/HI)$ is much greater than $P(O/\text{theism})$.

IV   THE SIGNIFICANCE OF THE PROBLEM

In *The Origin of Species*, Charles Darwin argued that his theory of the evolution of species by means of natural selection explains numerous facts (e.g., the geographical distribution of species and the existence of atrophied organs in animals) much better than the alternative hypothesis that each species of plant and animal was independently created by God. (Let us call this latter hypothesis "special creationism.") Darwin's results were significant partly because special creationists at Darwin's time did not have nor were they able to obtain any evidence favoring special creationism over evolution theory that outweighed or at least offset Darwin's evidence favoring evolution theory over special creationism. For this reason, many theists, while continuing to believe in creationism, which is consistent with Darwin's theory, rejected special creationism. And those theists who were familiar with Darwin's arguments and yet remained special creationists did so at a cost: their belief in special creationism was no longer an epistemically rational one.

Similarly, how significant my results are depends, in part, on how many theists have or could obtain propositional or non-propositional evidence favoring theism over HI that offsets the propositional evidence, provided by my argument for C, favoring HI over theism.[11] Any theist confronted with my argument for C that lacks such evidence and is unable to obtain it cannot rationally continue to believe that theism is true. It is beyond the scope of this essay to determine how many theists would be in such a position. But I will make four sets of comments that I hope indicate how difficult a theist's search for the needed evidence might be.

First, I do not see how it could be shown that HI is an *ad hoc* hypothesis or that theism is *intrinsically* more probable than HI. For HI is consistent with a wide variety of both naturalistic and supernaturalistic hypotheses, and it has no positive ontological commitments. Theism, on the other hand, is a very specific supernaturalistic claim with a very strong ontological commitment. Indeed, such differences between theism and HI might very well provide additional evidence favoring HI over theism.

Second, traditional and contemporary arguments for theism are far from compelling – that is, they are far from being so persuasive as to coerce the acceptance of all or even most rational theists. Thus, even if some such argument were sound, most theists, including many philosophically sophisticated ones, would not recognize this, and hence the argument would not provide them with evidence favoring theism over HI. (The evidence would exist, but they would not *have* it.)

Third, many traditional and contemporary arguments for theism, including many versions of the cosmological argument, the teleological argument, and the argument from consciousness, may not solve the theist's problem even if they are sound and recognized by the theist to be so. For they at most purport to show that an omnipotent and omniscient being exists – not that that being is morally perfect. Suppose then that some such argument is sound. My argument for C would work just as well if HI were replaced with the following hypothesis, which I will call "the Indifferent Deity Hypothesis":

> There exists an omnipotent and omniscient person who created the Universe and who has no intrinsic concern about the pain or pleasure of other beings.

Like theism, this hypothesis entails that an omnipotent and omniscient being exists. So establishing that such a being exists would help the theist only if the theist also has strong evidence favoring theism over the Indifferent Deity Hypothesis.[12]

Finally, religious experiences of the kind appealed to by "Reformed Epistemologists" like Alvin Plantinga (1983) are ambiguous with respect to the moral attributes of the creator. While Plantinga is correct in claiming that theists typically do feel inclined in certain circumstances (e.g., "when life is sweet and satisfying") to think that the creator is morally good, sensitive theists also feel inclined in other circumstances – namely, when they experience poignant evil – to believe that the creator is indifferent to their good or to the good of others. And many atheists have very powerful experiences in which they seem to be aware of the ultimate indifference of nature. These experiences are very common and are very similar phenomenologically to the experiences Plantinga mentions. Moreover, C implies that these "experiences of indifference" are better corroborated than the "theistic experiences" to which Plantinga appeals. Thus, even if Plantinga is correct in thinking that theistic experiences confer *prima facie* justification on the theist's belief in God, experiences of indifference defeat this justification. Therefore, theistic experiences do not provide non-propositional evidence that favors theism over HI, or at least none that outweighs the propositional evidence favoring HI over theism provided by my argument for C.[13]

REFERENCES

Adams, Robert M. 1977. Middle Knowledge and the Problem of Evil, *American Philosophical Quarterly* 14, 109–117.
—— 1985. Plantinga on the Problem of Evil, in *Alvin Plantinga*, James E. Tomberlin and Peter van Inwagen, eds., *Profiles*, Dordrecht: D. Reidel, pp. 225–55.
Ahern, M. B. 1971. *The Problem of Evil*, London: Routledge and Kegan Paul.
Boorse, Christopher. 1976. Wright on Functions, *The Philosophical Review* 85, 70–86.
Hare, Peter H. and Madden, Edward H. 1968. *Evil and the Concept of God*, Springfield: Charles C. Thomas.
—— 1972. Evil and Inconclusiveness, *Sophia* 11, 8–12.
Hick, John. 1966. *Evil and the God of Love*, New York: Harper and Row.
Hume, David. 1980. *Dialogues Concerning Natural Religion*, Richard Popkin, ed., Indianapolis: Hackett Publishing Co.
Kane, Stanley. 1970. Theism and Evil, *Sophia* 9, 14–21.
Mavrodes, George I. 1970. *Belief in God: A Study in the Epistemology of Religion*, New York: Random House.
Moser, Paul K. 1984. Natural Evil and the Free Will Defense, *International Journal for the Philosophy of Religion* 15, 49–56.
Pargetter, Robert. 1976. Evil as Evidence Against the Existence of God, *Mind* 85, 242–5.
Plantinga, Alvin. 1979. The Probabilistic Argument From Evil, *Philosophical Studies* 35, 1–53.
—— 1983. Reason and Belief in God, in *Faith and Rationality: Reason and Belief in God*, Alvin Plantinga and Nicholas Wolterstorff, eds., Notre Dame: University of Notre Dame Press, pp. 16–93.
Reichenbach, Bruce. 1980. The Inductive Argument From Evil, *American Philosophical Quarterly* 17, 221–7.
Ruse, Michael. 1973. *The Philosophy of Biology*, London: Hutchingson & Co.
Sircello, Guy. 1975. *A New Theory of Beauty*, Princeton: Princeton University Press.
Stump, Elcomore. 1983. Knowledge. Freedom and the Problem of Evil, *International Journal for the Philosophy of Religion* 14, 49–58.
Swinburne, Richard. 1979. *The Existence of God*, Oxford: Clarendon Press.
Wykstra, Steven. 1984. The Humean Obstacle to Evidential Arguments From Suffering: On Avoiding the Evils of "Appearance," *International Journal for the Philosophy of Religion* 16, 73–93.
Yandell, Keith E. 1969a. Ethics, Evils, and Theism, *Sophia* 8, 18–28.
—— 1969b. A Premature Farewell to Theism, *Religious Studies* 5, 251–5.
—— 1972. Theism and Evil: A Reply, *Sophia* 11, 1–7.

LEEDS TRINITY UNIVERSITY

NOTES

1 I agree with most philosophers of religion that theists face no serious logical problem of evil. This paper challenges the increasingly popular view (defended recently by Pargetter, 1976, Plantinga, 1979, and Reichenbach, 1980) that theists face no serious evidential problem of evil.

2 The concept of epistemic probability is an ordinary concept of probability for which no adequate philosophical analysis has, in my opinion, been proposed. As a first approximation, however, perhaps the following analysis will do:

> Relative to K, p is epistemically more probable than q, where K is an epistemic situation and p and q are propositions, just in case any fully rational person in K would have a higher degree of belief in p than in q.

3 One difficulty with the claim that this theorem of the probability calculus is true for epistemic probability is that, since multiplication and addition can only be performed on numbers, it follows that the theorem presupposes that probabilities have numerical values. But most epistemic probabilities have only comparative values. This difficulty can be overcome by intepreting the claim that this theorem is true for epistemic probability as the claim that (i) if each of the probabilities in the theorem have numerical values, then the theorem states the numerical relationships which hold between them, and (ii) if at least one probability in the theorem does not have a numerical value, then all statements of comparative probability entailed by that theorem are true. My reason for believing that this theorem is true for epistemic probability in this sense is that I can find no counterexample to it. I do not place a lot of emphasis on the mere fact that it is a theorem of the probability calculus. For I do not believe that all theorems of the probability calculus are true for epistemic probability.

4 I am grateful to a *Noûs* referee for this objection.

5 Even the enjoyment of perceiving beauty may be biologically appropriate. For our enjoyment of clear perception is plausibly thought to be biolgically useful, and Guy Sircello (1975, pp. 129–34) gives a very interesting argument for the conclusion that perceiving beauty is a special case of clear perception.

6 The term "theodicy" is often defined as "an attempt to state what God's actual reason for permitting evil is." This definition implies that, in order to show that some theodicy is successful, one must show that God exists. I

prefer a definition of "theodicy" that avoids this implication. By a "theodicy" I mean an attempt to give a plausible theistic explanation of some fact about evil.

7   More generally, it follows from the probability calculus that $P(O/\text{theism}) = (P(T_n/\text{theism}) \times P(O/\text{theism \& } T_n)) + (P(\sim T_n/\text{theism}) \times P(O/\text{theism \& } \sim T_n))$. WAP replaces $P(O/\text{theism \& } T_n)$ with $P(O/T_n)$ because T_n is an expansion of theism and hence is known to be logically equivalent to theism & T_n.

8   Robert Adams (1977) argues that God, despite being omniscient, would not know what free* choice a particular human would make in a certain situation prior to deciding both to place that human in that situation and to allow him to make that choice. Adams also argues, however, that God would have prior knowledge of what free* choices humans would be likely to make in various situations.

9   A slightly different version of this theodicy employs the following expansion of theism:

T_1^*:   God exists, and one of His final ends is a favorable balance of morally good humans whose moral goodness was freely* acquired over morally bad humans.

I suspect that $P(T_1^*/\text{theism})$ is greater than $P(T_1/\text{theism})$ because God would be more likely to be concerned about persons than about actions. However, I need not evaluate T_1^* separately because I will assume that $P(T_1/\text{theism})$ is high and my arguments concerning $P(O/T_1)$ would work just as well if T_1 were replaced with T_1^*.

10   One might challenge this assumption and thereby attack theodicies that employ T_2 in the following way. Choosing whether or not to produce a large amount of pleasure is, all else held equal, a more important moral decision than choosing whether or not to produce a small amount of pain. Hence, it would seem that by increasing our capacity to produce or prevent pleasure, God could give us the power to make moral decisions about pleasure that are as important as any that we now make concerning pain. But it is antecedently likely that such a world would be a better world than one in which humans have the ability to cause others to suffer. Therefore, it is antecedently unlikely that God would use pain to accomplish His goal of giving humans important moral choices.

11   One way of attempting to show that such evidence exists would be to (i) identify an appropriate body of evidence (call it O*) that is broader than O (e.g., a statement reporting the relevant observations and testimony, not just about pain and pleasure, but about all intrinsic goods and evils) and then (ii) attempt to show that, independent of the

observations and testimony O* reports, O* is at least as likely on theism as it is on HI.

12 Swinburne (1979, ch. 5) argues that quasi-theistic hypotheses like the Indifferent Deity Hypothesis are intrinsically much less probable than theism. I do not believe his argument is sound, but if it were, then strong evidence favoring theism over the Indifferent Deity Hypothesis would be available.

13 For criticisms of previous versions of this essay, I am grateful to Gary Gutting, C. Stephen Layman, Nelson Pike, Alvin Plantinga, Philip L. Quinn, and an anonymous *Noûs* referee.

10

PETER VAN INWAGEN

The Problem of Evil, the Problem of Air, and the Problem of Silence

It used to be widely held that evil – which for present purposes we may identify with undeserved pain and suffering – was incompatible with the existence of God: that no possible world contained both God and evil. So far as I am able to tell, this thesis is no longer defended. But arguments for the following weaker thesis continue to be very popular: Evil (or at least evil of the amounts and kinds we actually observe) constitutes evidence against the existence of God, evidence that seems decisively to outweigh the totality of available evidence *for* the existence of God.

In this essay, I wish to discuss what seems to me to be the most powerful version of the "evidential argument from evil." The argument takes the following form. There is a serious hypothesis h that is inconsistent with theism and on which the amounts and kinds of suffering that the world contains are far more easily explained than they are on the hypothesis of theism. This fact constitutes a *prima facie* case for preferring h to theism. Examination shows that there is no known way of answering this case, and there is good reason to think that no way of answering it will be forthcoming. Therefore, the hypothesis h is (relative to the epistemic situation of someone who has followed the argument this far) preferable to theism. But if p and q are inconsistent and p is (relative to one's epistemic situation) epistemically preferable to q, then it is not rational for one to accept q. (Of course, it does not follow either that it is rational for one to accept p or that it is rational for one to reject q.) It is, therefore, not rational for one who has followed the argument up to this point to accept theism.[1]

Original publication: Pp. 135–65, James E. Tamberlin (ed.), *Philosophical Perspectives*, 5, Philosophy of Religion, 1991 (Atascaderg, CA: Ridgeview, 1991).

In section I, I shall present the version of the evidential argument from evil I wish to discuss. In section II, I shall explain why I find the argument unconvincing. These two sections could stand on their own, and this paper might have consisted simply of the proposed refutation of the evidential argument from evil that they contain. But many philosophers will find the proposed refutation implausible, owing to the fact that it turns on controversial theses about the epistemology of metaphysical possibility and intrinsic value. And perhaps there will also be philosophers who find my reasoning unconvincing because of a deep conviction that, since evil just *obviously* creates an insoluble evidential problem for the theist, a reply to any version of the evidential argument can be nothing more than a desperate attempt to render the obvious obscure. Now if philosophers are unconvinced by one's diagnosis of the faults of a certain argument, one can attempt to make the diagnosis seem more plausible to them by the following method. One can try to find a "parallel" argument that is obviously faulty, and try to show that a parallel diagnosis of the faults of the parallel argument can be given, a diagnosis that seems plausible, and hope that some of the plausibility of the parallel diagnosis will rub off on the original. For example, if philosophers find one's diagnosis of the faults of the ontological argument unconvincing, one can construct an obviously faulty argument that "runs parallel to" the ontological argument – in the classical case, an argument for the existence of a perfect island. And one can then attempt to show that a diagnosis parallel to one's diagnosis of the faults of the ontological argument is a correct diagnosis of the faults (which, one hopes, will be so evident as to be uncontroversial) of the parallel argument. It is worth noting that even if an application of this procedure did not convince one's audience of the correctness of one's diagnosis of the faults of the original argument, the parallel argument might by itself be enough to convince them that there must be *something* wrong with the original argument.

This is the plan I shall follow. In fact, I shall consider *two* arguments that run parallel to the evidential argument from evil. In section III, I shall present an evidential argument, which I feign is addressed to an ancient Greek atomist by one of his contemporaries, for the conclusion that the observed properties of air render a belief in atoms irrational. In section IV, I shall present an evidential argument for the conclusion that the observed fact of "cosmic silence" renders a belief in "extra-terrestrial intelligence" irrational. Neither of these parallel arguments – at least this seems clear to me – succeeds in establishing its conclusion.

In each case, I shall offer a diagnosis of the faults of the parallel argument that parallels my diagnosis of the faults of the evidential argument from evil.

Finally, in section V, I shall make some remarks in aid of a proposed distinction between facts that raise *difficulties* for a theory, and facts that constitute *evidence* against a theory.

I

Let 'S' stand for a proposition that describes in some detail the amount, kinds, and distribution of suffering – the suffering not only of human beings, but of all the sentient terrestrial creatures that there are or ever have been.[2] (We assume that the content of S is about what one would expect, given our own experience, the newspapers, history books, textbooks of natural history and paleontology, and so on. For example, we assume that the world was not created five minutes ago – or six thousand years ago – "complete with memories of an unreal past," and we assume that Descartes was wrong and that cats really do feel pain.)

Let "theism" be the proposition that the universe was created by an omniscient, omnipotent, and morally perfect being.[3]

The core of the evidential argument from evil is the contention that there is a serious hypothesis, inconsistent with theism, on which S is more probable than S is on theism. (The probabilities that figure in this discussion are epistemic. Without making a serious attempt to clarify this notion, we may say this much: p has a higher epistemic probability on h than q does, just in the case that, given h, q is more *surprising* than p. And here 'surprising' must be understood as having an epistemic, rather than a merely psychological, sense. It is evident that the epistemic probability of a proposition is relative to the "epistemic background" or "epistemic situation" of an individual or a community: the epistemic probability of p on h need not be the same for two persons or for the same person at two times.[4]) That hypothesis is "the hypothesis of indifference" (HI):

> Neither the nature nor the condition of sentient beings on earth is the result of benevolent or malevolent actions performed by non-human persons.[5]

Here is a brief statement of the argument that is built round this core. We begin with an epistemic challenge to the theist, the presentation of a *prima facie* case against theism: The truth of S is not at all surprising, given HI, but the truth of S is very surprising, given theism. (For the following propositions, if they are not beyond all dispute, are at least highly plausible. Suffering is an intrinsic evil; A morally perfect being will see to it that, insofar as it is possible, intrinsic evils, if they are allowed to exist at all, are distributed according to desert; An omniscient and omnipotent being will be able so to arrange matters that the world contains sentient beings among whom suffering, if it exists at all, is apportioned according to desert; the pattern of suffering recorded in S is well explained – insofar as it can be explained: many instances of suffering are obviously due to chance – by the biological utility of pain, which is just what one would expect on HI, and has little if anything to do with desert.) We have, therefore, a good *prima facie* reason to prefer HI to theism.

How shall the theist respond to this challenge? The "evidentialist" (as I shall call the proponent of the evidential argument from evil) maintains that any response must be of one of the following three types:

- the theist may argue that S is much more surprising, given HI, than one might suppose
- the theist may argue that S is much less surprising, given theism, than one might suppose
- the theist may argue that there are reasons for preferring theism to HI that outweigh the *prima facie* reason for preferring HI to theism that we have provided.

The first of these options (the evidentialist continues) is unlikely to appeal to anyone. The third is also unappealing, at least if "reasons" is taken to mean "arguments for the existence of God" in the traditional or philosophy-of-religion-text sense. Whatever the individual merits or defects of those arguments, none of them but the "moral argument" (and perhaps the ontological argument) purports to prove the existence of a morally perfect being. And neither the moral argument nor the ontological argument has many defenders these days. None of the "theistic" arguments that are currently regarded as at all promising is, therefore, really an argument for *theism*.[6] And, therefore, none of them can supply a reason for preferring theism to HI.

The second option is that taken by philosophers who construct *theodicies*. A theodicy, let us say, is the conjunction of theism with some "auxiliary hypothesis" *h* that purports to explain how S could be true, given theism. Let us think for a moment in terms of the probability calculus. It is clear that if a theodicy is to be at all interesting, the probability of S on the conjunction of theism and *h* (that is, on the theodicy) will have to be high – or at least not too low. But whether a theodicy is interesting depends not only on the probability of S on the conjunction of theism and *h*, but also on the probability of *h* on theism. Note that the higher P(*h*/theism), the more closely P(S/theism) will approximate P(S/theism & *h*). On the other hand, if P(*h*/theism) is low, P(S/theism) could be low even if P(S/theism & *h*) were high. (Consider, for example, the case in which *h* is S itself: even if P(S/theism) is low, P(S/theism & S) will be 1 – as high as a probability gets.) The task of the theodicist, therefore, may be represented as follows: find an hypothesis *h* such that P(S/theism & *h*) is high, or at least not too low, and P(*h*/theism) is high. In other words, the theodicist is to reason as follows. "Although S might initially seem surprising on the assumption of theism, this initial appearance, like many initial appearances, is misleading. For consider the hypothesis *h*. The truth of this hypothesis is just what one would expect given theism, and S is just what one would expect [would not be all that surprising] given both theism and *h*. Therefore, S is just what one would expect [would not be all that surprising] given theism. And, therefore, we do not have a *prima facie* reason to prefer HI to theism, and the evidential argument from evil fails."[7]

But (the evidentialist concludes) the prospects of finding a theodicy that satisfies these conditions are not very promising. For any auxiliary hypothesis *h* that has actually been offered by the defenders of theism, it would seem that either no real case has been made for P(*h*/theism) being high, or else no real case has been made for P(S/theism & *h*) being high – or even not too low. Consider, for example, the celebrated Free Will Defense (FWD). Even if it is granted that P(FWD/theism) is high, there is every reason to think that P(S/theism & FWD) is low, since of all cases of suffering (a phenomenon that has existed for hundreds of millions of years), only a minuscule proportion involve, even in the most indirect way, beings with free will. And no one has the faintest idea of how to find a proposition that is probable on theism *and*, in conjunction with theism, renders S probable. Therefore, given the present state of the available evidence, our original judgment stands:

we have a good *prima facie* reason to prefer HI to theism. And, as we have seen, we have no reason to prefer theism to HI that outweighs this *prima facie* reason. It is, therefore, irrational to accept theism in the present state of our knowledge.

II

It will be noted that the evidential argument consists not only of an argument for the conclusion that there is a *prima facie* case for preferring HI to theism, but also of a list of options open to the theist who wishes to reply to that argument: the defender of theism must either refute the argument or else make a case for preferring theism to HI that out-weighs the *prima facie* case for preferring HI to theism; if the defender chooses to refute the argument, he must do this by producing a theodicy in the sense explained in section I.

This list of options seems to me to be incomplete. Suppose that one were successfully to argue that S was not surprising on theism – and not because S was "just what one should expect" if theism were true, but because no one is in a position to know whether S is what one should expect if theism were true. (Suppose I have never seen, or heard a description of, Egyptian hieroglyphs, although I am familiar with Chinese characters and Babylonian cuneiform and many other exotic scripts. I am shown a sheet of paper reproducing an ancient Egyptian inscription, having been told that it displays a script used in ancient Egypt. What I see cannot be described as "looking just the way one should expect a script used in ancient Egypt to look," but the fact that the script looks the way it does is not epistemically surprising on the hypothesis that it was a script used in ancient Egypt. I am simply not in a position to know whether *this* is the way one should expect a script that was used in ancient Egypt to look.[8]) If one could successfully argue that one simply could not know whether to expect patterns of suffering like those contained in the actual world in a world created by an omniscient, omnipotent, and morally perfect being, this would refute the evidentia-list's case for the thesis that there is a *prima facie* reason for preferring HI to theism. If one is not in a position to assign any epistemic probability to S on theism – if one is not in a position even to assign a probability-range like 'high' or 'low' or 'middling' to S on theism –, then, obviously, one is not in a position to say that the epistemic probability of S on HI is higher than the probability of S on theism.[9]

The evidentialist's statement of the way in which the defender of theism must conduct his defense is therefore overly restrictive: it is false that the defender must either make a case for theism or devise a theodicy. At any rate, another option exists as a formal possibility. But how might the defender of theism avail himself of this other option? Are there reasons for thinking that the assumption of theism yields no *prima facie* grounds for expecting a pattern of suffering different from that recorded by S?

I would suggest that it is the function of what have come to be called "defenses" to provide just such reasons. The word 'defense' was first employed as a technical term in discussions of the "logical" version of the argument from evil. In that context, a defense is a story according to which both God and suffering exist, and which is possible "in the broadly logical sense" – or which is such that there is no reason to believe that it is impossible in the broadly logical sense. Let us adapt the notion of a defense to the requirements of a discussion of the evidential argument: a defense is a story according to which God and suffering of the sort contained in the actual world both exist, and which is such that (given the existence of God) there is no reason to think that it is false, a story that is not surprising on the hypothesis that God exists. A defense obviously need not be a theodicy in the evidentialist's sense, for the probability of a defense need not be high on theism.[10] (That is, a defense need not be such that its denial is surprising on theism.) In practice, of course, the probability of a defense will never be high on theism: if the defender of theism knew of a story that accounted for the sufferings of the actual world and which was highly probable on theism, he would employ it as a theodicy. We may therefore say that, in practice, a defense is a story that accounts for the sufferings of the actual world and which (given the existence of God) is true "for all anyone knows."

What does the defender of theism accomplish by constructing a defense? Well, it's like this. Suppose that Jane wishes to defend the character of Richard III, and that she must contend with evidence that has convinced many people that Richard murdered the two princes in the Tower. Suppose that she proceeds by telling a story – which she does not claim to be true, or even more probable than not – that accounts for the evidence that has come down to us, a story according to which Richard did not murder the princes. If my reaction to her story is, "For all I know, that's true. I shouldn't be at all surprised if that's how things happened," I shall be less willing to accept a negative evaluation of Richard's character than I might otherwise have been. (Note that Jane need not try to show that her story is highly probable on the hypothesis that Richard was of good character.) It would, moreover, strengthen Jane's case if she could produce not one story but many stories that "exonerated" Richard – stories that were not trivial variants on one another but which were importantly different.

This analogy suggests that one course that is open to the defender of theism is to construct stories that are true for all anyone knows – given that there is a God – and which entail both S and the existence of God. If the defender can do that, this accomplishment will undermine the evidentialist's case for the proposition that the probability of S is lower on theism than on HI. Of course, these stories will (presumably) be *false* for all anyone knows, so they will not, or should not, create any tendency to believe that the probability of S on theism is *not* lower than it is on HI, that it is about the same or higher. Rather, the stories will, or should, lead a person in our epistemic situation to refuse to make any judgment about the relation between the probabilities of S on theism and on HI.

I shall presently offer such a story. But I propose to simplify my task in a way that I hope is legitimate. It seems to me that the theist should not assume that there is a single reason, or tightly interrelated set of reasons, for the sufferings of all sentient creatures. In particular, the theist should not assume that God's reasons for decreeing, or allowing, the sufferings of non-rational creatures have much in common with His reasons for decreeing or allowing the sufferings of human beings. The most satisfactory "defenses" that have so far been offered by theists purport to account only for the sufferings of human beings. In the sequel, I will offer a defense that is directed towards the sufferings of non-rational creatures – "beasts," I shall call them. If this defense were a success, it could be combined with defenses directed towards the sufferings of human beings (like the Free Will Defense) to produce a "total" defense. This "separation of cases" does not seem to me to be an arbitrary procedure. Human beings are radically different from all other animals, and a "total" defense that explained the sufferings of beasts in one way and the sufferings of human beings in a radically different way would not be implausible on that account. Although it is not strictly to our purpose, I will point out that this is consonant with the most usual Christian view of suffering. Typically, Christians have held that human suffering is not a part of God's plan for the world, but exists only because that plan has gone awry. On the other hand:

Thou makest darkness that it may be night; wherein all the beasts of the
forest do move.

The lions, roaring after their prey, do seek their meat from God.

The sun ariseth, and they get them away together, and lay them down in
their dens. (Ps. 104: 20–22)

This and many other Biblical texts seem to imply that the whole
subrational natural world proceeds according to God's plan (except
insofar as we human beings have corrupted nature). And this, as the
Psalmist tells us in his great hymn of praise to the order that God has
established in nature, includes the phenomenon of predation.

I will now tell a story, a story that is true for all I know, that accounts
for the sufferings of beasts. The story consists of the following three
propositions:

(1) Every possible world that contains higher-level sentient creatures
either contains patterns of suffering morally equivalent to those
recorded by S, or else is massively irregular.

(2) Some important intrinsic or extrinsic good depends on the existence of higher-level sentient creatures; this good is of sufficient
magnitude that it outweighs the patterns of suffering recorded by S.

(3) Being massively irregular is a defect in a world, a defect at least as
great as the defect of containing patterns of suffering morally
equivalent to those recorded by S.

The four key terms contained in this story may be explained as
follows.

Higher-level sentient creatures are animals that are *conscious* in the way in
which (*pace* Descartes) the higher non-human mammals are conscious.

Two patterns of suffering are *morally equivalent* if there are no morally
decisive reasons for preferring one to the other: if there are no
morally decisive reasons for creating a world that embodies one pattern
rather than the other. To say that A and B are in this sense morally
equivalent is not to say that they are in any interesting sense comparable. Suppose, for example, that the Benthamite dream of a universal
hedonic calculus is an illusion, and that there is no answer to the
question whether the suffering caused by war is less than, the same
as, or greater than the suffering caused by cancer. It does not follow
that these two patterns of suffering are not morally equivalent. On the
contrary: unless there is some "non-hedonic" morally relevant distinction to be made between a world that contains war and no cancer and a

world that contains cancer and no war (i.e., a distinction that does not depend on comparing the amounts of suffering caused by war and cancer), it would seem to follow that the suffering caused by war and the suffering caused by cancer *are*, in the present technical sense, morally equivalent.

It is important to note that A and B may be morally equivalent even if they are comparable and one of them involves *less* suffering than the other. By way of analogy, consider the fact that there is no morally decisive reason to prefer a jail term of ten years as a penalty for armed assault to a term of ten years and a day, despite the indubitable facts that these two penalties would have the same deterrent effect and that one is lighter than the other. I have argued elsewhere that, for any amount of suffering that somehow serves God's purposes, it may be that some smaller amount of suffering would have served them as well.[11] It may be, therefore, that God has had to choose *some* amount of suffering as the amount contained in the actual world, and could, consistently with His purposes, have chosen any of a vast array of smaller or greater amounts, and that all of the members of this vast array of alternative amounts of suffering are morally equivalent. (Similarly, a legislature has to choose *some* penalty as the penalty for armed assault, and – think of penalties as jail terms measured in minutes – must choose among the members of a vast array of morally equivalent penalties.) Or it may be that God has decreed, with respect to this vast array of alternative, morally equivalent amounts of suffering, that *some* member of this array shall be the actual amount of suffering, but has left it up to chance which member that is.[12]

A *massively irregular world* is a world in which the laws of nature fail in some massive way. A world containing all of the miracles recorded in the New Testament would not, on that account, be massively irregular, for those miracles were too small (if size is measured in terms of the amounts of matter directly affected) and too few and far between. But a world would be massively irregular if it contained the following state of affairs:

> God, by means of a continuous series of ubiquitous miracles, causes a planet inhabited by the same animal life as the actual earth to be a hedonic utopia. On this planet, fawns are (like Shadrach, Meshach, and Abednego) saved by angels when they are in danger of being burnt alive. Harmful parasites and microorganisms suffer immediate supernatural dissolution if they enter a higher animal's body. Lambs are miraculously hidden from lions, and the lions are compensated for the resulting

restriction on their diets by physically impossible falls of high-protein manna. On this planet, either God created every species by a separate miracle, or else, although all living things evolved from a common ancestor, a hedonic utopia has existed at every stage of the evolutionary process. (The latter alternative implies that God has, by means of a vast and intricately coordinated sequence of supernatural adjustments to the machinery of nature, guided the evolutionary process in such a way as to compensate for the fact that a hedonic utopia exerts no selection pressure.)

It would also be possible for a world to be massively irregular in a more systematic or "wholesale" way. A world that came into existence five minutes ago, complete with memories of an unreal past, would be on that account alone massively irregular – if indeed such a world was metaphysically possible. A world in which beasts (beasts having the physical structure and exhibiting the pain-behavior of actual beasts) felt no pain would be on that account alone massively irregular – if indeed such a world was metaphysically possible.

A *defect in a world* is a feature of a world that (whatever its extrinsic value might be in various worlds) a world is intrinsically better for not having.

Our story comprises propositions (1), (2), and (3). I believe that we have no reason to assign any probability or range of probabilities to this story. (With the following possible exception: if we have a reason to regard the existence of God as improbable, then we shall have a reason to regard the story as improbable.)

We should have reason to reject this story if we had reason to believe that there were possible worlds – worlds that were not massively irregular – in which higher-level sentient creatures inhabited a hedonic utopia. Is there any reason to think that there are such worlds? I suppose that the only kind of reason one could have for believing that there was a possible world having a certain feature would be the reason provided by a plausible attempt to "design" a world having that feature. How does one go about designing a world?

One should start by describing in some detail the laws of nature that govern that world. (Physicists' actual formulations of quantum field theories and the general theory of relativity provide the standard of required "detail.") One should then go on to describe the boundary conditions under which those laws operate: the topology of the world's spacetime, its relativistic mass, the number of particle families, and so on. Then one should tell in convincing detail the story of cosmic evolution in that world: the story of the development of large objects like galaxies and stars and of small objects like carbon atoms. Finally, one should tell the story of the evolution of life. These stories, of course, must be coherent, given one's specification of laws and boundary conditions. Unless one proceeds in this manner, one's statements about what is intrinsically or metaphysically possible – and thus one's statements about an omnipotent being's "options" in creating a world – will be entirely subjective, and therefore without value. But I have argued for this view of the epistemology of modal statements (that is, of modal statements concerning major departures from actuality) elsewhere, and the reader is referred to those arguments. In fact, the argument of those papers should be considered a part of the argument of the present essay.[13]

Our own universe provides the only model we have for the formidable task of designing a world. (For all we know, in every possible world that exhibits any degree of complexity, the laws of nature are the actual laws, or at least have the same structure as the actual laws. There are, in fact, philosophically minded physicists who believe that there is only one possible set of laws of nature, and it is epistemically possible that they are right.) Our universe apparently evolved out of an initial singularity in accordance with certain laws of nature.[14] This evolution is not without its mysteries: the very early stages of the unfolding of the universe (the incredibly brief instant during which the laws of nature operated under conditions of perfect symmetry), the formation of the galaxies, and the origin of life on the earth are, in the present state of natural knowledge, deep mysteries. Nevertheless, it seems reasonable to assume that all of these processes involved only the non-miraculous operation of the laws of nature. One important thing that is known about the evolution of the universe into its present state is that it has been a very tightly structured process. A large number of physical parameters have apparently arbitrary values such that if those values had been only slightly different (very, *very* slightly different) the universe would contain no life, and *a fortiori* no intelligent life.[15] It may or may not be the "purpose" of the cosmos to constitute an arena in which the evolution of intelligent life takes place, but it is certainly true that this evolution did take place, and that if the universe had been different by an all but unimaginably minute degree it wouldn't have. My purpose in citing this fact – it is reasonable to believe that it is a fact – is not to produce an up-to-date version of the Design Argument. It is, rather, to suggest that (at least, for all we know) only in a universe very much like ours could intelligent life, or even sentient life, develop by the non-miraculous operation of the laws of nature. And the natural evolution of higher sentient life in a universe like ours essentially involves suffering, or there is every reason to believe it does. The mechanisms underlying biological evolution may be just what most biologists seem to suppose – the production of new genes by random mutation and the culling of gene pools by environmental selection pressure – or they may be more subtle. But no one, I believe, would take seriously the idea that conscious animals, animals conscious as a dog is conscious, could evolve naturally without hundreds of millions of years of ancestral suffering. Pain is an indispensable component of the evolutionary process after organisms have reached a certain stage of complexity. And, for all we know, the amount of pain that organisms have experienced in the actual world, or some amount morally equivalent to that amount, is necessary for the natural evolution of conscious animals. I conclude that the first part of our defense is true for all we know: Every possible world that contains higher-level sentient creatures either contains patterns of suffering morally equivalent to those recorded by S, or else is massively irregular.

Let us now consider the second part of our defense: Some important intrinsic or extrinsic good depends on the existence of higher-level sentient creatures; this good is of sufficient magnitude that it outweighs the patterns of suffering recorded by S. It is not very hard to believe (is it?) that a world that was as the earth was just before the appearance of human beings would contain a much larger amount of intrinsic good, and would, in fact, contain a better balance of good over evil, than a world in which there were no organisms higher than worms. (Which is not to say that there could not be worlds lacking intelligent life that contained a still better balance of good over evil – say, worlds containing the same organisms, but significantly less suffering.) And then there is the question of extrinsic value. One consideration immediately suggests itself: intelligent life – creatures made in the image and likeness of God – could not evolve directly from worms or oysters; the immediate evolutionary predecessors of intelligent animals must possess higher-level sentience.

We now turn to the third part of our defense: Being massively irregular is a defect in a world, a defect at least as great as the defect of containing patterns of suffering morally equivalent to those recorded by S. We should recall that a defense is not a theodicy, and that we are not required to argue at this point that it is *plausible to suppose* that massive irregularity is a defect in a world, a defect so grave that creating a world containing animal suffering morally equivalent to the animal suffering of the actual world is a reasonable price to pay to avoid it. We are required to argue only that *for all we know* this judgment is correct.

The third part of our defense is objectionable only if we have some *prima facie* reason for believing that the actual sufferings of beasts are a graver defect in a world than massive irregularity would be. Have we any such reason? It seems to me that we do not. To begin with, it does seem that massive irregularity is a defect in a world. One minor point in favor of this thesis is the witness of deists and other thinkers who have deprecated the miraculous on the ground that *any* degree of irregularity in a world is a defect, a sort of unlovely jury-rigging of things that is altogether unworthy of the power and wisdom of God. Presumably such thinkers would regard *massive* irregularity as a very grave defect indeed. And perhaps there is something to this reaction. It does seem that there is something right about the idea that God would include no more irregularity than was necessary in His creation. A second point is that many, if not all, massively irregular worlds are not only massively irregular but massively *deceptive*. This is obviously true of a world that looks like the actual world but which began five minutes ago, or a world that looks like the actual world but in which beasts feel no pain. (And this is not surprising, for our beliefs about the world depend in large measure on our habit of drawing conclusions that are based on the assumption that the world is regular.) But it is plausible to suppose that deception, and, *a fortiori*, massive deception, is inconsistent with the nature of a perfect being. These points, however, are no more than suggestive, and, even if they amounted to proof, they would prove only that massive irregularity was a defect; they would not prove that it was a defect in any way comparable with the actual suffering of beasts. In any case, proof is not the present question: the question is whether there is a *prima facie* case for the thesis that the actual sufferings of beasts constitute a graver defect in a world than does massive irregularity.

What would such a case be based on? I would suppose that someone who maintained that there was such a case would have to rely on his moral intuitions, or, more generally, on his intuitions of value. He would have to say something like this: "I have held the two states of affairs – the actual sufferings of beasts and massive irregularity – before my mind and carefully compared them. My considered judgment is that the former is worse than the latter." This judgment presupposes that these two states of affairs are, in the sense that was explained above, comparable: one of them is worse than the other, or else they are of the same value (or disvalue). It is not clear to me that there is any reason to suppose that this is so. If it is *not* so, then, as we have seen, it can plausibly be maintained that the two states of affairs are morally equivalent, and a Creator could not be faulted on moral grounds for choosing either over the other. But let us suppose that the two states of affairs are comparable. In that case, if the value-judgment we are considering is to be trusted, then human beings possess a faculty that enables them correctly to judge the relative values of states of affairs of literally cosmic magnitude, states of affairs, moreover, that are in no way (as some states of affairs of cosmic magnitude may be) connected with the practical concerns of human beings. Why should one suppose that one's inclinations to make judgments of value are reliable in this area? One's intuitions about value are either a gift from God or a product of evolution or socially inculcated or stem from some combination of these sources. Why should we suppose that any of these sources would provide us with the means to make correct value-judgments in matters that have nothing to do with the practical concerns of everyday life? (I do think we must be able to speak of *correct* value-judgments if the Problem of Evil is to be of any interest. An eminent philosopher of biology has said in one place that God, if He existed, would be indescribably wicked for having created a world like this one, and, in another place, that morality is an illusion, an illusion that we are subject to because of the evolutionary advantage it confers. These two theses do not seem to me to add up to a coherent position.) Earlier I advocated a form of modal skepticism: our modal intuitions, while they are no doubt to be trusted when they tell us that the table could have been placed on the other side of the room, are not to be trusted on such matters as whether there could be transparent iron or whether there could be a "regular" universe in which there were higher sentient creatures that did not suffer. And if this true, it is not surprising. Assuming that there are "modal facts of the matter," why should we assume that God or evolution or social training has given us access to modal facts knowledge of which is of no interest to anyone but the metaphysician? God or evolution has provided us with a capacity for making judgments about size and distance that is very useful in hunting mammoths and driving cars, but which is of no use at all in astronomy. It seems that an analogous restriction applies to our capacity for making modal judgments. How can we be sure that an analogous restriction does not also apply to our capacity for making *value*-judgments? My position is that we cannot be sure, and that for all we know our inclinations to make value-judgments are not veridical when they are applied to cosmic matters unrelated to the concerns of everyday life. (Not that our inclinations in this area are at all uniform. I myself experience no inclination to come down on one side or the other of the question whether massive irregularity or vast amounts of animal suffering is the graver defect in a world. I suspect that others do experience such inclinations. If they don't, of course, then I'm preaching to the converted.) But then there is no *prima facie* case for the thesis that the actual sufferings of beasts constitute a graver defect in a world than does massive irregularity. Or, at least, there is no case that is grounded in our intuitions about value. And in what else could such a case be grounded?

These considerations have to do with intrinsic value, with comparison of the intrinsic disvalue of two states of affairs. There is also the matter of extrinsic value. Who can say what the effects of creating a massively irregular world might be? What things of intrinsic value might be frustrated or rendered impossible in a massively irregular world? We cannot say. Christians have generally held that at a certain point God plans to hand over the government of the world to humanity. Would a massively irregular world be the sort of world that could be "handed over"? Perhaps a massively irregular world would immediately dissolve into chaos if an infinite being were not constantly making adjustments to it. We simply cannot say. If anyone insists that he has good reason to believe that nothing of any great value depends on the world's being regular, we must ask him why he thinks he is in a position to know things of that sort. We might remind him of the counsel of epistemic humility that was spoken to Job out of the whirlwind:

> Gird up now thy loins like a man; for I will demand of thee, and answer
> thou me.
> Where wast thou when I laid the foundations of the earth? Declare if
> thou hast understanding.
> Knowest thou it, because thou wast then born, or because the number
> of thy days is great?
> Canst thou bind the sweet influences of Pleiades, or loose the bands of
> Orion?
> Knowest thou the ordinances of heaven? Canst thou set the dominion
> thereof in the earth?[16]

I have urged extreme modal and moral skepticism (or, one might say, humility) in matters unrelated to the concerns of everyday life. If such skepticism is accepted, then we have no reason to accept the evidentialist's premise that "an omniscient and omnipotent being will be able so to arrange matters that the world contains sentient beings among whom suffering, if it exists at all, is apportioned according to desert." More exactly, we have no reason to suppose that an omniscient and omnipotent being could do this without creating a massively irregular world; and, for all we know, the intrinsic or extrinsic disvalue of a massively irregular world is greater than the intrinsic disvalue of vast amounts of animal suffering (which, presumably, are not apportioned according to desert). If these consequences of modal and moral skepticism are accepted, then there is no reason to believe that the probability of S on HI is higher than the probability of S on theism, and the evidential argument from evil cannot get started. Even if we assume that the probability of S on HI is high (that the denial of S is very surprising on HI), this assumption gives us no reason to prefer HI to theism. If there were such a reason, it could be presented as an argument:

> The probability of S on HI is high
> We do not know what to say about the probability of S on theism
> HI and theism are inconsistent
> Therefore, for anyone in our epistemic situation, the truth of S constitutes a *prima facie* case for preferring HI to theism.

This argument is far from compelling. If there is any doubt about this, it can be dispelled by considering a parallel argument. Let L be the proposition that intelligent life exists, and let G be the proposition that God wants intelligent life to exist. We argue as follows:

> The probability of L on G is high
> We do not know what to say about the probability of L on atheism
> G and atheism are inconsistent
> Therefore, for anyone in our epistemic situation, the truth of L constitutes a *prima facie* case for preferring G to atheism.

The premises of this argument are true. (As to the second premise, there has been considerable debate in the scientific community as to whether the natural evolution of intelligent life is inevitable or extremely unlikely or something in between; let us suppose that "we" are a group of people who have tried to follow this debate and have been hopelessly confused by it.) But I should be very surprised to learn of someone who believed that the premises of the argument entailed its conclusion.

I will close this section by pointing out something that is not strictly relevant to the argument it contains, but is, in my view, of more than merely autobiographical interest. I have not accepted the extreme modal skepticism that figures so prominently in the argument of this section as a result of epistemic pressures exerted by the evidential argument from evil. I was an extreme modal skeptic before I was a theist, and I have, on the basis of this skepticism, argued (and would still argue) against both Swinburne's attempt to show that the concept of God is coherent, and Plantinga's attempt to use the modal version of the ontological argument to show that theism is rational.[17]

III

Imagine an ancient Greek, an atomist who believes that the whole world is made of tiny, indestructible, immutable solids. Imagine that an opponent of atomism (call him Aristotle) presents our atomist with the following argument: "If fire were made of tiny solids, the same solids earth is made of, or ones that differ from them only in shape, then fire would not be Absolutely Light – it would not rise toward the heavens of its own nature. But that fire is not Absolutely Light is contrary to observation."[18] From our lofty twentieth-century vantage-point, we might be inclined to regard Aristotle's argument as merely quaint. But this impression of quaintness rests on two features of the argument that can be removed without damage to what is, from one point of view anyway, its essential force. The two quaint features of Aristotle's argument, the idea that fire is a stuff, and the idea of the Absolutely Light, can be removed from the argument by substituting air for fire and by substituting the behavior we nowadays associate with the gaseous state for the defining behavior of the Absolutely Light (that is, a natural tendency to move upwards). The resulting argument would look something like this:

> Suppose air were made of tiny solid bodies as you say. Then air would behave like fine dust: it would eventually settle to the ground and

become a mere dusty coating on the surface of the earth. But this is
contrary to observation.

Well, what is wrong with this argument? Why *don't* the O_2, N_2, CO_2,
and other molecules that make up the atmosphere simply settle to the
ground like dust particles? The answer is that air molecules, unlike dust
particles, push on one another; they are kept at average distances that
are large in comparison with their own sizes by repulsive forces (electromagnetic in nature), the strength of these forces in a given region
being a function of the local temperature. At the temperatures one finds
near the surface of the earth (temperatures maintained by solar radiation and the internal heat of the earth), the aggregate action of these
intermolecular forces produces the kind of aggregate molecular behavior that, at the macroscopic level of description, we call the gaseous
state.

We can see where the improved version of Aristotle's argument goes
wrong. (We can also see that in one minor respect it's better than an
ancient Greek could know: if it weren't for intermolecular forces, air
molecules would not simply settle slowly to the ground; they would
drop like rocks.) But what about our imaginary ancient atomist, who
not only doesn't know all these things about intermolecular forces and
temperature and so on, but who couldn't even conceive of them as
epistemic possibilities? What shall he say in response to the improved
version of Aristotle's argument?

In order to sharpen this question, let us imagine that a Greek
philosopher called A-prime has actually presented our atomist with
the air-and-dust argument, and let us imagine that A-prime has at his
disposal the techniques of a late-twentieth-century analytical philosopher. Having presented the atomist with the simple argument that I
have given above (the primitive or "whence, then, is air?" version of the
Argument from Air), he presses his point by confronting the atomist
with a much more sophisticated argument, the *evidential* argument from
air. "Let HI, the Hypothesis of Independence, be the thesis that there
are four independent and continuous elements, air among them, each
of which has *sui generis* properties (you can find a list of them in any
reputable physics text) that determine its characteristic behavior. Let S
be a proposition that records the properties of air. The simple air-and-
dust argument is sufficient to establish that S is not surprising given HI,
but is very surprising given atomism. There are only three ways for you
to respond to this *prima facie* case against atomism: you may argue that S

is much more surprising, given HI than one might suppose; or that S is much less surprising, given atomism, than one might suppose; or that there are reasons for preferring atomism to HI that outweigh the *prima facie* reason for preferring HI to atomism that is provided by the air-and-dust argument. The first I shall not discuss. The third is unpromising, unless you can come up with something better than the very abstract metaphysical arguments with which you have attempted to support atomism in the past, for they certainly do not outweigh the clear and concrete air-and-dust argument. The only course open to you is to construct an *atomodicy*. That is, you must find some auxiliary hypothesis *h* that explains how S could be true, given atomism. And you will have to show both that the probability of S is high (or at least not too low) on the conjunction of atomism and *h* and that the probability of *h* on atomism is high. While you may be able to find an hypothesis that satisfies the former condition, I think it very unlikely that you will be able to find one that satisfies the latter. In any case, unless you *can* find an hypothesis that satisfies both conditions, you cannot rationally continue to be an atomist."

Whatever else may be said about this argument, A-prime is certainly right about one thing: it is unlikely that the atomist will be able to produce a successful atomodicy. Even if he were told the modern story about air, he could not do it. At least, I don't think he could. What is the epistemic probability on atomism (relative to the epistemic situation of an ancient Greek) of our complicated modern story of intermolecular forces and the gaseous state? What probability should someone who knew nothing about the micro structure of the material world except that it was composed of atoms (it is, of course, our "elementary particles" and not our "atoms" or our "molecules" that correspond to the atoms of the Greeks) assign to the modern story? As far as I am able to judge, the only rational thing such a person could do would be to decline to assign any probability to the modern story on atomism. (The answer of modern science to the air-and-dust argument does not take the form of a story that, relative to the epistemic situation of an ancient Greek, is highly probable on atomism.)

Fortunately for the atomist, A-prime's demand that he produce an atomodicy is unreasonable. The atomist need do nothing more in response to the evidential argument from air than find a defense – or, better, several independent defenses. A defense, of course, is a story that explains how there could be a stuff that has the properties of air (those known to an ancient Greek), given that the material world is made entirely of atoms. A defense need *not* be highly probable on atomism. It is required only that, given atomism, the defense be true for all anyone (*sc.* any ancient Greek) knows.

Here is one example of a defense: air atoms (unlike earth atoms) are spheres covered with a "fur" of long, thin, flexible spikes that are, unless flexed by contact with another atom, perpendicular to the surface of the atom's "nucleus" (i.e., its central sphere); the length of the spikes is large in comparison with the diameters of nuclei, and their presence thus tends to keep nuclei far apart. Since, for all anyone (anyone in the epistemic situation of an ancient Greek) knows, some atoms have such features – if there are atoms at all – the observed properties of air are not surprising on the assumption of atomism. Since there are defenses that are true for all anyone (anyone in the epistemic situation of an ancient Greek) knows, no ancient Greek was in a position to say anything about the probability on atomism of S, the proposition that sums up the properties of air that were known to him. A-prime, therefore, is left with no better argument than the following:

The probability of S on HI is high
We do not know what to say about the probability of S on atomism
HI and atomism are inconsistent
Therefore, for anyone in our epistemic situation, the truth of S constitutes a *prima facie* case for preferring HI to atomism.

And this argument is manifestly invalid.

IV

We know how it is that air can be composed of molecules and yet not drift to the ground like dust. This knowledge provides us with a certain rather Olympian perspective from which to view the "Problem of Air." I wish next to examine the epistemic situation of those of our contemporaries who believe that the Milky Way galaxy (ours) contains other intelligent species than humanity. (Since they are our contemporaries, we cannot view their situation from any such Olympian perspective.) Let us confront them with an argument analogous to the argument from evil and the argument from air. The essence of this argument is contained in a question of Enrico Fermi's, a question as pithy as 'Whence, then, is evil?': Where are they?

If there are other intelligent species in the galaxy, the overwhelming probability is that at least one intelligent species existed at least a hundred million years ago. There has been life on the earth for at least thirty times that long, and there is nothing magical about the present time. The universe was just as suitable for intelligent life a hundred million years ago, and if the pace of evolution on the earth had been just three or four percent faster, there would have been intelligent life *here* a hundred million years ago. An intelligent and technologically able species will attempt to send messages to other species elsewhere in the galaxy (as we have begun to do). The most efficient way to do this is to send out self-reproducing robotic probes to other stars: when such a probe reaches another star, it makes two or more duplicates of itself out of local materials, and these duplicates proceed to further stars. Then it waits, perhaps for hundreds of millions of years, till it detects locally produced radio signals, at which point it reveals itself and delivers its message. (There are no fundamental technological barriers to this program. At our present rate of scientific progress, we shall be able to set such a process in motion within the next century.) It is not hard to show that the descendants of the original probes will reach every star in the galaxy within fifty million years. (We assume that the probes are capable of reaching one-tenth the speed of light.) But no such probe has revealed itself to us. Therefore, any non-human intelligence in the galaxy came into existence less than fifty million years ago. But it is statistically very unlikely that there are non-human intelligences *all* of which came into existence within the last fifty million years. (The reasoning is like this: if you know that such people as there are in the Sahara Desert are distributed randomly, and if you know that there are no people in the Sahara except, possibly, within a circular area one hundred miles in diameter that is hidden from you, you can conclude that there are probably no people at all in the Sahara.) Furthermore, it is not merely the absence of robotic probes that should disturb the proponent of "extra-terrestrial intelligence." There are also the absence of radio signals from thousands of nearby stars and several of the nearer galaxies[19] and the absence of manifestations of "hypertechnology" like the wide-angle infrared source that would signal the presence of a star that has been surrounded with a "Dyson sphere." We may refer collectively to all of these "absences" as *cosmic silence*, or simply *silence*. (If there are other intelligent species in the galaxy, or even in nearby galaxies, they are *species absconditae*.) The obvious implication of these observations is that we are alone.[20]

Let us call the thesis that there is intelligent life elsewhere in the galaxy *noetism*. The above argument, the argument from cosmic silence, provides materials from which the anti-noetist may construct an evidential argument against noetism analogous to the evidential argument from evil: "Let the Hypothesis of Isolation (HI) be the hypothesis that humanity is the only intelligent species that exists or has ever existed in the Milky Way galaxy or any of the nearby galaxies. Let S be a proposition that records all of the observations that constitute a failure to discover any manifestation whatever of life, and, *a fortiori*, of intelligent life, elsewhere in the universe. The argument from cosmic silence is sufficient to establish that the truth of S (which, of course, is not at all surprising given HI) is very surprising, given noetism. There are only three ways for you to respond to the argument from cosmic silence: you may argue that S is much more surprising, given HI, than one might suppose; or that S is much less surprising, given noetism, than one might suppose; or that there are reasons for preferring noetism to HI that outweigh the *prima facie* reason for preferring HI to noetism that is provided by the argument from cosmic silence. The first is no more than a formal possibility. The third is unpromising, unless you can come up with something better than those facile arguments for the prevalence of life in the cosmos that are so popular with astronomers and physicists and so exasperating to evolutionary biologists.[21] The only course open to you is to construct a *noödicy*. That is, you must find some auxiliary hypothesis *h* that explains how S could be true, given noetism. And you will have to show both that the probability of S is high (or at least not too low) on the conjunction of noetism and *h* and that the probability of *h* on noetism is high. While you may be able to find an hypothesis that satisfies the former condition, I think it very unlikely that you will be able to find one that satisfies the latter. In any case, unless you *can* find an hypothesis that satisfies both conditions, you cannot rationally continue to be an noetist."

The anti-noetist is no doubt right in supposing that it is very unlikely that the noetist will be able to construct a successful noödicy. One example should suffice to make the point. Consider the elegantly simple, if rather depressing, Nuclear Destruction Scenario: intelligent species do not last long enough to make much of a mark on the cosmos; within at most a few decades of developing radio transmitters powerful enough to be detected across a distance of light-years (and long before they can make self-reproducing intersiderial robotic probes), they invariably destroy themselves in nuclear wars. It is clear that the

Nuclear Destruction Scenario is a failure as a noödicy, for it is not highly probable on noetism. (That intelligent species invariably destroy themselves in nuclear wars is not highly probable on the hypothesis that intelligent species exist.) The proponents of extra-terrestrial intelligence have provided a wide range of possible explanations of "cosmic silence" (intelligence does not necessarily imply technology; the desire to communicate with other intelligent species is a human idiosyncrasy; the most efficient means of intersiderial signaling, the one that all the extra-terrestrials actually employ, is one we haven't yet thought of), but it is clear that none of these possible explanations should be regarded as *highly probable* on noetism. We simply do not know enough to make any such probability judgment. Shall the noetist therefore concede that we have shown his position to be irrational? No, for the anti-noetist's demand that the noetist produce a noödicy is wholly unreasonable. The noetist need only produce one or more *defenses*, one or more explanations of the phenomenon of cosmic silence that entail noetism and are true for all we know. And this is just what the noetist has done. (I have already mentioned several of them.) Since there are defenses that for all anyone knows are true, no one knows what to say about the probability on noetism of S (the proposition that records all of our failed attempts to discover any manifestation of intelligent life elsewhere in the universe). The anti-noetist has therefore failed to show that the truth of S constitutes a *prima facie* case in favor of preferring HI to noetism.

V

"This is all very well. But evil *is* a difficulty for the theist, and the gaseous state *was* a difficulty for the ancient atomist, and cosmic silence *is* a difficulty for the noetist. You seem to be saying that they can just ignore these difficulties."

Not at all. I have said that these difficulties (I accept the term "difficulty") do not render their beliefs irrational – not even if they are unable to find arguments that raise the probabilities of their hypotheses relative to the probabilities of competing hypotheses that do not face the same difficulties, and are also unable to devise auxiliary hypotheses that enable them to construct "-dicies." It doesn't follow that they should simply ignore the difficulties.

"Well, what *should* they do?"

To begin with, they can acknowledge the difficulties. They can admit that the difficulties exist and that they're not sure what to say about them. They might go on to offer some speculations about the causes of the phenomena that raise the difficulties: mechanisms that would account for the gaseous state, possible conditions that would interfere with communications across light-years, reasons God might have for allowing evil. Such speculations need not be (they almost certainly will not be) highly probable on the "-ism" in whose defense they are employed. And they need not be probable on anything that is known to be true, although they should not be improbable on anything that is known to be true. They are to be offered as explanations of the difficult phenomena that are, *for all anyone knows*, the correct ones. In sum, the way to deal with such difficulties is to construct defenses.

"But if a phenomenon is a 'difficulty' for a certain theory, does that not mean that it is evidence against that theory? Or if it is not evidence against that theory, in what sense can it raise a 'difficulty' for the theory? Are you not saying that it can be right to accept a theory to which there is counterevidence when there are competing theories to which there is no counterevidence?"

That sounds good, but it is really a recipe for rejecting just about any interesting theory. Just about any interesting theory is faced with phenomena that make the advocates of the theory a bit uncomfortable, this discomfort being signalled by the tendency to speculate about circumstances consistent with the theory that might produce the phenomena. For any theory that faces such a difficulty, there will always be available another "theory," or at least another hypothesis, that does not face that difficulty: its denial. (The denial of an interesting theory will rarely if ever itself be an interesting theory; it will be too general and non-specific.) Your suggestion would therefore appear to constrain us never to accept any interesting theory, but always either to accept its denial or else neither the theory nor its denial. The latter will be the more common result, since the denial of a theory can usually be partitioned into interesting theories that face individual difficulties. (For example, the denial of atomism can be partitioned into the following hypotheses: matter is continuous; matter is neither continuous nor atomically structured; matter does not exist. Each of these hypotheses faces difficulties.) This result might be avoided if you placed some sort of restriction on what counted as a "competing theory," but it is not clear what sort of restriction would be required. It will not do simply to rule out the denial of a theory as a competing theory, for contraries of the theory that were very general and non-specific could produce equally counterintuitive results. If, moreover, you did produce a satisfactory solution to this problem, it is not clear what consequences your solution might have for the evidential argument from evil. Consider, for example, the Hypothesis of Indifference. This is not a very specific thesis: it tells us only that the nature and condition of sentient beings on earth do *not* have a certain (very narrowly delineated) cause. Perhaps it would not count as a proper "competitor" with the quite specific thesis we have called 'theism'. Perhaps it would be a consequence of your solution that only some proposition more specific than HI, some proposition that entailed but was not entailed by HI, could properly be in competition with theism. And this proposition might face difficulties of its own, difficulties not faced by HI.

But we may answer your question more directly and simply. A difficulty with a theory does not necessarily constitute evidence against it. To show that an acknowledged difficulty with a theory is not evidence against it, it suffices to construct a defense that accounts for the facts that raise the difficulty. (This thesis by no means provides an automatic "out" for a theory that is confronted with some recalcitrant observation, for a defense is not automatically available to the proponents of every theory that is confronted with a recalcitrant observation. A defense may not be improbable, either on the theory in whose cause it is employed, or on anything we know to be true. In a particular case, it may be that no one can think of any hypothesis that satisfies these two conditions, and what was a mere difficulty for a theory will thereby attain to the status of evidence against the theory. It is perhaps worth pointing out that two or more difficulties may jointly constitute evidence against a theory, even if none of them taken individually counts as evidence against it. This could be the case if the defenses that individually "handle" the difficulties are inconsistent, or if – despite the fact that none of the defenses taken individually is improbable – their conjunction is improbable.)

The central thesis of this paper may be usefully summarized in the terminology that has been introduced in the present section: While the patterns of suffering we find in the actual world constitute a *difficulty* for theism and do not constitute a difficulty for the competing hypothesis HI, they do not – owing to the availability of the defense[22] I have outlined – attain to the status of *evidence* that favors HI over theism. It follows that the evidential argument from evil fails, for it is essential to the evidential argument that those patterns of suffering be evidence that favors HI over theism.[23]

NOTES

1   My formulation of this argument owes a great deal to a recent article by Paul Draper ("Pain and Pleasure: An Evidential Problem for Theists," *Noûs* 23 (1989), 331–50). I do not, however, claim that the argument I shall present *is* Draper's intricate and subtle argument, or even a simplified version of it. (One important difference between the argument discussed in the present paper and Draper's argument is that the latter makes reference to the distribution of both pain and pleasure, while the former makes reference only to the distribution of pain.) Nevertheless, I hope that the version of the evidential argument from evil that I shall discuss is similar enough to Draper's that what I say about my version will at least suggest strategies that the theist can employ in dealing with Draper's argument. Draper (p. 332) credits Hume with being the first to ask the question whether there is "any serious hypothesis that is logically inconsistent with theism [and] explains some significant set of facts about evil...much better than theism does." (See *Dialogues Concerning Natural Religion*, Part XI.)

2   In Draper's argument, the role that corresponds to the role played by S in our argument is played by a proposition O that reports "both the observations one has made of humans and animals experiencing pain or pleasure and the testimony one has encountered concerning the observations others have made of sentient beings experiencing pain or pleasure" (p. 332). I find that the argument goes more easily if it is stated in terms of the probability (on various hypotheses) of the pattern of suffering that it is reasonable to believe the actual world exhibits, rather than in terms of the probability (on those hypotheses) of the observations and testimony on which our reasonable belief in that pattern rests. I do not think that this modification of Draper's strategy leaves me with an argument that is easier to refute than the argument that would have resulted if I had retained this feature of his strategy.

3   *Cf.* Draper, p. 331. Perhaps we should add that this being has not ceased to exist, and has never ceased to be omniscient, omnipotent, or morally perfect.

4   *Cf.* Draper, pp. 333 and 349 (note 2). Some difficulties with the notion of epistemic probability are discussed in note 7 below.

5   *Cf.* Draper, p. 332.

6   It is a currently popular view that one can have reasons for believing in God that are of a quite different kind from "arguments for the existence of

God." For a sampling of versions of this view, see the essays by the editors and the essay by William P. Alston in Alvin Plantinga and Nicholas Wolterstorff, eds., *Faith and Rationality: Reason and Belief in God* (South Bend, Indiana: the University of Notre Dame Press, 1983). My own position on this matter is that some version of this view is right, and that there are reasons for believing in God that are of the general kind described by Plantinga, Wolterstorff, and Alston. I believe, moreover, that these reasons not only can provide one with adequate justification for being a theist in the absence of a *prima facie* case against theism, but are strong enough to override any conceivable *prima facie* case against theism. (For a contrary view – which I believe rests on a misunderstanding – see Draper, pp. 347–8.) But I shall not defend this thesis here, since the point of the present paper is that the patterns of suffering that exist in the actual world do not constitute even a *prima facie* case against theism.

7   I prefer to formulate the evidential argument from evil in terms of epistemic surprise, rather than in terms of high and low epistemic probability. (Draper's essay suggested this use of the concept of "surprise" to me. Although his "official" formulation of his argument is in terms of epistemic probability, he frequently employs the notion of "surprise" in his informal commentary on the argument. Indeed, at one place – see p. 333 – he comes very close to explaining epistemic probability as I did in the text: by equating 'has a lower epistemic probability' with 'is more surprising'.) Let me attempt to explain why I am uneasy about formulating the argument in terms of probabilities. If the argument is so formulated, it would appear to depend on the validity of the following inference-form: p; the probability of p on q is much higher than the probability of p on r; q and r are inconsistent; therefore, there exists a *prima facie* reason (*viz*, that p) for preferring q to r. The trouble with this inference-form is that the probability of p may be very low on q despite the fact that p is not at all *surprising* on q. For example, the probability of the hypothesis that the unobservable card that Alice is holding is the four of clubs is quite low on the hypothesis that she drew the card at random from a standard deck, but the former hypothesis is not at all surprising on the latter. Now let S be some true proposition that has a low probability on theism, but is not at all surprising on theism. I should think that the proposition that states the exact number of dogs would do: in "most" possible worlds in which God exists, the number of dogs is not the actual number. It is clear that the following facts do not comprise a *prima facie* case for preferring 'S and God does not exist' to 'God exists': S; the probability of S on 'S and God does not exist' is much higher than the probability of S on 'God exists'; 'S and God does not exist' and 'God exists' are inconsistent.

These considerations show that the use of the language of high and low probabilities in formulating the evidential argument from evil is a source of possible confusion. Since, however, my criticisms of the argument have nothing to do with this point, I shall continue to employ this language. But I shall employ it only as a stylistic device: anything I say in this language could easily be restated in terms of epistemic surprise.

8   I can have *some* epistemically warranted expectations about how what I see displayed on the sheet of paper will look: it must in some sense "look like writing" – it can't be a detailed drawing of a cat or a series of a thousand identical marks. Similarly, I can have *some* epistemically warranted expectations about how suffering will be distributed if there is a God. I would suppose, for example, that it is highly improbable on theism that there be sentient creatures and that all of them be in excruciating pain at every moment of their existence.

9   Well, one might somehow know the probability of S on theism as a function of the probability of S on HI; one might know that the former probability was one-tenth the latter, and yet have no idea what either probability was. But that is not the present case. The evidentialist's argument essentially involves two independent probability-judgments: that the probability of S on HI is at least not too low, and that the probability of S on theism is very low.

10 Indeed, in *one* sense of probability, the probability of a defense may be very low on theism. We have said that a defense may not be *surprising* on theism, but, as we saw in note 7, there is a perfectly good sense of probability in which a proposition that is not at all surprising on theism may nevertheless be very improbable on theism. If the defender of theism had at his disposal a very large number of defenses, all of them inconsistent with the others, and none of them epistemically preferable to any of the others, it is hard to see why he should not conclude that (relative to his epistemic situation) the probability of any given one of them was very low on theism.

11 "The Magnitude, Duration, and Distribution of Evil: A Theodicy," *Philosophical Topics*, Vol. 16, no. 2 (1988), pp. 161–87. See especially pp. 167–8. Failure to appreciate this consideration is a weak point in many versions of the evidential argument from evil. Consider, for example, William L. Rowe's much-discussed article, "The Problem of Evil and Some Varieties of Atheism" (*American Philosophical Quarterly* 16 (1979) pp. 335–41). In this article, Rowe employs the following premise:

> An omniscient, wholly good being would prevent the occurrence of any intense suffering it could, unless it could not do so without losing some greater good or permitting some evil equally bad or worse.

If there are alternative, morally equivalent amounts of (intense) suffering, then this premise is false. To make this point more concrete, let us consider Rowe's famous case of a fawn that dies in prolonged agony of burns that it suffers in a forest fire caused by lightning. God, I concede, could have miraculously prevented the fire, or miraculously saved the fawn, or miraculously caused its agony to be cut short by death. And, I will concede for the sake of argument, if He had done so, this would have thwarted no significant good and permitted no significant evil. But what of the hundreds of millions (at least) of similar incidents that have, no doubt, occurred during the long history of life? Well, I concede, He could have prevented any one of them, or any two of them, or any three of them . . . without thwarting any significant good or permitting any significant evil. But could he have prevented all of them? No – not without causing the world to be massively irregular. And, of course, there is no sharp cut-off point between a world that is massively irregular and a world that is not – just as there is no sharp cut-off point between a penalty that is an effective deterrent for armed assault and a penalty that is not. There is, therefore, no *minimum* number of cases of intense suffering that God could allow without forfeiting the good of a world that is not massively irregular – just as there is no shortest sentence that a legislature can establish as the penalty for armed assault without forfeiting the good of effective deterrence.

12   See my essay "The Place of Chance in a World Sustained by God" in Thomas V. Morris, ed., *Divine and Human Action: Essays in the Metaphysics of Theism* (Ithaca, N.Y.: Cornell University Press, 1988), pp. 211–35.

13   "Ontological Arguments," *Noûs* 11 (1977) pp. 375–95; Review of *The Coherence of Theism* by Richard Swinburne, *The Philosophical Review* LXXXVII (1979), pp. 668–72. See also George Seddon, "Logical Possibility," *Mind* LXXXI (1972), pp. 481–94.

14   These laws, being quantum-mechanical, are indeterministic. God could not, therefore, have "fine-tuned" the initial state of a universe like ours so as to render an eventual universal hedonic utopia causally inevitable. It would seem to be almost certain that, owing to quantum-mechanical indeterminacy, a universe that was a duplicate of ours when ours was, say, 10^{-45} seconds old could have evolved into a very different universe from our present universe. (There is also the point to be considered that there probably *was* no initial state of the universe.) Would it be possible for an omniscient and omnipotent being to create a universe that evolved deterministically out of a carefully selected initial state into an hedonic utopia? This question raises many further questions, questions that mostly cannot be answered. Nevertheless, the following facts would seem to be relevant to an attempt to answer it: life depends on chemistry, and chemistry depends on atoms, and atoms depend on quantum mechanics (classically speaking, an atom cannot exist: the electrons of a "classical" atom would spiral inward, shedding their potential energy in

the form of electromagnetic radiation, till they collided with the nucleus), and quantum mechanics is essentially indeterministic.

15   This fact has been widely remarked on. See, e.g., John Leslie, "Modern Cosmology and the Creation of Life" in Ernan McMullin, ed., *Evolution and Creation* (South Bend, Indiana: the University of Notre Dame Press, 1985), pp. 91–120.

16   This is not properly speaking a quotation; it is, rather, a selection of verses from Chapter 38 of the Book of Job. It comprises verses 3, 4, 21, 31, and 33.

17   See the article and review cited in note 13.

18   *Cf. De Cælo* IV, especially 309^a 18–310^a 13.

19   This latter fact is very important in the debate about extra-terrestrial intelligence. If someone in our galaxy aimed a powerful signal at, say, the Andromeda galaxy, then, two million years later, anyone in the Andromeda galaxy who aimed a sensitive receiver precisely at our galaxy would detect that signal. When we aim a sensitive receiver precisely at the Andromeda galaxy, however, we detect no signal. Therefore, no one on any planet circling any of the hundred billion or more stars in the Andromeda galaxy was aiming a signal at the Milky Way galaxy two million years ago. (This argument actually depends on the false assumption that all of the stars in the Andromeda galaxy are equally distant from us, but the essential point of the argument is sound.)

20   For an excellent popular article on the search for extra-terrestrial intelligence, see Gregg Easterbrook, "Are We Alone?", *The Atlantic*, August 1988, pp. 25–38.

21   See for example, Ernst Mayr, "The Probability of Extraterrestrial Intelligent Life," in Michael Ruse, ed., *Philosophy of Biology* (New York: Macmillan, 1989), pp. 279–85.

22   Are there other defenses – other defenses that cover the same ground as the defense I have presented in Section II? I should like to think so, although I have not had any very interesting ideas about how additional defenses might be constructed. I should welcome suggestions.

23   This paper was read at Brandeis University. The author wishes to thank the members of the Brandeis Philosophy Department, and especially Eli Hirsch, for their helpful comments and criticisms.

PART IV

THEODICIES

Clearly, if God exists and, therefore, permits all the evils in our world, he must have good reasons for doing so. And since evils are themselves bad, God's reasons must involve goods that he can realize only if he permits those evils to occur. A theodicy is an attempt to enumerate some goods whose realization may be God's reasons for permitting the horrendous evils that afflict our world. Provided it is reasonable to believe that these goods, if realized, would justify God in permitting all these evils, and provided we have no good reasons to think these goods won't be realized, we will have reason to believe that the occurrence of all these evils doesn't count significantly against the existence of God. In order for a theodicy to be successful it is not required that the postulated goods be the actual goods that justify God, if he exists, in permitting all these evils. All that is required is that they be such that it is reasonable to think that they could be the goods that justify God in permitting the evils in our world. Of course, if we see that these goods aren't good enough, or likely could be realized by God without his having to permit those evils, then the theodicy is a failure. Providing a plausible theodicy, therefore, is an important task for theists to pursue. For insofar as we possess a *plausible* theodicy, the problem of evil does not count significantly against theism. So, it is important to consider some major efforts to develop a plausible theodicy.

Richard Swinburne cites certain good states of affairs which he thinks God might well try to bring about and argues that they could not be brought about without certain evils occurring or its being in the power of some created beings to produce those evils. He cites *enjoyment* and *pleasure* owing to the satisfaction of desires as good states of affairs. But he notes that a state of affairs such as *one's being pleased on contemplating the sufferings of others* is not a good state of affairs. He then claims that the mere having of desires is good, whether ever satisfied or not. "Desires in themselves are good, except when they are desires for the bad." This enables Swinburne to claim that it is good to have permanently frustrated desires. It will seem to some, however, that a desire we are incapable of satisfying, is at best only *instrumentally* good or an *essential* part of some state that is *intrinsically* good. It is not itself something *intrinsically* good, as is, for example, the satisfaction of desire. And once we enter the realm of instrumental goods it is important to raise the question of whether an infinitely good, infinitely wise deity cannot achieve the good ends with better means. Swinburne notes that *compassion* is a good state that requires the existence of the bad state of suffering. And perhaps the unique goodness of compassion may justify God's permission of some degree of suffering in the world. But can we reasonably think that the compassion of others for the victims of the holocaust justifies a loving being's permission of that human tragedy? Swinburne is aware of this common objection to his theodicy. His opponents may agree with him that certain good states require the existence of bad states. They may also agree with him that we should not neglect the intrinsic value of being of help to those who suffer, as well as the intrinsic value of experiencing being helped and comforted. What his opponents reject is the idea that these goods require God to permit the *extraordinary amount* of horrendous suffering we know to exist in the world. Swinburne's response: "Yet it must be stressed that each evil or possible evil removed takes away one more actual good," will strike many readers as doubtful. Surely, they will say, not every fawn's death by fire serves the good of teaching other deer to avoid fires. And would many great goods have been lost if only four million, rather than six, perished in the Holocaust? The connections between evils and goods do not appear to be as fine-tuned as Swinburne believes them to be.

    John Hick's response to the perennial challenge of the problem of evil is to develop and defend a theodicy stemming from Irenaeus, a theodicy in which the divine purpose is to create imperfect creatures within an environment in which they can freely develop themselves into moral and spiritual beings and eventually enter into an eternal life of love and fellowship with God. For this to happen, Hick argues, there must be an epistemic distance between us and God. For if we were directly aware of God as an infinitely powerful, infinitely loving being we would be overwhelmed, unable to freely choose our own path through life. Hick's soul-making theodicy, like Swinburne's, does seem to make it understandable why God would permit the existence of moral and natural evil in the world. For unless there are real obstacles in nature to overcome, and unless human beings are capable of doing real harm to one another, freely attained moral and spiritual growth would be practically, if not theoretically, impossible.

Although Hick's soul-making theodicy can explain why the world contains both moral and natural evil, it initially seems incapable of accounting for the apparently excessive amount of evil in our world and the fact that much of this evil seems quite unrelated to moral and spiritual development. Hick is aware of this major difficulty for his theodicy. Indeed, what seems obvious to Hick and to us is (1) that the amount and intensity of evil in our world far exceeds what is needed for soul-making, and (2) that the evils in our world are distributed in a haphazard fashion, apparently unrelated to anyone's stage of development in soul-making. In light of this, how can anyone seriously propose the good of soul-making as the reason for God's permission of all the pain and suffering in our world? In response, Hick asks us to consider a world in which no evil occurs in an amount beyond what is needed to play a role in significant soul-making. Moreover, he asks us to suppose that we all know that this is so. He then argues that the result would be that we would make no significant efforts to overcome evil. But it is precisely such efforts (or the need for them) that lead to significant moral growth and development. A similar line of argument is developed for the haphazard, random distribution of evil. In a world in which suffering by a person is permitted only if it is merited or needed for soul-making, then if we further suppose that we all know this to be so, no one would make efforts to relieve the suffering of others. Paradoxically, then, soul-making would be considerably limited in a world in which we all knew or rationally believed that suffering is permitted only as it is required for soul-making. The point of Hick's argument seems to be this. Significant soul-making requires not only the existence of evils; it also requires that it be rational for us to believe that evils occur in excess of what is needed for soul-making. For if we were to believe that each evil that occurs is one that even an omnipotent being could not prevent without loss of soul-making, we would make no significant efforts to overcome evils. And, as we've noted, it is precisely such efforts that are crucial to significant moral growth and development. And what this implies is that the amount, intensity, and distribution of evil in our world must be such as to create and sustain our belief that evils occur in excess of what an omnipotent being would need to permit for our moral and spiritual growth. But isn't it apparent to us that evils occur in excess of what is needed to sustain our belief that evils occur in excess of what an omnipotent being would need to permit for our moral and spiritual growth. Suppose again that only four million Jews were to have perished in the Holocaust. Would anyone then have concluded that it is no longer rational to believe that evils occur in excess of what an omnipotent being would need to permit for our moral and spiritual growth? It does not seem so. Thus the problem of evils not needed by God to accomplish his purposes appears to come back to haunt Hick's theodicy.

Marilyn Adams thinks that those who discuss the problem of evil need to realize that a *theistic* worldview will hold a distinctive set of values on which to draw in discussing the evils of the world, a set of values not all of which will be shared by nontheists. But she also thinks that a particular theism may hold views that make the problem of evil more difficult to resolve. She proposes to discuss the problem of evil from the perspective of a particular version of theism, Christian theism, acknowledging the distinctive values of Christian theism as well its dark side, "the postmortem evil of hell, in which the omnipotent creator turns effectively and finally against a creature's good." As a Christian philosopher, her own view is that God's goodness to the creatures he creates is such that he will provide to each person a life that is a great good to that person on the whole. Of course, if the doctrine of an eternal hell is true it certainly isn't true that each person's life is a great good to that person on the whole. Accordingly, she argues that the doctrine of an eternal hell should be rejected in favor of a doctrine of universal salvation. In the course of developing her view she carefully discusses the alternative view that some creatures so misuse their free will that God has no choice but to condemn them to an eternal life in hell, a place of constant torment whose inhabitants would be better off had they not been born. Her view is that a careful look at how some people exist in the world – kids brought up in crack houses, abused, etc. – makes it simply unrealistic to suppose that each person *freely chooses* an evil life or a good life. It must be admitted, I think, that there is a good deal of plain commonsense in Adams's view of the world. She insists on seeing God as the loving, forgiving father, rather than as the vengeful lord bent on punishing those who disobey his rules. To the objection that withdrawing the threat of eternal punishment leads to moral and religious laxity, she replies that her pastoral experience as an Anglican priest suggests otherwise: "the disproportionate threat of hell produces despair that masquerades as skepticism, rebellion, and unbelief. If your father threatens to kill you if you disobey him, you may cower in terrorized submission, but you may also (reasonably) run away from home." Of course, since it is abundantly clear that the majority of mankind fail in this life to grow into true children of God, Adams must suppose that there are post-mortem lives in which the slow progression in growth continues until all become true children of God. She also must suppose that undergoing suffering is somehow an important step to fully entering into a life with a God.

11

RICHARD SWINBURNE

Some Major Strands of Theodicy

God is by definition omnipotent and perfectly good. Yet manifestly there is evil of many diverse kinds. It would appear that an omnipotent being can prevent evil if he tries to do so, and that a perfectly good being will try. The existence of such evil appears, therefore, to be inconsistent with the existence of God, or at least to render it improbable.[1] Theodicy is the enterprise of showing that appearances are misleading: that evils of the kind and quantity we find on Earth are neither incompatible with nor render improbable the existence of God.[2] Even if the evils around us do render improbable the existence of God, we may still have stronger evidence to show that there is a God which outweighs the counterevidence, which suffices to make it rational for us to believe that there is a God. My own view, however, is that theodicy is a viable enterprise, that we do not need to rely on stronger evidence for the existence of God to outweigh counterevidence from evil. This essay is a contribution to theodicy. I accept that an omnipotent being can prevent any evil he chooses, but I deny that a perfectly good being will always try to do so. If a perfectly good being is to allow evil to occur, he must have the right to do so, and there must be some good which is brought about by allowing the evil to occur and could not be brought about by him in any better way, and so great that it is worth allowing the evil to occur. If the perfectly good being is also omnipotent (i.e., can do anything logically possible), then it must be logically impossible for him to bring about the greater good in any better way. The condition about the right is important: even if my allowing you to suffer will do you great good, unless I am in some

Original Publication: Pp. 30–48, Daniel Howard-Snyder (ed.), *The Evidential Argument from Evil* (Bloomington and Indianapolis: Indiana University Press, 1996).

special position in regard to you (e.g., I am your parent), I do not have the right to allow you to suffer. I believe that God does have the right to allow humans (and animals) to suffer for the sake of greater good – to a limited extent and for a limited period (e.g., 100 years per human) – but I shall not argue for that here for reason of space.[3] My concern will be rather with contributing toward showing that evils of the kind and quantity we find on Earth serve greater goods.

I believe that theodicy seems to many people an impossible task because they have a very narrow conception of good and evil – e.g., in extremis, that the only goods are sensory pleasures and the only evils sensory pains. If that conception were correct, then obviously God could create sensory pleasures without creating sensory pains. But that conception is not merely too narrow, it is absurdly too narrow – someone whose conception of the good was thus limited would be a moral pygmy. But when you start having a wider conception of good and evil, theodicy does not seem so impossible a task; it just seems difficult. The difficulty arises because of the variety of the goods and evils and the complexity of the logical relations between them.

My approach in this essay will be to list various good states of affairs (understood in a wide sense, which includes events and actions), which a good God might well seek to bring about and which do in fact occur on Earth, and show how so many of them could not be realized without the occurrence (or possible occurrence) of corresponding evils. (By the "possible occurrence" of some evil I mean some agent, animate or inanimate, having the power to bring about the evil which nothing inside or outside the agent causes the agent either to exercise or not to exercise.) In the course of running through the good states, I shall mention the major evils we find on Earth – both those involving humans and those involving animals – and show that they contribute to goods, in that the goods could not be realized without their actual or possible occurrence or the actual or possible occurrence of evils equally bad. That I hope I shall show fairly conclusively. What I shall also begin to show but could not within the compass of a philosophical essay of normal length possibly show conclusively to those without considerable sympathies toward certain general moral views is that the good states of affairs are so good that it is worth allowing the evils to occur in order to make possible the good states. There are two main reasons why I cannot show the latter conclusively within the stated space. The first of these reasons is that, I believe, there are so many different kinds of good states and so many different ways in which evil is required for their occurrence. For example, I believe that the occurrence of natural evils (i.e., evils such as disease and accidents unpredictable by humans) is required for humans to have the power to choose between doing significant good or evil to their fellows, for the reason that the observation of the processes which produce natural evil is required for humans to have the knowledge of how to do significant evil to their fellows. Without that knowledge the choice between good and evil will not be available. We learn how to poison by observing someone accidentally eating a berry and being poisoned by it; that then puts us in a position deliberately to poison others (by giving them similar berries), or through negligence to allow others to be poisoned, or alternatively to prevent their being poisoned. I believe that what goes for this schematically simple example goes generally, and that evils of the kind and quantity we find around us are required if humans are to have the power to choose between doing good or evil of varied significant kinds to their fellows. It is good that they have this latter choice, as I shall be arguing in due course. But the demonstration that natural evil is required to give us the requisite knowledge is a complicated one which I have expounded elsewhere,[4] and a fuller defense of it would require at least an article of its own. I therefore deprive myself of the strand of theodicy provided by "the argument from the need for knowledge," and rely on other strands.

The second and major reason, however, why I cannot show conclusively within the allotted space that the goods are so great that it is worth allowing the evils which they require to occur is that my assessment of the relative worth of the goods depends on more general moral views which are not fashionable today. Now, people only come to see the strength of a moral position rather different from their initial one as a result of reflection upon their experiences of life or description at some considerable length of real or fictional incidents. The philosopher can assist in the process of reflection or description; but convincing conclusions will not be reached solely by a few pages of rigorous deductive argument, aided by numbered propositions. For those of my readers who have considerable initial sympathy with the general moral views which I shall be expounding, I hope that I shall say enough to clarify and to strengthen those views in such a way as to enable the readers to see that they lead to a viable theodicy. But for the readers without much initial sympathy with the views in question, I hope that I shall say enough to make the readers more sympathetic, and so enable them to see that there are prospects for a theodicy of the kind I shall expound, that theodicy could well be a viable enterprise.[5]

So let's begin to list some goods. I have no general formula for picking out good states of affairs – I believe them to be too diverse to fall under any formula – but I list quite a number of them relevant to theodicy. Perhaps the most basic good of all is the good of the satisfaction of desire, basic in the sense that its goodness makes for the greater goodness of many other states of affairs. A desire, as I understand it, is an involuntary inclination with which an agent finds himself to do some action or to have something happen.[6] Desires may be for almost anything – for mental states, including sensory states, for bodily states, for states of the world far distant from the agent. I may desire to have a certain tingling sensation, or for a piece of poetry to run through my mind, to waggle my ears, to be president of the United States. Or my desires may be focused on others – that my children be happy or successful or inherit my wealth when I am dead.

Enjoyment or pleasure consists in the known satisfaction of present desire. It consists in doing what you are inclined to do, or letting happen what you are inclined to let happen, when you know that you are doing the action or letting the state occur. I enjoy eating cake or playing golf if I'm inclined to do so, do so while inclined, and know that I am doing so. I get pleasure out of sitting in the sun if I let myself continue to sit in the sun when inclined so to do (do not struggle against sitting there) and know that is what I am doing. I get pleasure out of being president if I am inclined to be president, and am, and know that I am president. The most primitive kind of pleasure is sensory pleasure, pleasure in the having of certain sensations, the occurrence of which I cannot be mistaken. But the more remote from my immediate environment is the state of affairs on which my inclinations are focused, the more serious is the possibility that I may believe some inclination to be satisfied when it is not. I may believe that I am president when I am not; in that case what I get pleasure from is not being president but believing that I am. I am in one state in which I desire to be – believing that I am president – but not in another such one – being president. When I am disabused of my false belief, there is nothing left out of which I can get pleasure.

Pleasure is the known satisfaction of present desire. Is there good in the present satisfaction of past desire? I suggest so, if it is uncanceled desire (i.e., the agent hasn't given it up). If, aged five, I long to be an engine driver but I give up this desire when I am aged ten, when I desire to be a naval captain instead; I am then declared medically unfit for the navy when conscription arrives and drafted to become an engine driver instead, there would seem little (if any) good in this. But this is because my earlier desire has been replaced by a different desire. Yet contrast this with the desire of a man for being buried here rather than there when he is dead. Surely it is good that his relatives should bury him here rather than there, even if but for the dead man's known past desire, there would be nothing particularly good about burial here rather than there.

As such, the satisfaction of desire, and above all pleasure, is a good thing. But the satisfaction of certain desires is not a good thing. The satisfaction of desires for things bad in themselves is not good. The satisfaction of a desire that others, or even one's later self, suffer pain, lose their reputation, fortune, or family is a bad thing; and any pleasure derived from these things is not merely not a good, but very much an evil. Only the pervert rejoices at the sufferings of others. Also, I suggest, pleasure is not a good where the belief needed to sustain it is false. The pleasure which a man gets from believing his son to be a successful businessman when in fact he is unemployed is not a good thing. We can see this when we consider that if we had the opportunity to plug into an "experience machine" which would inculcate in us the false beliefs that our desires were currently being satisfied, we would – almost all of us – refrain, under normal circumstances (i.e., unless life without the machine was so intolerable that "plugging in" was the lesser of two evils).

The satisfaction of a strong desire is as such a greater good than the satisfaction of a weak desire. Further, the satisfaction of a desire is the better if it is a desire for a state of affairs good for other reasons. Desires to drink good wine rather than Coca-Cola, to read great novels rather than pornography, to understand quantum physics, or to develop a correct theodicy rather than know Wisden's Almanac by heart are like this, because of the subtlety of the sensitivity we desire to indulge in the former cases, and width and depth of the knowledge we desire to attain in the latter cases. The satisfaction of joint desires – e.g., the desires of two creatures for the common end of their nest being built – is very good because of the goodness of sharing and cooperation. It is better to have a desire for the satisfaction of desire as such – viz., the desire for pleasure in whatever way it can be achieved rather than the desire for a particular sensation – for it shows sensitivity to what is good in the satisfaction of desire. And it is yet better that the desire of one for the satisfaction of the desire of another – e.g., my desire that your desire to eat cream cake be satisfied; or more generally that the desire of a mother for the satisfaction of her offspring's desire be satisfied – than that the desire of each of us to eat cream cake be satisfied. This is because of the goodness of mutual concern and involvement. Much better that my desire that your desire to eat cream cake be satisfied than that the desire of each of us to eat cream cake be satisfied. It follows, because of the goodness of mutual concern, that even better is the satisfaction of joint desires for the satisfaction of the desire of a third creature, e.g., the satisfaction of the desire of both parents for the desired success in examinations of their child. Even better still is the satisfaction of desires to perform actions of certain sorts benefiting oneself and others, to the goodness of which actions (desired or not) I shall come in due course.

In cases such as those just described, where one person, A, desires the satisfaction of the desire of a second person, B, and the desire is satisfied, there is a triple good. There is the primitive good of the satisfaction of B's desire. There is the greater good of the satisfaction of A's desire, greater because A's desire focused on the fulfillment of another's desire (as such, quite apart from what it is) is a desire for a better good than B's desire. And there is the further good for B that A desired his (B's) desire to be satisfied. It is a good for us when other people mind about us. We are fortunate if our happiness gives happiness to others – even if we don't know that it does. We can see this by the fact that we regard ourselves as fortunate when we discover that another was made happy by our being happy; but although the discovery causes us so to regard ourselves, what we regard ourselves as fortunate in respect of is what we discover (not the fact of our discovering it) – and that is something which could occur without our having discovered it.

Just as the satisfaction of desire is good, so is its frustration (i.e., the desire continuing when it is for a present state of affairs but is not known to be satisfied)[7] an evil. Pains are evils because they involve desires for the nonoccurrence of a sensation, which are not satisfied. And an unfulfilled longing to be president is an evil for the same reason.

God has reason to bring about the existence of creatures with desires for good states of affairs which are satisfied. He can do so without any evil occurring so long as the satisfaction is known and immediate. But if the creature continues to exist with his desire unsatisfied or not known to be satisfied, we have immediately the evil of frustrated desire. Yet there is special good in the satisfaction of persisting desire. For a desire which persists through varied experiences and new desires is a thought-through and committed desire. Hence the special good of the satisfaction of an animal's desire for the return of its offspring lost for hours or days, of the satisfaction of the desire for a mate the longing for which has deterred the animal from the search for other goods such as food, and of the satisfaction of the desire for food by those hungry for some hours. The greater good of the satisfaction of persisting desire is greater when what is desired is the success of some action of some kind. It is good that someone persists in attempting to search for food and doesn't just grab it off the table; to stick at trying to learn to type or drive or swim and finally succeed. But the eventual satisfaction of persisting desires involves on the way the evil of temporary frustrations: pangs of hunger on the way to getting food, feelings of exhaustion in the course of the long search for a mate, etc. And note of course that in these as in other cases, the good of the satisfaction of desire does not lie solely in its known satisfaction. It follows that there is significant good in the satisfaction of a persisting desire after the desirer's death. The greater good of the satisfaction of persisting desires is yet greater, the better their object; and so there is special good in the satisfaction of shared persisting desires for the satisfaction of the persisting desire of a third individual, a good which involves more evil on the way. The goodness of the satisfaction of persisting desire is the first aspect of that logical straightjacket which means that good cannot be achieved save through evil and which provides the key to theodicy. God has reason to give to creatures the good of persistent desires, despite the agony of their temporary frustration.

It is not just the satisfaction of desire which is in general a good, and especially when it is of a desire for a state of affairs good for other reasons. The mere having of desire is good, especially when it is desire for a state of affairs good for other reasons. It is good that I want things, long for things, am inclined to try to bring about things. It is better that I be someone to whom things matter rather than a "cold fish" who acts under the guidance of reason alone. Desires in themselves are good, except when they are desires for what is bad; but they are better, the better the states desired. And if my desires are focused on your well-being, that is a good not merely for me but also for you – how lucky we are if people care about us. But there are some desires for what is good which can never be satisfied. The desire to be monogamously married to beautiful Jane for all her adult life is a desire for what is good, and so it is good that both John and George have it. But of course both of their desires cannot be satisfied. Likewise, it is good to desire to be president of the United States for the next four years, to hold a great office of public service; but we can't all occupy the office. A world in which all our desires were satisfied at some time would be a world in which we were deprived of desires for certain great goods, just because we couldn't get them. If God wants to make creatures sensitive to all that is good, He will allow them to have desires which are permanently frustrated. So we are rightly sentenced to ambitions that we cannot achieve, and to the consequent deprivation, and (because of the goodness of true beliefs about these matters) to feelings of failure.

There is also great good in certain emotional states, including desire as well as other elements. It is good that I love all creatures, but especially those with whom I have contact and in particular those greatly dependent on me or on whom I am greatly dependent. It is good that I love these latter more than others – otherwise I do not pay proper tribute to their connection with myself; I trivialize our personal relations. And again, the love that persists despite inadequate response or is evoked by bad states has its own special greatness. It is good that I feel compassion for the sufferer, sadness at failure, and grief at the loss of the departed.[8] Again, these attitudes are good both for him who has these right attitudes and good for him on whom they are focused – very good if the latter knows about them and that gives him some pleasure, but good even if he doesn't – for the reason given earlier. What gives him pleasure is the knowledge of the existence of a good state (e.g., someone else's compassion for him), and that state can exist without his knowing about it. We are fortunate if others mourn for us when we are dead; we can see this by the fact that we regard people as unfortunate if no one is sorry when they die. So too it lessens the evil of the suffering of a fawn caught in a forest fire if others know about this and respond with compassion – both other deer at the time and humans centuries later. Our compassion for sentient creatures is often far too narrow; it needs to extend far over space and time.

A natural reaction to examples such as these is to urge that while compassion may be a good state, which mitigates the evil of suffering, a world would be much better without either of them; and likewise for the other two examples. That reaction seems to me overgeneral – a world without any suffering or in consequence any compassion would not be better than a world with a little suffering and its proper response (other things being equal), and likewise for the other two examples. For compassion is an involvement in the inner life of another in a deep kind of way, which simply cannot be provided by a sharing of their joy. This is because the sufferer is one whose desires are frustrated. He is at his most naked. He has little to cling to by way of a structure of desire being fulfilled or which he may hope can be fulfilled. Our involvement with him is therefore an involvement with him as he is in himself, not as someone who has as it were exteriorized himself in the fulfillment of plans for himself or others, but someone with a unique opportunity to cope with his nakedness. "Sorrow shared is sorrow halved," says the proverb, and it is only doing the sums insofar as they affect the original sufferer who knows of the compassion. If we add the benefit (not altogether an enjoyed benefit) to the sympathizer, the sums may well sometimes come out level. God will not give us endless pain, failure, and felt loss of dear ones in order to allow us to show proper compassion, sadness, and grief; but he may well give us some pain, failure, and felt loss in order to allow us to be involved with each other in ways and at levels we could not otherwise have.

So far I've been concerned largely with the goodness of passive states. But doing is more important than having happen. Causing matters, and above all, intentional actions matter, in particular actions of promoting the goods so far described, and certainly not just because it is good that those goods come about. A good (intentional) action is good to the extent to which it is done intentionally (under the description under which it is good), efficaciously, freely, spontaneously, or contrary to temptation. An action can have all of the first three characteristics, and a free intentional action will be either spontaneous or contrary to temptation, but to the extent to which it has one of the latter characteristics it will lack the other. Performing some intentional action (e.g., I buy your house), I may unintentionally do something else good (e.g., I save you from bankruptcy). Such a good action will derive its goodness not from its intention but from its effect (so long as the effect is closely connected to the intentional action and not a remote effect dependent also on many other and very different causes). What is achieved is a good, and it is also a good for the agent who effected it, even if unintentionally; he is lucky to be a vehicle of benefit. Conversely, an unsuccessful action which aimed at something good is also a good for the agent.[9] It is good that people try to help the starving, even if they don't succeed. We can see the good of unintended success better than in my earlier example by bringing in this latter point, and considering an action which is aimed at a good but fails and is better for having an unintended good result than it would be otherwise. I toil to save a life and fail, but the record of my efforts makes possible the development of a technique for saving other lives in the future. Is that better than if I failed and by chance someone else hit on the new technique? Yes, because my efforts are crowned, and therefore it is a good for me, not merely for those whose lives were ultimately saved. But clearly things are better if the good which I achieve is intended. While it is good that I try to feed the starving, even if I don't succeed, it is better if I do succeed – but not just because it is good that the starving have enough to eat; it is a good for me that I am privileged to help them, that I am of use.

An intended good action is the better if done freely in the sense of not being fully caused.[10] An agent's freely bringing about the good is indeed a good for the agent. It is a good for any agent to have a free choice, for that makes him an ultimate source of the way things happen in the universe. He is no longer totally at the mercy of forces from without, but himself an autonomous minicreator. And if he exercises that choice in forwarding the good, that is a further good for him. But the good of forwarding the good is a lot better if the agent has a free choice between good and evil, not just between alternative goods, for then his choice is deeply significant for the way the world goes. Yet if he is to have a choice between good and evil, he must be subject to temptation, i.e., desires for the evil. An action would not be intentional unless it was done for a reason, i.e., seen as in some way a good thing (either in itself or because of its consequences). And if reasons alone influence actions, that regarded by the subject as most important will determine what is done; an agent under the influence of reason alone will inevitably do the action which he regards as overall the best (or one of the actions, if there are such, which he regards as overall equal best). If an agent is to have a free choice of whether to do an action which he regards as overall best, factors other than reason must exert an influence on him. In other words, desires for what he regards as good only in a certain respect, but not overall and so on balance evil, must be influencing him. Then he has a choice of whether to yield to desire or to pursue the best, despite contrary desire, i.e., temptation. Just as if reasons alone influence action, an agent inevitably does what he believes to be the best; so if desires alone influence action, an agent will inevitably follow his strongest desire. Free choice of action only comes in when there is a choice between two actions which the agent regards as equally good, or between two actions which he desires to do equally, or – the serious free choice – between two actions, one of which he desires to do more, and the other of which he believes it is better to do.[11] An agent's free choice of good despite contrary temptation is indeed a good – for the agent. For he has determined the flow of events in favor of the good rather than the bad. And he will have exerted more influence on that flow, the greater the temptation to the bad.

But while the pursuit of the good, despite serious contrary temptation, is a good, so too is the spontaneous pursuit of the good, the pursuit of the good which the agent fully desires to pursue. We value the willingly generous action, the naturally honest, spontaneously loving action. The spontaneous ready pursuit of the good has its own special kind of goodness, which – given the risk that, if he is tempted, the subject will yield to temptation, and a bad act be done and bad consequences follow. I cannot rank as either better or worse than the pursuit of the good, despite contrary temptation. (The spontaneous pursuit of the good may or may not involve a free choice. There may be a free choice between two actions seen as equally good and equally desired; or desire and reason may combine to make one choice inevitable.)

A good action is better, the greater the goals sought and attained. Especially good are supererogatory acts of helping people in great need. And just as it is good that there be a crisscrossing of desires and their satisfaction, so it is good that we seek each other's good and cooperate in seeking the good of others.

Just as having the desire and not merely its fulfillment is a good, so is having the opportunity to pursue the good, even if the opportunity is not taken. As I wrote earlier, having the opportunity to pursue the good intentionally, efficaciously, and freely is indeed a good for the agent; and if he has a free choice between good and evil, that makes him an ultimate source of how things go in the world in a very significant way. That, as we have seen, will involve his being subject to temptation to pursue the evil. The greater the choice of goods and evils we have, and (up to a limit) the greater the genuine freedom provided by serious temptation to pursue the bad instead, the more how the world goes is up to us and so the greater the privilege of our position. It is this which leads to the "free-will" defense of theodicy in respect of moral evil, the evil knowingly caused or constituted by the actions or negligence of human beings. God cannot give us the great good of the possibility of intentional, efficacious, free action, involving a choice between good and evil without at the same time providing the natural possibility (i.e., possibility allowed by natural laws) of evil which he will not prevent (not "cannot prevent" but "will not prevent," in order that the freedom he gives us may be efficacious freedom). The "free-will defense," carefully spelled out, must be a central core of theodicy, as it has been for the last two or three thousand years. But one point of this paper is to stress that the incompatibility of significant efficacious freedom and the absence of a natural possibility of evil is but one aspect of the logical straightjacket of goods which cannot be realized without actual or possible evils.

It is good that the free choices of humans between good and evil should include choices which make a difference to other humans for good or ill. A world where agents can benefit but not harm each other is a world where they have only very limited responsibility for each other. But the good of responsibility for each other is a very great good. We recognize this when we recognize it as a good gift to our own children to give them the responsibility for things, animals, and even other humans, and do not pressure them too much as to how they are to act. But if my responsibility for you is limited to whether or not to give you some quite unexpected new piece of photographic equipment, but I cannot make you unhappy, stunt your growth, or limit your education, then I do not have a great deal of responsibility for you. If God gave agents only such limited responsibility for their fellows, He would not have given much. He would be like a father asking his elder son to look after the younger son, and adding that he would be watching the elder son's every move and would intervene the moment the elder son did a thing wrong. The elder son might justly retort that while he would be happy to share his father's work, he could only really do so if he was left to make his own judgments as to what to do within a significant range of the options available to the father. God, like a good father, has reason to delegate responsibility. In order to allow creatures a share in creation, he has reason to allow them the choice of hurting and maiming, of frustrating the divine plan. Given that human choices are free ones (and I believe that there are reasons for supposing so),[12] then our world is one where humans have deep responsibility for each other.

This responsibility is not limited to the short term. By choices now I can affect the welfare of my own children in years to come; and I and others can make great differences for good or ill to life on this earth in decades to come. And by our choices now – to pursue certain kinds of scientific research and invest our wealth in certain sorts of technology – we may be able in centuries to come to influence for how long the human race lives and on which planet. My claim is that so good a thing is that deep responsibility that there is justification for God's allowing the evils caused by humans to each other (and themselves) to occur.

If an agent is to choose freely between good and evil, he needs, we have seen, to have contrary desires, evil inclinations; and these are themselves evils. I cannot choose freely to give money to the starving rather than hoard it unless I have some inherent miserly inclination, and my having that is itself an evil. For that reason, as well as for the reason of the evil which will be brought about if the agent yields to temptation, there is, as I noted earlier, a special kind of goodness in the good act done naturally and spontaneously without contrary tempta- tion. God has reason to create creatures simpler than ourselves who naturally pursue the good. God has reason to make higher animals who often act spontaneously (without, I assume, free will) to benefit them- selves (not just by acquiring food, but by playing and exploring) and others of their kind (mates and offspring whom they feed, clean, protect, etc.) and indeed often other kinds too (e.g., humans). And it is good too that humans often spontaneously pursue the good of their fellows.

What is known as the "higher-order goods defense" draws to our attention the good of performing certain sorts of good action, viz., those done in the face of evils, and of having the opportunity freely to choose to do such actions. There are certain actions which cannot be done unless there is pain and suffering (which I suggest centrally involve frustration of desire) to which they react. Showing sympathy (as opposed to the passive state of feeling compassion), helping the suffer- ing, and showing courage of a certain sort are like this. I cannot show you sympathy unless you are suffering, nor help the suffering unless there is suffering nor bravely bear my pain unless I have pain to bear. The evil of pain is the grit which makes possible the growth of the pearl. Of course, no benevolent creator would multiply pains without limit in order to give creatures the opportunity to show courage, sympathy, and help of this sort. But he might well give us some pain in order to give us the opportunity to perform some actions good in the special way that these actions are good.

In these cases, as with feeling compassion, we are involved with the sufferer (ourself or another) at his lowest. But here we can do something about the situation, not merely have the appropriate feelings. It is good that an agent do good actions, and he expresses his most substantial commitment to the good when he does such actions when it is hardest, when he gets no encouragement from the success of other plans and things are happening to him which he does not desire. He does so when he shows courage of a certain sort. And it is good that others should be involved with people at their most naked making the hard choices, when the sufferer can see the others as concerned for him and not anything slightly exterior to him (aspects of his appearance of success which make him attractive), doing what they can for him and helping him to make the right choices. Help is most significant when it is most needed, and it is most needed when its recipient is suffering and deprived. Whatever it is good that we do, it is good that others help us to do – even if sometimes it is also good that we have available the ever harder choice of showing courage on our own.

Showing sympathy and showing courage are good actions which may be done in the face of the simple natural evil of frustration of desire involved in pain and suffering. But there are good actions of other kinds which can only be done in the face of evil actions of various kinds. I can only make reparation if I have wronged you, or forgive you if you have wronged me. In these cases, while of course it is not overall a good that wrong be done, reparation made and it be forgiven, still these actions do in part compensate for the wrong done. And while the possibility of its misuse provides a reason for God not to create creatures with significant freedom, the possibility of such compensation for misuse reduces the force of that reason. There is some truth, though not as much as the writer of the Exultet supposed, in "O Felix Culpa, quae talem ac tantum meruit habere redemptorem."[13] There are good actions of certain kinds which can only be done in the face of good actions of various kinds – such as showing gratitude, recognition of achievement, and reward; and the possibility of these responses to actions which may themselves be responses to pain and suffering (e.g., showing gratitude to doctors who have worked hard to relieve pain) provides further reason for permitting the pain and suffering.[14]

It is good that some actions, including the actions of animals lacking free will, should be serious actions which involve benefiting despite loss or foreseen risk of loss to themselves and so actions of looking for a mate, despite failure to find; or decoying predators or exploring despite risk of loss of life. But again an action good in this kind of way cannot be done without evil. You cannot intentionally avoid forest fires, or take trouble to rescue your offspring from forest fires, unless there exists a serious danger of getting caught in a forest fire. The action of rescuing despite danger simply cannot be done unless the danger exists – and the danger will not exist unless there is a significant natural probability of being caught in the fire. To the extent that the world is deterministic, that involves creatures actually being caught in the fire;[15] and to the extent that the world is indeterministic, that involves an inclination of nature to produce that effect unprevented by God. Fawns are bound to get caught in forest fires sometimes if other fawns are to have the opportunity of intentionally avoiding fires and if deer are to have the opportunities of rescuing other fawns from fires.[16]

Not all evil actions are actions of agents with free will and so to be justified by the free-will defense. Animals sometimes reject their off-spring or hurt other animals.[17] Yet these actions, like physical pain, provide opportunities for good actions to be done in response to them, e.g., make possible adoption of the rejected offspring by other animals, or rescue of the injured by other animals, or the animal courageously coping with his injury or rejection.

I have argued so far for the great good of the having and satisfaction of desire, and shown how the satisfaction of persisting desires and the having of compassionate desires involves the occurrence of various evils. I then went on to show how the great good of having significant free choice involves actual bad desires and the possible occurrence of further significant harm to ourselves and others; and how having the opportunity to show courage or compassion involves the actual occurrence of pain and suffering. I also brought out the lesser value of serious beneficiary action by animals lacking free will.

As with desire, so with action, I have stressed the good for the subject of desire and action of having and satisfying good desires and performing or trying to perform good actions, especially ones whose object is someone else. It is a great good for me to bring the goods of life to others. Helping, contributing, being of use to others, even more than to ourselves, is a great good, a blessing, a privilege – especially if it is by free action, but also if it is by a spontaneous action, a significantly greater good than are the goods (which are indeed goods) of having tingles of sensory pleasure. And, as we have seen, there is special value in helping those who most need help. That helping is an immense good for the helper has always been difficult for humans to see, but it is especially hard for twentieth-century secularized Western people to see. It is however, something quite often near the surface of New Testament writings; and it was aptly summarized by Saint Paul in his farewell sermon to the church at Ephesus when he urged them "to remember the words of the Lord Jesus, how he himself said, It is more blessed to give than to receive" (Acts 20: 35).

We don't, most of us, think that most of the time. We think that our well-being consists in the things that we possess or the experiences we enjoy. Sometimes, true, all men find themselves in circumstances in which they ought to give – alas, the starving appear on our doorstep and we ought to give them some of our wealth, perhaps something large which will deprive us of future enjoyments. But that, the common thinking goes, is our misfortune, good for the starving but bad for us. Life would have been better for us if they hadn't turned up on the doorstep. But what the words of Christ say, taken literally, is "not so." We are lucky that they turned up on the doorstep. It would have been our misfortune if there had been no starving to whom to give; life would have been worse for us.

And even twentieth-century people can begin to see that – sometimes – when they seek to help prisoners not by providing more comfortable quarters but by letting prisoners help the handicapped; or when they pity rather than envy the "poor little rich girl" who has everything and does nothing for anyone else. And one phenomenon prevalent in end-of-century Britain draws this especially to our attention – the evil of unemployment. Because of our system of social security the unemployed on the whole have enough money to live without too much discomfort; certainly they are a lot better off than are many employed in Africa or Asia or Victorian Britain. What is evil about unemployment is not so much any resulting poverty but the uselessness of the unemployed. They often report feeling unvalued by society, of no use, "on the scrap heap." They rightly think it would be a good for them to contribute, but they can't.

It is not only intentional actions freely chosen, but also ones performed involuntarily, which have good consequences which constitute a good for the person who does them. If the unemployed were compelled to work for some useful purpose, they would still – most of them – regard that as a good for them in comparison with being useless. Or consider the conscript killed in a just and ultimately successful war in defense of his country against a tyrannous aggressor. Almost all peoples, apart from those of the Western world in our generation, have recognized that dying for one's country is a great good for him who dies, even if he was conscripted.[18] And it is not only intentional actions but experiences undergone involuntarily (or involuntary curtailment of good experiences, as by death) which have good consequences – so long as those experienced are closely connected with their consequences – which constitute a good for him who has them (even if a lesser good than that of a free intentional action causing those consequences, and a good often outweighed by the evil of the experience in question). Consider someone hurt or killed in an accident, where the accident leads to some reform which prevents the occurrence of similar accidents in the future (e.g., someone killed in a rail crash which leads to the installation of a new system of railway signaling which avoids similar accidents in the future). He and his relatives may comment in such a situation that at any rate the victim did not suffer or die in vain. They would have regarded it as a greater misfortune even for the victim if his suffering or death served no useful purpose. It is a good for us if our experiences are not wasted but are used for the good of others, if they are the means of a benefit which would not have come to others without them, which will at least in part compensate for those experiences. It follows from this insight that it is a blessing for a person if the possibility of his suffering makes possible the good for others of having the free choice of hurting or harming him; and if his actual suffering makes possible the good for others of feeling compassion for him, and of choosing to show or not show sympathy or provides knowledge for others. Thus it is a good for the fawn caught in the thicket in the forest fire that its suffering provides knowledge for the deer and other animals who see it to avoid the fire and deter their other offspring from being caught in it. The supreme good of being of use is worth paying a lot to get. It is much better if the being-of-use is chosen voluntarily, but it is good even if it isn't. Blessed is the man or woman whose life is of use.

If A desires the satisfaction of B's desire, the satisfaction of this desire is, I argued, a good for B in having his desire satisfied, a good for A in that his especially good desire is satisfied, and also an additional good for B in that the satisfaction of his desire was something that A cared about. Similarly, and much more so, with intentional actions. If A secures the fulfillment of some desire of B, not merely is it a good for B that his desire is fulfilled, and a good for A that he is the instrument of this, but it is a further good for B that the fulfillment of desire did not come by chance but by A actively seeking his well-being. We are lucky if people mind about us, and the natural expression of minding is seeking well-being. Sometimes those who "don't like to be beholden to others" don't see this. "I wish that I were not so dependent on my parents for money," says the undergraduate. But "so" is the crucial word – dependence can come in irksome forms or be too complete; but how awful it would be if nobody ever cared for us enough to give us anything. Fortunately, if God exists, no human or animal is ever in that position.

In the course of this paper I have run through many good states which we find on Earth and which God might seek to bring about. I have shown how often various evils (or their possibility) are (logically) necessary for their attainment. The evils include moral evils – the harm we humans do to each other or negligently allow to occur – the natural evils of various kinds, both animal and human suffering. The same goods could exist in a world different from ours in which there was less natural evil and more moral evil – e.g., there was so much moral evil in virtue of stronger human desires for evil – that there was no need for so much natural evil if humans were to have the same opportunity for courage in face of pain. But it is far from obvious that such a world would be a better world than ours. In general we need a similar amount of evil if we are to have the similar amount of good by way of the having and satisfaction of desire, and of significant choice and serious beneficiary action. There are also, I believe, other goods and other ways in which evil is necessary for good which I have not described.

None of the goods which I have listed are such that their production would justify God in causing endless suffering, but he does not do that. There is a limit of intensity and above all time (the length of a human life) to the suffering caused to any individual. In the perspective of eternity, the evils of this world are very limited in number and duration; and the issue concerns only whether God would allow such narrowly limited evils to occur for the sake of the great goods they make possible. A central theme of this paper is to draw attention to goods of two kinds which the modern world tends not to notice. It is when you take them into serious account, I suggest, that you begin to realize that not merely are certain evils necessary for certain goods, but they are necessary for goods at least as great as the evils are evil. There is first the good of being of use, or helping, and secondly the good of being helped. God will seek to bestow generously these great blessings.

I have almost always found in discussion of these matters that my opponents are usually happy to grant me, when I bring the suggestion to their attention, that the states which I describe as "goods" cannot be had without the corresponding evils, and quite often happy to grant that the former states are indeed good states and even that a world is not on balance worse for containing a few of these goods in the mildest of forms with the corresponding evils than it would otherwise be. But my opponents usually object to the scale – there are, they claim, too many, too various, and too serious evils to justify bringing about the goods which they make possible. Yet it must be stressed that each evil or possible evil removed takes away one more actual good.

If the fawn does not suffer in the thicket, other deer will not so readily have the opportunity of intentionally avoiding fires; he will not through his suffering be able to show courage or have the privilege of providing knowledge for other deer of how to avoid such tragedies; other deer and humans centuries later will not be able to show compassion for his suffering, etc. The sort of world where so many such evils are removed and which in effect my opponents think that God's goodness requires him to make, turns out – as regards the kinds of good to which I have drawn attention – to be a toy world. Things matter in the kinds of respect which I mention, but they don't matter very much. I cannot see that God would be less than perfectly good if he gave us a world where things matter a lot more than that.

I suggest that the reluctance of my opponents to see that arises primarily from overestimating the goodness of mere pleasure and the evil of mere pain, and grossly underestimating the value of being of use and being helped. Our culture has dulled our moral sensitivities in these respects. Yet even if an opponent allows the formal point that there is great value for the subject in being of use and being helped, he may fail to see that that has the consequence for theodicy which I commend because of two characteristic human vices – short-term and short-distance thinking. He tends to think of the worth of a sentient life as dependent on things that happen during that life and fairly close in space to the life. But once you grant the formal point that things outside a life, e.g., its causes and effects, make a great difference to the value of that life, it seems totally arbitrary to confine those things to ones near to the life in space and time. The sufferings of the Jewish victims of the Nazi concentration camps were the result of a web of choices that stretched back over centuries and continents and caused or made possible a whole web of actions and reactions that will stretch forward over centuries and continents (and the same goes to a lesser extent for the suffering of the fawn). Such sufferings made heroic choices possible for people normally too timid to make them (e.g., to harbor the prospective victims) and for people normally too hardhearted (as a result of previous bad choices) to make them (e.g., for a concentration camp guard not to obey orders). And they make possible reactions of courage (e.g., by the victims), of compassion, sympathy, penitence, forgiveness, reform, avoidance of repetition, etc., stretching down time and space. In saying this, I am not of course saying that those Nazi officials who sent Jews to the concentration camps were justified in doing so. For they had no right whatever to do that to others. But I am saying that God, who has rights over us that we do not have over others, is not less than perfectly good if he allowed the Jews for a short period to be subjected to these terrible evils through the evil free choice of others – in virtue of the hard heroic value of their lives of suffering.

There is no other way to get the evils of this world into the right perspective, except to reflect at length on innumerable very detailed thought experiments (in addition to actual experiences of life) in which we postulate very different sorts of worlds from our own, then ask ourselves whether the perfect goodness of God would require him to create one of these (or no world at all) rather than our own.[19] But I conclude with a very small thought experiment, which may help my opponents to begin this process. Suppose that you exist in another world before your birth in this one and are given a choice as to the sort of life you are to lead. You are told that you are to have only a short life, maybe of only a few minutes, although it will be an adult life in the sense that you will have the richness of sensation and belief characteristic of adults. You have a choice as to the sort of life you will have. You can have either a few minutes of very considerable pleasure of the kind produced by some drug such as heroin, which you will experience by yourself and will have no effects at all in the world (e.g., no one else will know about it); or you can have a few minutes of considerable pain, such as the pain of childbirth, which will have (unknown to you at the time of pain) considerable good effects on others over a few years. You are told that if you do not make the second choice, those others will never exist – and so you are under no moral obligation to make the second choice. But you seek to make the choice which will make your own life the best life for you to have led. How will you choose? The choice is, I hope, obvious. You must choose the second alternative. And it would of course make no difference to your choice if the good effects are to be very distant in time and space from your life.[20]

If we go on to meditate on how we should choose between other alternatives with longer lives or different lives – incarnation as a fawn or a suffering child[21] maybe – against a background of many centuries of effect and cause and place in the web of human and animal society, we may begin to look at things a little more sub specie aeternitatis. If God

is generously to give to creatures the privilege of forming other creatures, developing their desires and freedom of choice and informing
them about the possible choices open to them, he cannot (for logical
reasons) ask the latter before they are born what sort of life they would
like to live. He has to make the choice on their behalf, and he will
therefore seek to make a choice which, if rational, we might make for
ourselves. He sometimes pays us the compliment of supposing that we
would choose to be heroes.

For someone who remains unconvinced by my claims about the
relative strengths of the goods and evils involved, holding that great
though the goods are they do not justify the evils which they involve,
there is a fall-back position. My arguments may have convinced the
reader of the greatness of the goods involved sufficiently for him to
allow that God would be justified in bringing about the evils for the
sake of the goods which they make possible, if and only if God also
provides compensation in the form of happiness after death to the
victims whose sufferings make possible the goods. Someone whose
theodicy requires buttressing in this way will need independent reason
for believing that God does provide such life after death if he is to be
justified in holding his theodicy, and he may well have such reason.[22]
While believing that God does provide at any rate for many humans
such life after death, I have expounded a theodicy without relying on
this assumption. But I can understand someone thinking that the
assumption is needed. If, for example, the goods making possible free
choice for the Nazi concentration camp guards (in choosing whether to
disobey orders), for the Jewish victims (in deciding how to bear their
suffering), and for many others involved are not goods great enough to
justify God's allowing the Nazis to choose to exterminate Jews, maybe
they would be if the evil is compensated by some years of happy
afterlife for the Jews involved.

It remains the case, however, that evil is evil, and there is a substantial price to pay for the goods of our world. God would not be less
than perfectly good if he created instead a world without pain and
suffering, and so without the particular goods which they make possible. Christian tradition claims that God has created worlds of both
kinds – our world, and the heaven of the blessed. The latter is a
marvelous world with a vast range of possible deep goods, but it lacks
a few goods which our world contains, including the good of being able
to reject the good. Out of generosity, God might well choose to give
some of us the choice of rejecting the good in a world like ours, before

giving to those who accept it a wonderful world in which that possibility no longer exists.[23]

NOTES

1   Given that an omnipotent being can prevent and that a perfectly good being will always try to prevent evils of the kind and quantity we find on Earth, the argument from such evils is a conclusive deductive argument against the existence of God. But insofar as it is only probable that an omnipotent being can prevent or that a perfectly good being will try to prevent evils of the kind and quantity we find on Earth, then the conclusion that there is no God will only be probable.

2   Some writers have used "theodicy" as the name of the enterprise of showing God's actual reasons for allowing evil to occur and have contrasted it with a "defense" to the argument from evil to the nonexistence of God which merely shows that the argument doesn't work. See, e.g., Alvin Plantinga, *The Nature of Necessity* (Oxford: Clarendon Press, 1974), 192. Given this contrast, what I am seeking to do is provide a "defense" rather than a "theodicy," but I do so by showing what reasons God could have for allowing evil to occur; I am not, however, claiming that the reasons which I give are God's actual reasons. I believe, however, that my use of "theodicy" is that normal to the tradition of discussion of these issues.

3   For argument on this, see my book *The Existence of God* (Oxford: Clarendon Press, 1979), 216–18.

4   See *The Existence of God*, 202–14. I present the argument at greater length and defend it against objections in "Knowledge from Experience, and the Problem of Evil" in Wm. Abraham and S. Holtzer, eds., *The Rationality of Religious Belief* (Oxford: Clarendon Press, 1987). While I accept the need for yet further tightening of the argument, to do so would require at least an article devoted entirely to that topic.

5   I plan to write a full-length book on Providence, in which I shall defend the moral views in question at much greater length than I do in this paper.

6   For a fuller account of desire, see my book *The Evolution of the Soul* (Oxford: Clarendon Press, 1986), chap. 6.

7   I stress that the desire is only "frustrated" when it is a (believedly) unfulfilled desire for something to happen now. A desire to go to London tomorrow is today neither satisfied nor frustrated. Of course, some frustrations are so mild that we might hesitate to call them that in ordinary speech – but my unfulfilled mild desire for cream cake is on a continuum with my strong desire that a certain sensation go away, or that peace come to the Middle East; and hence it is appropriate in philosophical discussion to call the former also a case of frustration of desire.

8   The evil is not the death of the loved ones but our being deprived of intercourse with them. Death is simply in itself the point at which the finite good of life comes to an end. Death is only an evil for the dead one if it occurs under certain circumstances (e.g., prematurely, when life's ambitions are suddenly frustrated). That death is not as such an evil (i.e., for the dead one under normal circumstances) but that in many respects it is good that the world contain death, see *The Existence of God*, 193–96.

9   In discussing intentional actions, I am assuming that the agent's moral beliefs are correct. It would complicate the discussion too much to bring in the goodness of actions aimed at some end falsely believed to be good. But I do not believe that this simplification in any way affects the main points of the argument.

10 That is, the agent has libertarian free will – his choices are not fully determined; not just compatibilist free will – no one puts psychological or physical pressure on him to act as he does. Of course, libertarian free will only belongs to an agent choosing intentionally between alternatives; it doesn't belong to any nonmental events, such as the random swervings of atoms, which are not fully caused.

11 There is a further circumstance under which free choice is possible. That is where an agent has a choice between an infinite number of good actions, each of which is, he believes, worse than some other such action; there is, he believes, no best or equal best action. However, since only a being whose power is unlimited in some respect will be in such a situation, humans or animals are never in such a situation; and so for the sake of simplicity of exposition, I ignore this possibility.

12 I have given my reasons for my belief, that they do have such free will elsewhere – see my *Evolution of the Soul*, chap. 13. Insofar as there is reason to suppose that they do not have such free will, the free-will defense will fail.

13 This is the comment of the Exultet, the hymn of the traditional Easter Eve Liturgy, on the sin of Adam: "O happy fault which merited a redeemer so great and of such a kind."

14 For analysis of such notions as reparation, forgiveness, gratitude, and reward, see my *Responsibility and Atonement* (Oxford: Clarendon Press, 1989), chaps. 4 and 5.

15 If the behavior of tossed coins is deterministic, talk about a natural probability of a coin landing heads can only be intelligibly construed as talk about proportions of coins tossed in typical setups which result in heads. ("Natural probability" or "physical probability" is probability in nature in contrast to "epistemic probability," which is probability relative to our knowledge.) See my *Introduction to Confirmation Theory* (Oxford: Methuen, 1973), chaps. 1 and 2.

16 Those familiar with recent philosophical writing on the problem of evil will realize that I choose the example of a fawn caught in a forest fire

because of its prevalence in that literature. It was put forward by William Rowe as an example of apparently pointless evil.

17 It is a mistake, in my view, to regard the killing of one animal by another for food as in itself an evil. To be killed and eaten by another animal is as natural an end to life as would be death by other natural causes at the same age. For, given that animals lack free will and moral concepts, the killing of one by another is as much part of the natural order as is accident or disease not involving its transmission by other animals. And if death by such natural causes is not as such an evil, as I have urged (see note 8), but simply the end of a good, so too with death by predator. Evil comes insofar as there is pain involved in the killing, or offspring are knowingly deprived of a parent. I do not see any very good reason to suppose that invertebrates who do not have a central nervous system similar to that of humans suffer pain, let alone have knowledge. The evil of suffering arises, I suspect, only with the vertebrates and possibly only with mammals. Plausibly, too, since the central nervous systems of other vertebrates and mammals are less developed than ours, their sufferings are less than ours.

18 This good, others have recognized, exists as a this-worldly good, quite apart from any reward for patriotic behavior which might accrue in the afterlife. The hope of such reward was not a major motive among Romans and Greeks who died for their country: "The doctrine of a future life was far too vague among the pagans to exercise any powerful general influence," writes W. E. H. Lecky in his *History of European Morals from Augustus to Charlemagne*, vol. 2 (1899), 3. And he states that "the Spartan and the Roman died for his country because he loved it. The martyr's ecstasy of hope had no place in his dying hour. He gave up all he had, he closed his eyes, as he believed for ever, and he asked for no reward in this world or in the next" (vol. 1, 178). The lines of Horace, "dulce et decorum propatria mori" (it is sweet and proper to die for one's country) in his *Odes* (3.2.13), were written by a man whose belief in personal immortality was negligible – see 3.30, in which Horace sees his "immortality" as consisting in his subsequent reputation and seems to convey the view that dying for one's country was a good for the one who died. It was of course a Socratic view that doing just acts was a good for the one who does them; see Plato, *Gorgias* 479.

19 Note that the issue is not whether this world is the best of all possible worlds. There cannot, I suggest, be a best of all possible worlds, because any world could always be bettered in some respect – see *The Existence of God*, 113–14. The issue is whether there is too much evil in this world, despite the goods it makes possible, for God to create it at all. He may of course create other worlds as well.

20   The thought experiment is only meant to bring out the value of such a life for the sufferer. It is not put forward as a case when God could not produce the good effect in any other way. But it is meant to begin to help us to assess correctly cases of the latter kind.

21   See Ivan's speech in Dostoyevsky's *Brothers Karamazov*, bk. 5, chap. 4.

22   This may, for example, be provided by revelation. On the evidence for revealed truth, see my *Revelation* (Oxford: Clarendon Press, 1992).

23   For comments on earlier drafts of this essay, I thank C. Stephen Layman, Bruce Russell, Eleonore Stump, and Mark O. Webb.

12

JOHN HICK

Soul-Making Theodicy

Can a world in which sadistic cruelty often has its way, in which selfish lovelessness is so rife, in which there are debilitating diseases, crippling accidents, bodily and mental decay, insanity, and all manner of natural disasters be regarded as the expression of infinite creative goodness? Certainly all this could never by itself lead anyone to believe in the existence of a limitlessly powerful God. And yet even in a world which contains these things innumerable men and women have believed and do believe in the reality of an infinite creative goodness, which they call God. The theodicy project starts at this point, with an already operating belief in God, embodied in human living, and attempts to show that this belief is not rendered irrational by the fact of evil. It attempts to explain how it is that the universe, assumed to be created and ultimately ruled by a limitlessly good and limitlessly powerful Being, is as it is, including all the pain and suffering and all the wickedness and folly that we find around us and within us. The theodicy project is thus an exercise in metaphysical construction, in the sense that it consists in the formation and criticism of large-scale hypotheses concerning the nature and process of the universe.

Since a theodicy both starts from and tests belief in the reality of God, it naturally takes different forms in relation to different concepts of God. In this essay I shall be discussing the project of a specifically Christian theodicy; I shall not be attempting the further and even more difficult work of comparative theodicy, leading in turn to the question of a global theodicy.

Original publication: Pp. 39–52, Stephen T. Davis (ed.), *Encountering Evil: Live Options in Theodicy* (Atlanta: Westminster/John Knox, 1981).

The two main demands upon a theodicy-hypothesis are (1) that it be internally coherent, and (2) that it be consistent with the data both of the religious tradition on which it is based, and of the world, in respect both of the latter's general character as revealed by scientific enquiry and of the specific facts of moral and natural evil. These two criteria demand, respectively, possibility and plausibility.

Traditionally, Christian theology has centered upon the concept of God as both limitlessly powerful and limitlessly good and loving; and it is this concept of deity that gives rise to the problem of evil as a threat to theistic faith. The threat was definitively expressed in Stendhal's bombshell, "The only excuse for God is that he does not exist!" The theodicy project is the attempt to offer a different view of the universe which is both possible and plausible and which does not ignite Stendhal's bombshell.

Christian thought has always included a certain range of variety, and in the area of theodicy it offers two broad types of approach. The Augustinian approach, representing until fairly recently the majority report of the Christian mind, hinges upon the idea of the fall, which has in turn brought about the disharmony of nature. This type of theodicy is developed today as "the free-will defense." The Irenaean approach, representing in the past a minority report, hinges upon the creation of humankind through the evolutionary process as an immature creature living in a challenging and therefore person-making world. I shall indicate very briefly why I do not find the first type of theodicy satisfactory, and then spend the remainder of this essay in exploring the second type.

In recent years the philosophical discussion of the problem of evil has been dominated by the free-will defense. A major effort has been made by Alvin Plantinga and a number of other Christian philosophers to show that it is logically possible that a limitlessly powerful and limitlessly good God is responsible for the existence of this world. For all evil may ultimately be due to misuses of creaturely freedom. But it may nevertheless be better for God to have created free than unfree beings; and it is logically possible that any and all free beings whom God might create would, as a matter of contingent fact, misuse their freedom by falling into sin. In that case it would be logically impossible for God to have created a world containing free beings and yet not containing sin and the suffering which sin brings with it. Thus it is logically possible, despite the fact of evil, that the existing universe is the work of a limitlessly good creator.

These writers are in effect arguing that the traditional Augustinian type of theodicy, based upon the fall from grace of free finite creatures – first angels and then human beings – and a consequent going wrong of the physical world, is not logically impossible. I am in fact doubtful whether their argument is sound, and will return to the question later. But even if it should be sound, I suggest that their argument wins only a Pyrrhic victory, since the logical possibility that it would establish is one which, for very many people today, is fatally lacking in plausibility. For most educated inhabitants of the modern world regard the biblical story of Adam and Eve, and their temptation by the devil, as myth rather than as history; and they believe that so far from having been created finitely perfect and then falling, humanity evolved out of lower forms of life, emerging in a morally, spiritually, and culturally primitive state. Further, they reject as incredible the idea that earthquake and flood, disease, decay, and death are consequences either of a human fall, or of a prior fall of angelic beings who are now exerting an evil influence upon the earth. They see all this as part of a pre-scientific world view, along with the stories of the world having been created in six days and of the sun standing still for twenty-four hours at Joshua's command. One cannot, strictly speaking, disprove any of these ancient biblical myths and sagas, or refute their confident elaboration in the medieval Christian picture of the universe. But those of us for whom the resulting theodicy, even if logically possible, is radically implausible, must look elsewhere for light on the problem of evil.

I believe that we find the light that we need in the main alternative strand of Christian thinking, which goes back to important constructive suggestions by the early Hellenistic Fathers of the Church, particularly St. Irenaeus (AD 120–202). Irenaeus himself did not develop a theodicy, but he did – together with other Greek-speaking Christian writers of that period, such as Clement of Alexandria – build a framework of thought within which a theodicy became possible which does not depend upon the idea of the fall, and which is consonant with modern knowledge concerning the origins of the human race. This theodicy cannot, as such, be attributed to Irenaeus. We should rather speak of a type of theodicy, presented in varying ways by different subsequent thinkers (the greatest of whom has been Friedrich Schleiermacher), of which Irenaeus can properly be regarded as the patron saint.

The central theme out of which this Irenaean type of theodicy has arisen is the two-stage conception of the creation of humankind, first in the "image" and then in the "likeness" of God. Re-expressing this in modern terms, the first stage was the gradual production of *Homo sapiens*, through the long evolutionary process, as intelligent ethical and religious animals. The human being is an animal, one of the varied forms of earthly life and continuous as such with the whole realm of animal existence. But the human being is uniquely intelligent, having evolved a large and immensely complex brain. Further, the human being is ethical – that is, a gregarious as well as an intelligent animal, able to realize and respond to the complex demands of social life. And the human being is a religious animal, with an innate tendency to experience the world in terms of the presence and activity of super-natural beings and powers. This then is early *Homo sapiens*, the intelli-gent social animal capable of awareness of the divine. But early *Homo sapiens* is not the Adam and Eve of Augustinian theology, living in perfect harmony with self, with nature, and with God. On the contrary, the life of this being must have been a constant struggle against a hostile environment, and capable of savage violence against one's fellow human beings, particularly outside one's own immediate group; and this being's concepts of the divine were primitive and often blood-thirsty. Thus existence "in the image of God" was a potentiality for knowledge of and relationship with one's Maker rather than such knowledge and relationship as a fully realized state. In other words, people were created as spiritually and morally immature crea-tures, at the beginning of a long process of further growth and devel-opment, which constitutes the second stage of God's creative work. In this second stage, of which we are a part, the intelligent, ethical, and religious animal is being brought through one's own free responses into what Irenaeus called the divine "likeness." The human animal is being created into a child of God. Irenaeus' own terminology (*eikon, homoiosis; imago, similitudo*) has no particular merit, based as it is on a misunder-standing of the Hebrew parallelism in Genesis 1:26; but his conception of a two-stage creation of the human, with perfection lying in the future rather than in the past, is of fundamental importance. The notion of the fall was not basic to this picture, although it was to become basic to the great drama of salvation depicted by St. Augustine and accepted within western Christendom, including the churches stemming from the Reformation, until well into the nineteenth century. Irenaeus him-self however could not, in the historical knowledge of his time, question the fact of the fall; though he treated it as a relatively minor lapse, a youthful error, rather than as the infinite crime and cosmic disaster which has ruined the whole creation. But today we can acknowledge that there is no evidence at all of a period in the distant past when humankind was in the ideal state of a fully realized "child of God." We can accept that, so far as actual events in time are concerned, there never was a fall from an original righteousness and grace. If we want to continue to use the term fall, because of its hallowed place in the Christian tradition, we must use it to refer to the immense gap between what we actually are and what in the divine intention is eventually to be. But we must not blur our awareness that the ideal state is not something already enjoyed and lost, but is a future and as yet unrealized goal. The reality is not a perfect creation which has gone tragically wrong, but a still continuing creative process whose completion lies in the eschaton.

Let us now try to formulate a contemporary version of the Irenaean type of theodicy, based on this suggestion of the initial creation of humankind, not as a finitely perfect, but as an immature creature at the beginning of a long process of further growth and development. We may begin by asking why one should have been created as an imperfect and developing creature rather than as the perfect being whom God is presumably intending to create? The answer, I think, consists in two considerations which converge in their practical implications, one concerned with the human's relationship to God and the other with the relationship to other human beings. As to the first, we could have the picture of God creating finite beings, whether angels or persons, directly in his own presence, so that in being conscious of that which is other than one's self the creature is automatically conscious of God, the limitless divine reality and power, goodness and love, knowledge and wisdom, towering above one's self. In such a situation the disproportion between Creator and creatures would be so great that the latter would have no freedom in relation to God; they would indeed not exist as independent autonomous persons. For what freedom could finite beings have in an immediate consciousness of the presence of the one who has created them, who knows them through and through, who is limitlessly powerful as well as limitlessly loving and good, and who claims their total obedience? In order to be a person, exercising some measure of genuine freedom, the creature must be brought into existence, not in the immediate divine presence, but at a "distance" from God. This "distance" cannot of course be spatial; for God is omnipresent. It must be an epistemic distance, a distance in the cognitive dimension. And the Irenaean hypothesis is that this "distance" consists, in the case of humans, in their existence within and as part of a world which functions as an autonomous system and from within which God is not overwhelmingly evident. It is a world, in Bonhoeffer's phrase, *etsi deus non daretur*, as if there were no God. Or rather, it is religiously ambiguous, capable both of being seen as a purely natural phenomenon and of being seen as God's creation and experienced as mediating his presence. In such a world one can exist as a person over against the Creator. One has space to exist as a finite being, a space created by the epistemic distance from God and protected by one's basic cognitive freedom, one's freedom to open or close oneself to the dawning awareness of God which is experienced naturally by a religious animal. This Irenaean picture corresponds, I suggest, to our actual human situation. Emerging within the evolutionary process as part of the continuum of animal life, in a universe which functions in accordance with its own laws and whose workings can be investigated and described without reference to a creator, the human being has a genuine, even awesome, freedom in relation to one's Maker. The human being is free to acknowledge and worship God; and is free – particularly since the emergence of human individuality and the beginnings of critical consciousness during the first millennium BC – to doubt the reality of God.

Within such a situation there is the possibility of the human being coming freely to know and love one's Maker. Indeed, if the end-state which God is seeking to bring about is one in which finite persons have come in their own freedom to know and love him, this requires creating them initially in a state which is not that of their already knowing and loving him. For it is logically impossible to create beings already in a state of having come into that state by their own free choices.

The other consideration, which converges with this in pointing to something like the human situation as we experience it, concerns our human moral nature. We can approach it by asking why humans should not have been created at this epistemic distance from God, and yet at the same time as morally perfect beings? That persons could have been created morally perfect and yet free, so that they would always in fact choose rightly, has been argued by such critics of the free-will defense in theodicy as Antony Flew and J. L. Mackie, and argued against by Alvin Plantinga and other upholders of that form of theodicy. On the specific issue defined in the debate between them, it appears to me that the criticism of the free-will defense stands. It appears to me that a perfectly good being, although formally free to sin, would in fact never do so. If we imagine such a being in a morally frictionless environment, involving no stresses or temptation, then we must assume that one would exemplify the ethical equivalent of Newton's first law of motion, which states that a moving body will continue in uniform motion until interfered with by some outside force. By analogy, a perfectly good being would continue in the same moral course forever, there being nothing in the environment to throw one off it. But even if we suppose the morally perfect being to exist in an imperfect world, in which one is subject to temptations, it still follows that, in virtue of moral perfection, one will always overcome those temptations – as in the case, according to orthodox Christian belief, of Jesus Christ. It is, to be sure, logically possible, as Plantinga and others argue, that a free being, simply as such, may at any time contingently decide to sin. However, a responsible free being does not act randomly, but on the basis of moral nature. And a free being whose nature is wholly and unqualifiedly good will accordingly never in fact sin.

But if God could, without logical contradiction, have created humans as wholly good free beings, why did he not do so? Why was humanity not initially created in possession of all the virtues, instead of having to acquire them through the long hard struggle of life as we know it? The answer, I suggest, appeals to the principle that virtues which have been formed within the agent as a hard won deposit of his own right decisions in situations of challenge and temptation, are intrinsically more valuable than virtues created within him ready made and without any effort on his own part. This principle expresses a basic value-judgment, which cannot be established by argument but which one can only present, in the hope that it will be as morally plausible, and indeed compelling, to others as to oneself. It is, to repeat, the judgment that a moral goodness which exists as the agent's initial given nature, without ever having been chosen by him in the face of temptations to the contrary, is intrinsically less valuable than a moral goodness which has been built up through the agent's own responsible choices through time in the face of alternative possibilities.

If, then, God's purpose was to create finite persons embodying the most valuable kind of moral goodness, he would have to create them, not as already perfect beings but rather as imperfect creatures who can then attain to the more valuable kind of goodness through their own free choices as in the course of their personal and social history new responses prompt new insights, opening up new moral possibilities, and providing a milieu in which the most valuable kind of moral nature can be developed.

We have thus far, then, the hypothesis that one is created at an epistemic distance from God in order to come freely to know and love the Maker; and that one is at the same time created as a morally immature and imperfect being in order to attain through freedom the most valuable quality of goodness. The end sought, according to this hypothesis, is the full realization of the human potentialities in a unitary spiritual and moral perfection in the divine kingdom. And the question we have to ask is whether humans as we know them, and the world as we know it, are compatible with this hypothesis.

Clearly we cannot expect to be able to deduce our actual world in its concrete character, and our actual human nature as part of it, from the general concept of spiritually and morally immature creatures developing ethically in an appropriate environment. No doubt there is an immense range of possible worlds, any one of which, if actualized, would exemplify this concept. All that we can hope to do is to show that our actual world is one of these. And when we look at our human situation as part of the evolving life of this planet we can, I think, see that it fits this specification. As animal organisms, integral to the whole ecology of life, we are programmed for survival. In pursuit of survival, primitives not only killed other animals for food but fought other human beings when their vital interests conflicted. The life of prehistoric persons must indeed have been a constant struggle to stay alive, prolonging an existence which was, in Hobbes' phrase, "poor, nasty, brutish and short." And in his basic animal self-regardingness humankind was, and is, morally imperfect. In saying this I am assuming that the essence of moral evil is selfishness, the sacrificing of others to one's own interests. It consists, in Kantian terminology, in treating others, not as ends in themselves, but as means to one's own ends. This is what the survival instinct demands. And yet we are also capable of love, of self-giving in a common cause, of a conscience which responds to others in their needs and dangers. And with the development of civilization we see the growth of moral insight, the glimpsing and gradual assimilation of higher ideals, and tension between our animality and our ethical values. But that the human being has a lower as well as a higher nature, that one is an animal as well as a potential child of God, and that one's moral goodness is won from a struggle with one's own innate selfishness, is inevitable given one's continuity with the other forms of animal life. Further, the human animal is not responsible for having come into existence as an animal. The ultimate responsibility for humankind's existence, as a morally imperfect creature, can only rest with the Creator. The human does not, in one's own degree of freedom and responsibility, choose one's origin, but rather one's destiny.

This then, in brief outline, is the answer of the Irenaean type of theodicy to the question of the origin of moral evil: the general fact of humankind's basic self-regarding animality is an aspect of creation as part of the realm of organic life; and this basic self-regardingness has been expressed over the centuries both in sins of individual selfishness and in the much more massive sins of corporate selfishness, institutionalized in slavery and exploitation and all the many and complex forms of social injustice.

But nevertheless our sinful nature in a sinful world is the matrix within which God is gradually creating children for himself out of human animals. For it is as men and women freely respond to the claim of God upon their lives, transmuting their animality into the structure of divine worship, that the creation of humanity is taking place. And in its concrete character this response consists in every form of moral goodness, from unselfish love in individual personal relationships to the dedicated and selfless striving to end exploitation and to create justice within and between societies.

But one cannot discuss moral evil without at the same time discussing the non-moral evil of pain and suffering. (I propose to mean by "pain" physical pain, including the pains of hunger and thirst; and by "suffering" the mental and emotional pain of loneliness, anxiety, remorse, lack of love, fear, grief, envy, etc.). For what constitutes moral evil as evil is the fact that it causes pain and suffering. It is impossible to conceive of an instance of moral evil, or sin, which is not productive of pain or suffering to anyone at any time. But in addition to moral evil there is another source of pain and suffering in the structure of the physical world, which produces storms, earthquakes, and floods and which afflicts the human body with diseases – cholera, epilepsy, cancer, malaria, arthritis, rickets, meningitis, etc. – as well as with broken bones and other outcomes of physical accident. It is true that a great deal both of pain and of suffering is humanly caused, not only by the inhumanity of man to man but also by the stresses of our individual and corporate life-styles, causing many disorders – not only lung cancer and cirrhosis of the liver but many cases of heart disease, stomach and other ulcers, strokes, etc. – as well as accidents. But there remain nevertheless, in the natural world itself, permanent causes of human pain and suffering. And we have to ask why an unlimitedly good and unlimitedly powerful God should have created so dangerous a world, both as regards its purely natural hazards of earthquake and flood etc., and as regards the liability of the human body to so many ills, both psychosomatic and purely somatic.

The answer offered by the Irenaean type of theodicy follows from and is indeed integrally bound up with its account of the origin of moral evil. We have the hypothesis of humankind being brought into being within the evolutionary process as a spiritually and morally immature creature, and then growing and developing through the exercise of freedom in this religiously ambiguous world. We can now ask what sort of a world would constitute an appropriate environment for this second stage of creation? The development of human personality – moral, spiritual, and intellectual – is a product of challenge and response. It does not occur in a static situation demanding no exertion and no choices. So far as intellectual development is concerned, this is a well-established principle which underlies the whole modern educational process, from pre-school nurseries designed to provide a rich and stimulating environment, to all forms of higher education designed to challenge the intellect. At a basic level the essential part played in learning by the learner's own active response to environment was strikingly demonstrated by the Held and Heim experiment with kittens.[1] Of two litter-mate kittens in the same artificial environment one was free to exercise its own freedom and intelligence in exploring the environment, whilst the other was suspended in a kind of "gondola" which moved whenever and wherever the free kitten moved. Thus the second kitten had a similar succession of visual experiences as the first, but did not exert itself or make any choices in obtaining them. And whereas the first kitten learned in the normal way to conduct itself safely within its environment, the second did not. With no interaction with a challenging environment there was no development in its behavioral patterns. And I think we can safely say that the intellectual development of humanity has been due to interaction with an objective environment functioning in accordance with its own laws, an environment which we have had actively to explore and to co-operate with in order to escape its perils and exploit its benefits. In a world devoid both of dangers to be avoided and rewards to be won we may assume that there would have been virtually no development of the human intellect and imagination, and hence of either the sciences or the arts, and hence of human civilization or culture.

The fact of an objective world within which one has to learn to live, on penalty of pain or death, is also basic to the development of one's moral nature. For it is because the world is one in which men and women can suffer harm – by violence, disease, accident, starvation, etc. – that our actions affecting one another have moral significance. A morally wrong act is, basically, one which harms some part of the human community; whilst a morally right action is, on the contrary, one which prevents or neutralizes harm or which preserves or increases human well being. Now we can imagine a paradise in which no one can ever come to any harm. It could be a world which, instead of having its own fixed structure, would be plastic to human wishes. Or it could be a world with a fixed structure, and hence the possibility of damage and pain, but whose structure is suspended or adjusted by special divine action whenever necessary to avoid human pain. Thus, for example, in such a miraculously pain-free world one who falls accidentally off a high building would presumably float unharmed to the ground; bullets would become insubstantial when fired at a human body; poisons would cease to poison; water to drown, and so on. We can at least begin to imagine such a world. And a good deal of the older discussion of the problem of evil – for example in Part XI of Hume's *Dialogues Concerning Natural Religion* – assumed that it must be the intention of a limitlessly good and powerful Creator to make for human creatures a pain-free environment; so that the very existence of pain is evidence against the existence of God. But such an assumption overlooks the fact that a world in which there can be no pain or suffering would also be one in which there can be no moral choices and hence no possibility of moral growth and development. For in a situation in which no one can ever suffer injury or be liable to pain or suffering there would be no distinction between right and wrong action. No action would be morally wrong, because no action could have harmful consequences; and likewise no action would be morally right in contrast to wrong. Whatever the values of such a world, it clearly could not serve a purpose of the development of its inhabitants from self-regarding animality to self-giving love.

Thus the hypothesis of a divine purpose in which finite persons are created at an epistemic distance from God, in order that they may gradually become children of God through their own moral and spiritual choices, requires that their environment, instead of being a pain-free and stress-free paradise, be broadly the kind of world of which we find ourselves to be a part. It requires that it be such as to provoke the theological problem of evil. For it requires that it be an environment which offers challenges to be met, problems to be solved, dangers

to be faced, and which accordingly involves real possibilities of hardship, disaster, failure, defeat, and misery as well as of delight and
happiness, success, triumph and achievement. For it is by grappling
with the real problems of a real environment, in which a person is one
form of life among many, and which is not designed to minister
exclusively to one's well-being, that one can develop in intelligence
and in such qualities as courage and determination. And it is in the
relationships of human beings with one another, in the context of this
struggle to survive and flourish, that they can develop the higher values
of mutual love and care, of self-sacrifice for others, and of commitment
to a common good.

To summarize thus far:

(1)   The divine intention in relation to humankind, according to our
      hypothesis, is to create perfect finite personal beings in filial rela-
      tionship with their Maker.
(2)   It is logically impossible for humans to be created already in this
      perfect state, because in its spiritual aspect it involves coming freely
      to an uncoerced consciousness of God from a situation of epistemic
      distance, and in its moral aspect, freely choosing the good in
      preference to evil.
(3)   Accordingly the human being was initially created through the
      evolutionary process, as a spiritually and morally immature crea-
      ture, and as part of a world which is both religiously ambiguous
      and ethically demanding.
(4)   Thus that one is morally imperfect (i.e., that there is moral evil),
      and that the world is a challenging and even dangerous environ-
      ment (i.e., that there is natural evil), are necessary aspects of the
      present stage of the process through which God is gradually creat-
      ing perfected finite persons.

In terms of this hypothesis, as we have developed it thus far, then,
both the basic moral evil in the human heart and the natural evils of the
world are compatible with the existence of a Creator who is unlimited
in both goodness and power. But is the hypothesis plausible as well as
possible? The principal threat to its plausibility comes, I think, from the
sheer amount and intensity of both moral and natural evil. One can
accept the principle that in order to arrive at a freely chosen goodness
one must start out in a state of moral immaturity and imperfection. But
is it necessary that there should be the depths of demonic malice and
cruelty which each generation has experienced, and which we have

seen above all in recent history in the Nazi attempt to exterminate the Jewish population of Europe? Can any future fulfillment be worth such horrors? This was Dostoevski's haunting question: "Imagine that you are creating a fabric of human destiny with the object of making men happy in the end, giving them peace and rest at last, but that it was essential and inevitable to torture to death only one tiny creature – that baby beating its breast with its fist, for instance – and to found that edifice on its unavenged tears, would you consent to be the architect on those conditions?"[2] The theistic answer is one which may be true but which takes so large a view that it baffles the imagination. Intellectually one may be able to see, but emotionally one cannot be expected to feel, its truth; and in that sense it cannot satisfy us. For the theistic answer is that if we take with full seriousness the value of human freedom and responsibility, as essential to the eventual creation of perfected children of God, then we cannot consistently want God to revoke that freedom when its wrong exercise becomes intolerable to us. From our vantage point within the historical process we may indeed cry out to God to revoke his gift of freedom, or to overrule it by some secret or open intervention. Such a cry must have come from millions caught in the Jewish Holocaust, or in the yet more recent laying waste of Korea and Vietnam, or from the victims of racism in many parts of the world. And the thought that humankind's moral freedom is indivisible, and can lead eventually to a consummation of limitless value which could never be attained without that freedom, and which is worth any finite suffering in the course of its creation, can be of no comfort to those who are now in the midst of that suffering. But whilst fully acknowledging this, I nevertheless want to insist that this eschatological answer may well be true. Expressed in religious language it tells us to trust in God even in the midst of deep suffering, for in the end we shall participate in his glorious kingdom.

Again, we may grant that a world which is to be a person-making environment cannot be a pain-free paradise but must contain challenges and dangers, with real possibilities of many kinds of accident and disaster, and the pain and suffering which they bring. But need it contain the worst forms of disease and catastrophe? And need misfortune fall upon us with such heartbreaking indiscriminateness? Once again there are answers, which may well be true, and yet once again the truth in this area may offer little in the way of pastoral balm. Concerning the intensity of natural evil, the truth is probably that our judgments of intensity are relative. We might identify some form of natural evil as the worst that there is – say the agony that can be caused by death from cancer – and claim that a loving God would not have allowed this to exist. But in a world in which there was no cancer, something else would then rank as the worst form of natural evil. If we then eliminate this, something else; and so on. And the process would continue until the world was free of all natural evil. For whatever form of evil for the time being remained would be intolerable to the inhabitants of that world. But in removing all occasions of pain and suffering, and hence all challenge and all need for mutual care, we should have converted the world from a person-making into a static environment, which could not elicit moral growth. In short, having accepted that a person-making world must have its dangers and therefore also its tragedies, we must accept that whatever form these take will be intolerable to the inhabitants of that world. There could not be a person-making world devoid of what we call evil; and evils are never tolerable – except for the sake of greater goods which may come out of them.

But accepting that a person-making environment must contain causes of pain and suffering, and that no pain or suffering is going to be acceptable, one of the most daunting and even terrifying features of the world is that calamity strikes indiscriminately. There is no justice in the incidence of disease, accident, disaster and tragedy. The righteous as well as the unrighteous are struck down by illness and afflicted by misfortune. There is no security in goodness, but the good are as likely as the wicked to suffer "the slings and arrows of outrageous fortune." From the time of Job this fact has set a glaring question mark against the goodness of God. But let us suppose that things were otherwise. Let us suppose that misfortune came upon humankind, not haphazardly and therefore unjustly, but justly and therefore not haphazardly. Let us suppose that instead of coming without regard to moral considerations, it was proportioned to desert, so that the sinner was punished and the virtuous rewarded. Would such a dispensation serve a person-making purpose? Surely not. For it would be evident that wrong deeds bring disaster upon the agent whilst good deeds bring health and prosperity; and in such a world truly moral action, action done because it is right, would be impossible. The fact that natural evil is not morally directed, but is a hazard which comes by chance, is thus an intrinsic feature of a person-making world.

In other words, the very mystery of natural evil, the very fact that disasters afflict human beings in contingent, undirected and haphazard ways, is itself a necessary feature of a world that calls forth mutual aid and builds up mutual caring and love. Thus on the one hand it would be completely wrong to say that God sends misfortune upon individuals, so that their death, maiming, starvation or ruin is God's will for them. But on the other hand God has set us in a world containing unpredictable contingencies and dangers, in which unexpected and undeserved calamities may occur to anyone; because only in such a world can mutual caring and love be elicited. As an abstract philosophical hypothesis this may offer little comfort. But translated into religious language it tells us that God's good purpose enfolds the entire process of this world, with all its good and bad contingencies, and that even amidst tragic calamity and suffering we are still within the sphere of his love and are moving towards his kingdom.

But there is one further all-important aspect of the Irenaean type of theodicy, without which all the foregoing would lose its plausibility. This is the eschatological aspect. Our hypothesis depicts persons as still in course of creation towards an end-state of perfected personal community in the divine kingdom. This end-state is conceived of as one in which individual egoity has been transcended in communal unity before God. And in the present phase of that creative process the naturally self-centered human animal has the opportunity freely to respond to God's non-coercive self-disclosures, through the work of prophets and saints, through the resulting religious traditions, and through the individual's religious experience. Such response always has an ethical aspect; for the growing awareness of God is at the same time a growing awareness of the moral claim which God's presence makes upon the way in which we live.

But it is very evident that this person-making process, leading eventually to perfect human community, is not completed on this earth. It is not completed in the life of the individual – or at best only in the few who have attained to sanctification, or moksha, or nirvana on this earth. Clearly the enormous majority of men and women die without having attained to this. As Eric Fromm has said, "The tragedy in the life of most of us is that we die before we are fully born."[3] And therefore if we are ever to reach the full realization of the potentialities of our human nature, this can only be in a continuation of our lives in another sphere of existence after bodily death. And it is equally evident that the perfect all-embracing human community, in which self-regarding concern has been transcended in mutual love, not only has not been realized in this world, but never can be, since hundreds of generations of human beings have already lived and died and accordingly could not be part of any ideal community established at some future moment of earthly history. Thus if the unity of humankind in God's presence is ever to be realized it will have to be in some sphere of existence other than our earth. In short, the fulfillment of the divine purpose, as it is postulated in the Irenaean type of theodicy, presupposes each person's survival, in some form of bodily death, and further living and growing towards that end-state. Without such an eschatological fulfillment, this theodicy would collapse.

A theodicy which presupposes and requires an eschatology will thereby be rendered implausible in the minds of many today. I nevertheless do not see how any coherent theodicy can avoid dependence upon an eschatology. Indeed I would go further and say that the belief in the reality of a limitlessly loving and powerful deity must incorporate some kind of eschatology according to which God holds in being the creatures whom he has made for fellowship with himself, beyond bodily death, and brings them into the eternal fellowship which he has intended for them. I have tried elsewhere to argue that such an eschatology is a necessary corollary of ethical monotheism; to argue for the realistic possibility of an after-life or lives, despite the philosophical and empirical arguments against this; and even to spell out some of the general features which human life after death may possibly have.[4] Since all this is a very large task, which would far exceed the bounds of this essay, I shall not attempt to repeat it here but must refer the reader to my existing discussion of it. It is that extended discussion that constitutes my answer to the question whether an Irenaean theodicy, with its eschatology, may not be as implausible as an Augustinian theodicy, with its human or angelic fall. (If it is, then the latter is doubly implausible; for it also involves an eschatology!)

There is however one particular aspect of eschatology which must receive some treatment here, however brief and inadequate. This is the issue of "universal salvation" versus "heaven and hell" (or perhaps annihilation instead of hell). If the justification of evil within the creative process lies in the limitless and eternal good of the end-state to which it leads, then the completeness of the justification must depend upon the completeness, or universality, of the salvation achieved. Only if it includes the entire human race can it justify the sins and sufferings of the entire human race throughout all history. But, having given human beings cognitive freedom, which in turn makes possible moral freedom, can the Creator bring it about that in the end all his human creatures freely turn to him in love and trust? The issue is a very difficult one; but I believe that it is in fact possible to reconcile a full affirmation of human freedom with a belief in the ultimate universal success of God's creative work. We have to accept that creaturely freedom always occurs within the limits of a basic nature that we did not ourselves choose; for this is entailed by the fact of having been created. If then a real though limited freedom does not preclude our being endowed with a certain nature, it does not preclude our being endowed with a basic Godward bias, so that, quoting from another side of St. Augustine's thought, "our hearts are restless until they find their rest in Thee."[5] If this is so, it can be predicted that sooner or later, in our own time and in our own way, we shall all freely come to God; and universal salvation can be affirmed, not as a logical necessity but as the contingent but predictable outcome of the process of the universe, interpreted theistically. Once again, I have tried to present this argument more fully elsewhere, and to consider various objections to it.[6]

On this view the human, endowed with a real though limited freedom, is basically formed for relationship with God and destined ultimately to find the fulfillment of his or her nature in that relationship. This does not seem to me excessively paradoxical. On the contrary, given the theistic postulate, it seems to me to offer a very probable account of our human situation. If so, it is a situation in which we can rejoice; for it gives meaning to our temporal existence as the long process through which we are being created, by our own free responses to life's mixture of good and evil, into "children of God" who "inherit eternal life."

NOTES

1 R. Held and A. Heim, "Movement-produced stimulation in the development of visually guided behaviour," *Journal of Comparative and Physiological Psychology* 56 (1963): 872–6.

2 Fyodor Dostoyevsky, *The Brothers Karamozov*, trans. Constance Garnett (New York: Modern Library, n.d.), Bk. V, ch. 4, p. 254.

3 Erich Fromm, "Values, Psychology, and Human Existence," in *New Knowledge of human Values*, ed. A. Maslow (New York: Harper & Row, 1959), p. 156.

4 John Hick, *Death and Eternal Life* (New York: Harper & Row; and London: Collins, 1976; revised, London: Macmillan, 1987).

5 *The Confessions of St. Augustine*, trans. F. J. Sheed (New York: Sheed and Ward, 1942) Bk. 1, ch.1, p. 3.

6 Hick, *Death and Eternal Life*, ch. 13.

13

Marilyn McCord Adams

The Problem of Hell:
A Problem of Evil for Christians

Since the 1950s, syllabi in analytic philosophy of religion have given the problem of evil pride of place. So-called atheologians have advanced as an argument against the existence of God the alleged logical incompossibility of the statements

(I) God exists, and is essentially omnipotent, omniscient, and perfectly good

and

(II) Evil exists.

The decision of Christian philosophers to reply from a posture of "defensive apologetics" and to let their (our) opponents define the value terms has carried both costs and benefits. For if it has limited the store of valuables available as defeaters of evil, it has also restricted the range of ills to be accounted for, to the ones secular philosophers believe in.

In my judgment, this bargain has proved bad, because it has been a distraction from the most important dimensions of the problem of evil. If what is fundamentally at stake – for David Hume and J. L. Mackie, as for Christian philosophers – is the consistency of *our* beliefs, then *our* value theory is the one that should come into play. Moreover, the agreement to try to solve the problem by exclusive appeal to this world's

Original publication: Pp. 301–27, Eleonore Stump (ed.), *Reasoned Faith: Essays in Philosophical Theology in Honor of Norman Kretzmann* (Ithaca and London: Cornell University Press, 1993).

(i.e., non-transcendent, created) goods has been curiously correlated with a reluctance to confront this world's worst evils (viz., horrors participation in which seems *prima facie* to suffice to ruin individual lives). The best-of-all-possible-worlds and free-will approaches try to finesse the existence of the worst evils by operating at a vague and global level. Elsewhere I have urged Christian philosophers to renounce secular value parsimony, to reach under the lid of our theological treasure chest for the only good big enough to defeat horrendous evils – viz., God Himself![1] On the other hand, our refusal to trade with our own store of valuables has allowed us to avoid dealing publicly with our own dark side.[2] For even if, as I argue, this-worldly horrors can be given positive meaning through integration into an overall beatific relation of loving intimacy with God, what about the postmortem evil of hell, in which the omnipotent creator turns effectively and finally against a creature's good?

My own view is that hell poses the principal problem of evil for Christians. Its challenge is so deep and decisive, that to spill bottles of ink defending the logical compossibility of (I) with this-worldly evils while holding a closeted belief that

(III)   Some created persons will be consigned to hell forever

is at best incongruous and at worst disingenuous. My purpose here is to engage the problem of hell at two levels: a theoretical level, concerning the logical compossibility of (I) and (III); and a pragmatic level, concerning whether or not a God who condemned some of His creatures to hell could be a logically appropriate object of standard Christian worship. My own verdict is no secret: statement (III) should be rejected in favor of a doctrine of universal salvation.

1   THE PROBLEM, FORMULATED

1.1   Theoretical dimension

The argument for the logical incompossibility of (I) with (III), mimics that for (I) with (II):

(1)   If God existed and were omnipotent, He would be able to avoid (III).

(2)   If God existed and were omniscient, He would know how to avoid (III).

(3)   If God existed and were perfectly good, He would want to avoid (III).

(4)   Therefore, if (I), not (III).

Obviously, the soundness of this argument depends on the construals given to the attribute terms and to 'hell'. As just noted, there is an important disanalogy between this and the parallel argument for the general problem of evil: viz., that if 'evil' takes on varying extensions in different value theories, nevertheless, (II) gets its bite from the fact that most people agree on a wide range of actually extant evils. By contrast, (III) enjoys no straightforward empirical support but rests on and must be in the first instance interpreted by the authorities that tell us so. Tradition counts Scripture among the witnesses. For example, the Gospel according to Matthew speaks in vivid imagery of the disobedient and unfaithful being "cast into outer darkness" where there is "weeping and gnashing of teeth" (Matt. 13:42, 50; 22:13) or being thrown into the "unquenchable fire" "prepared for the devil and all his angels" (Matt. 13:42, 50; 18:8–9; 22:13; cf. 3:10). Cashing the metaphors, it says of Judas that it would have been better for him never to have been born (Matt. 26:24). Mainstream medieval theology took such pictures at face value. Duns Scotus is typical in understanding that the reprobate will be forever given over to their guilt[3] and the torment of their inordinate appetites, deprived of both natural and supernatural happiness, and made to suffer perpetual fiery torture, which distracts their intellects so much that they can think of nothing else.[4]

Likewise, we can distinguish an *abstract* from a *concrete* version of the problem, depending on whether "some created persons" in statement (III) ranges over persons created in utopian antemortem environments and circumstances or only over persons in circumstances with combinations of obstacles and opportunities such as are found in the antemortem life experiences of persons in the actual world. Since the doctrine of hell is asserted by many Christians to be not merely logically possible but true, faith that embraces both (I) and (III) and seeks understanding will not complete its task unless it faces the concrete as well as the abstract version of the problem.

Premiss (1) is true because an omnipotent creator could altogether refrain from making any persons or could annihilate created persons any time He chose; either way, He could falsify (III). Again, many traditional theologians (e.g., Augustine, Duns Scotus, Ockham, Calvin) have understood divine sovereignty over creation – both nature and soteriology – to mean that nothing (certainly not creatures' rights) binds God as to what soteriological scheme (if any) He establishes. For example, God could have had a policy of not preserving human persons in existence after death, or He could have legislated temporary reform school followed by life in a utopian environment for all sinners. In these, and many other ways, God could avoid (III), and such was within His power.[5]

Likewise, (3) would be true if "perfectly good" is construed along the lines of person-relative goodness:

'God is good to a created person p' iff God guarantees to p a life that is a great good to p on the whole, and one in which p's participation in deep and horrendous evils (if any) is defeated within the context of p's life',

where

'Evil is horrendous' iff 'Participation in e by p (either as a victim or a perpetrator) gives everyone *prima facie* reason to believe that p's life cannot – given its inclusion of e – be a great good to p on the whole'.

The traditional hell is a paradigm horror, one which offers not merely prima facie but conclusive reason to believe that the life of the damned cannot be a great good to them on the whole. Any person who suffers eternal punishment in the traditional hell will, on the contrary, be one within whose life good is engulfed and/or defeated by evils.

For all we know, however, (3) may be false if divine goodness is evaluated in relation to God's role as producer of global goods. It is at least epistemically possible that (III) be true of a world that exhibits maximum variety with maximum unity or of a very good world that displays the best balance of moral good over moral evil which God could weakly actualize.[6] And in general, it is epistemically possible that the world have a maximally good overall order and still include the horrors of damnation for some created persons. Aquinas rationalizes this conclusion when he explains that since the purpose of creation is to show forth God's goodness, some must be damned to manifest his justice and others saved to advertise His mercy.[7]

1.2   Pragmatic implications

The pragmatic consequences of reconciling (I) with (III) by restricting divine goodness to its global dimension are severe. First of all, this assumption makes human life a bad bet. Consider (adapting John Rawls's device) persons in a preoriginal position, surveying possible worlds containing managers of varying power, wisdom, and character, and subjects with diverse fates. The subjects are to answer, from behind a veil of ignorance as to which position they would occupy, the question whether they would willingly enter a given world as a human being. Reason would, I submit, render a negative verdict already for worlds whose omniscient and omnipotent manager permits antemortem horrors that remain undefeated within the context of the human participant's life and a fortiori for worlds some or most of whose human occupants suffer eternal torment.[8]

Second, it would make pragmatically inconsistent any worship behavior that presupposes that God is good to the worshipper or to created persons generally. For given the traditional assumption that the identity of the elect is secret, so much so that there are no certain (or even very probabilifying) empirical signs by means of which humans can make an antemortem distinction between the saved and the damned, actual created persons are left to worry about whether this latter "fate-worse-than-death" is theirs. Nor would the knowledge that *we* were among the elect greatly relieve our pragmatic difficulty, given Christ's command to love our neighbors as ourselves.

If (III) were true, open-eyed worship would have to be of a God who mysteriously creates some persons for lives so horrendous on the whole and eternally, that it would have been better for them never to have been born, of a God who is at worst cruel (not that He had any obligation to be otherwise) and at best indifferent to our welfare. Christian Stoicism practices a species of such worship, one in which the believer (i) recognizes his or her insignificant place in the universe and (ii) by a series of spiritual exercises humbly accepts it (thereby submitting to God's inscrutable will), (iii) praises its Maker for His world-organizing activity, and (iv) finds dignity in this capacity for self-transcendence. Some even speak of divine love for them, in making them parts of His cosmic order and endowing them with the capacity for dignity, even when they are crushed by it. But the fact of such love carries no implication that God is *good to* them in the sense defined in section 1.1.[9] Notice, however, that Stoic worship that is honest (i.e., not based on denial and repression) is very difficult, indeed psychologically impossible for many, perhaps most, people. Avoiding pragmatic inconsistency requires vigilance against smuggling in the assumption to which none would be epistemically entitled, that after all God does care for me!

2 FREE WILL AND THE PROBLEM OF HELL

Many Christians find the Stoic bullet hard to bite but insist that it is unnecessary even if (III) is true. Mounting a kind of free-will defense, they claim that God has done a good thing in making incompatibilist free creatures. Like any good governor or parent, He has established a set of general conditional decrees, specifying sanctions and rewards for various sorts of free actions. His preference ("antecedent" or "perfect" will) is that everyone should be saved, but He has given us scope to work out our own destinies. Damnation would never happen but for the errant action of incompatibilist free creatures within the framework of divine regulations. It is not something God *does*, but rather allows; it is neither God's means, nor His end, but a middle-known but unintended side effect of the order He has created. Thus, (3) is true only regarding God's antecedent but not His all-things-considered preferences, and the incompossibility argument (in section 1.1) fails.

2.1 Exclusive salvation according to William Craig

William Craig offers a remarkably bold presentation of this position in his "'No Other Name': A Middle Knowledge Perspective on the Exclusivity of Salvation through Christ."[10] Motivated by his beliefs that (III) is asserted by Scripture and necessary to justify the missionary imperative, Craig takes Plantinga for his inspiration, and attempts to demonstrate the logical compossibility of (I) with

(III′) [a] Some persons do not receive Christ, and [b] are damned,

by finding another proposition that is compossible with (I) and that together with (I) entails (III′): viz.,

(IV)   God has actualized a world containing an optimal balance
       between saved and unsaved, and those who are unsaved suffer
       from trans-world damnation.[11]

By "optimal balance" Craig means the best that God could weakly
actualize and still fill heaven.[12] Nor need this ratio keep the number of
damned down to a few. For Craig thinks his defense also has the
makings of a theodicy[13] and insists that "if we take Scripture [Matt.
7:13–14] seriously, we must admit that *the vast majority of persons in the
world* are condemned and will be forever lost."[14]

Craig recognizes a need to defend his rejection of (3) for God's all-
things-considered preferences and his claim that (IV) is logically compossible with (I), against the charge that

(3′)   A perfectly good being would prefer not to create any persons at
       all rather than see some suffer in hell.

Once again, Craig has the courage of his convictions, insisting that
even if "the terrible price of filling heaven is also filling hell",[15] God's
decision to create free creatures – not merely a handful but enough to
fill heaven – and to accept this price does not count against His
benevolence or fairness,[16] provided God has done everything He
could (supplying grace to all). For their damnation is "of their own
free will", "the result of their own free choice".[17] They are "self-
condemned".[18] By the same token, the sufferings of the damned should
not tarnish the heavenly happiness of the saved, because they too will
recognize that the damned brought "this tragic circumstance" on
themselves as a "result of their own free choice."[19] And Craig insists
that divine distribution of graces through special and general revelation
does give each created person a chance to comply with God's will.

2.2   *Justice and commensuration*

Craig is concerned to maintain that God is neither "unjust"[20] nor
"unfair" in damning those who do not accept Christ.[21] Here it is
necessary to distinguish between (a) justice taken from the side of
God (whether God would be just in the sense of living up to His
obligations in weakly actualizing (III) or (III′)), and (b) justice considered in relation to created agents and their acts (whether weakly

actualizing (III) or (III′) would exemplify a policy of treating like cases alike, of rendering to each according to his or her deserts, or of setting expectations within reasonable reach). I want to argue that either way "justice" is the wrong concept, because justice trades in commensurables, whereas both God and eternal destinies are incommensurable with human beings and their acts.

2.2.1 Divine justice and the ontological gap.

I merely join the consensus of the great medieval and reformation theologians in recognizing that God and creatures are *ontologically incommensurate*. God is a being a greater than which cannot be conceived, the infinite being, in relation to which finite creatures are "almost nothing". Drawing on social analogies, Anselm contends that God is so far above, so different in kind from us, as not to be enmeshed in merely human networks of mutual rights and obligations; God is not the kind of thing that could be obligated to creatures in any way. Duns Scotus concurs, reasoning that God has no obligation to love creatures, because although the finite *goodness* of each provides *a* reason to love it, the fact of its *finitude* means that this reason is always defeasible, indeed negligible, almost nothing in comparison with the reason divine goodness has to love itself. Their conclusion from this ontological disproportion is that God will not be *unjust to* created persons no matter what He does.

2.2.2 Finite temporal agency versus eternal destiny

My earlier arguments[22] for the disproportion between human acts and eternal destinies centered on our limited capacities to do and suffer harm. Focusing on the "an-eye-for-an-eye" principle and its variants, I insisted that even if each human being were made to experience each of the harms she or he caused other humans, whether once, twice, or any finite multiple of times, the punishment thus mandated would eventually be over. I observed, however, that the notion of proportionate return already breaks down in ordinary cases where the numbers (though finite) get large, because in such cases we are irremediably unable to suffer precisely what we cause. For example, suppose I knock one tooth out of the mouth of each of thirty-two people each of whom has a full set of teeth. Is my losing one tooth thirty-two times and hence having no teeth not much worse than their each having thirty-one teeth? Or suppose I interrupt television transmission of the Superbowl game, thereby causing twenty million fans one hour of fury and frustration each. Surely, my suffering twenty million hours of fury and frustration is much worse. Harms are not atomic, their cumulative effect not simply additive; and so for large amounts, the notion of proportionate return already loses definition.

More recently, I have concentrated on the incommensuration between horrendous evils and human life and agency. For, on the one hand, *horrors have a power to defeat positive meaning disproportionate to their extension in the space-time worm of an individual's life.* And, on the other, *horrors are incommensurate with human cognitive capacities.* For (i) the human capacity to cause horrors unavoidably exceeds our ability to experience them. Many examples make this clear as to quantity: for example, on the traditional doctrine of the fall, Adam experiences one individual's worth of ignorance and difficulty, but his sin brought it on his many descendents; Hitler organized a holocaust of millions; small numbers of government leaders, scientists, and military personnel brought about the atomic explosions over Hiroshima and Nagasaki. Likewise for quality, it is probably true that, for example, a childless male soldier cannot experience anything like enough to the suffering of a mother whose child is murdered before her eyes. But (ii) where suffering is concerned, conceivability follows capacity to experience, in such a way that we cannot adequately conceive of what we cannot experience. Just as a blind person's color concepts are deficient because lack of acquaintance deprives him or her of the capacity for imaginative representation of colors, despite lots of abstract descriptive knowledge about them, so lack of experience deprives an agent of the capacity emphathetically to enter in to what it would be like to suffer this or that harm, despite more or less detailed abstract descriptive knowledge about such suffering. To these observations, I add the claim (iii) that agent responsibility is diminished in proportion to his or her unavoidable inability to conceive of the relevant dimensions of the action and its consequences, and I draw the conclusion that human agents cannot be fully responsible for the horrendous consequences of their actions.[23]

Returning to the problem of hell, I maintain that damnation is a horror that exceeds our conceptual powers. For even if we could experience for a finite period of time some aspect of hell's torments (e.g., the burning of the fire, deep depression, or consuming hatred) or heaven's bliss (e.g., St. Teresa's joyful glimpse of the Godhead), we are unavoidably unable to experience their cumulative effect in advance and so unable more than superficially to appreciate what is involved in either. It follows that human agents are unavoidably unable to exercise their free choice with fully open eyes, the way Craig implies we do.

2.2.3 Finite agency in the region of the divine

It may be objected that the ontological incommensuration between God and creatures redounds another way, however. For Anselm pointed out that the badness of sin is to be measured not simply in terms of what the creature is or does but in terms of the creature's relation to God, a being a greater/more worthy of honor, respect, and esteem than which cannot be conceived. Since God is infinitely worthy of honor, any offense against God is immeasurably indecent and hence infinitely culpable. Even if every created *harm* we caused were finite, at the very worst the ruin of finite created lives, Anselm's principle shows how we have the capacity to cause infinite *offense*. Any and every sin would turn out to be a horrendous evil. And if eternal torment for the creature is incommensurate with human agency taken in itself, it does not adequately measure the offensiveness of one small look contrary to God's will. Eternal torment is merely the closest approximation that creatures can make to experiencing the just punishment.

My reply is that it is not "fair" in Craig's sense (b) of setting reasonable expectations to put created agency (even if we think of its starting in utopian Eden with ideal competence of its kind) into a position where the consequences of its exercise are so disproportionate to its acts. Suppose the powers that be threaten a nuclear holocaust if I do not always put my pencil down no more than one inch from the paper on which I am writing. Although it is within my power to meet such a demand, such disproportionate consequences put my pencil-placing actions under unnatural strain. Although in some sense I *can* comply, I am also in some sense *bound* to "slip up" sooner or later. Hence, the demand is unreasonable, the responsibility too hard for me to bear. Interestingly, medieval adherents of free-will approaches to the problem of evil worried about this. In some works, Augustine confesses that the corruptibility of human nature makes failure virtually inevitable, incompatibilist freedom notwithstanding.[24] And Duns Scotus worries that it might be too risky for God to give us the liberty of indifference in heaven, because sooner or later the fall would be apt to recur.[25] Craig's own reading of Matthew – according to which the vast majority of created persons in the actual world are damned – lends credence to these probability estimates.

I do not say that were God to create persons with the intention of condemning to hell any who fail to honor him appropriately, he would be unjust in the sense (a) of violating his (non-existent) obligations to them (us). I do claim that such punishment would be *unusual*, because acting in the region of the divine levels out the differences among created act types (e.g., between peeking out at prayers and torturing babies). Moreover, God would be "unfair" in sense (b) and hence *cruel* in setting created persons conditions relative to which not only were they (we) unlikely to succeed, but also their (our) lives were as a consequence more apt than not to have all positive meaning swallowed up by horrendous evil.

2.3   The idol of human agency

Where soteriology is concerned, Christians have traditionally disagreed about human nature along two parameters. First, some hold that human nature was created in ideal condition and placed in a utopian environment: i.e., that *ab initio* humans had enough cognitive and emotional maturity to grasp and accurately apply relevant normative principles, while (on the occasion of their choice) their exercise of these abilities was unobstructed by unruly passions or external determinants of any kind. Others maintain, on the contrary, that humans are created immature and grow to adult competence through a messy developmental process. Second, where salvation is concerned, some take the human race collectively, while others consider humans individualistically. According to the Augustinian doctrine of the fall, Adam and Eve began as ideal agents in utopian Eden. The consequence of their sin is not only individual but collective: agency impaired by "ignorance" (clouded moral judgment) and "difficulty" (undisciplined emotions), which passes from the first parents to the whole family of their descendants. In his earlier works, Augustine insists that despite such inherited handicaps, the reprobate still bring damnation on themselves, because God has offered help sufficient to win the difficult struggle through faith in Christ.[26] In later anti-Pelagian works, Augustine abandons the idea that God confers on each fallen human grace sufficient for salvation; he concedes that damnation is the consequence of such divine omissions and Adam's original free choice to sin. Nevertheless, the damned deserve no pity, because the family collectively brought it on themselves through Adam's free choice of will.[27] Without being fully explicit, Craig seems to proceed individualistically, assuming that by the time we reach "the age of accountability", our agency is ideal enough for each to be entrusted with and held responsible for his or her own eternal destiny. Irenaeus stands on the other side as the patristic prototype of the developmental understanding of human nature.

In my judgment, the arguments from incommensuration offered in section 2.2 hold even where ideal human nature is concerned. For my own part, I reject the notion of a historical fall and read Genesis 2–3 the Irenaean way, as about the childhood of the human race. I deny not only that we human beings do have, but also that we ever had, ideal agency. Therefore, I conclude, that reasoning about it is relevant at most to the abstract and not to the concrete problem of hell.

By contrast, a realistic picture of human agency should recognize the following: (a) We human beings start life ignorant, weak, and help- less, psychologically so lacking in a self-concept as to be incapable of choice. (b) We learn to "construct" a picture of the world, ourselves, and other people only with difficulty over a long period of time and under the extensive influence of other non-ideal choosers. (c) Human development is the interactive product of human nature and its environment, and from early on we humans are confronted with problems that we cannot adequately grasp or cope with, and in response to which we mount (without fully conscious calculation) in- efficient adaptational strategies. (d) Yet, the human psyche forms habits in such a way that these reactive patterns, based as they are on a child's inaccurate view of the world and its strategic options, become entrenched in the individual's personality. (e) Typically, the habits are unconsciously "acted out" for years, causing much suffering to self and others before (if ever) they are recognized and undone through a difficult and painful process of therapy and/or spiritual formation. (f) Having thus begun *immature*, we arrive at adulthood in a state of *impaired freedom*, as our childhood adaptational strategies continue to distort our perceptions and behavior. (g) We adults with impaired freedom are responsible for our choices, actions, and even the character molded by our unconscious adaptational strategies, in the sense that we are the *agent causes* of them. (h) Our assessments of moral responsibility, praise, and blame cannot afford to take this impairment into account, because we are not as humans capable of organizing and regulating ourselves in that finetuned a way. And so, except for the most severe cases of impairment, we continue to hold ourselves *responsible to one another*.[28]

Taking these estimates of human nature to heart, I draw two conclusions: first, that such impaired adult human agency is no more
competent to be entrusted with its (individual or collective) eternal
destiny than two-year-old agency is to be allowed choices that could
result in its death or serious physical impairment; and second, that the
fact that the choices of such impaired agents come between the divine
creator of the environment and their infernal outcome no more reduces
divine responsibility for the damnation than two-year-old agency
reduces the responsibility of the adult caretaker. Suppose, for example,
that a parent introduces a two-year-old child into a room filled with gas
that is safe to breathe but will explode if ignited. Assume further that
the room contains a stove with brightly colored knobs, which if turned
will light the burners and ignite the gas. If the parent warns the child
not to turn the knobs and leaves, whereupon the child turns the knobs
and blows itself up, surely the child is at most marginally to blame, even
if it knew enough to obey the parent, while the parent is both primarily
responsible and highly culpable. Or suppose a terrorist announces his
intention to kill one hundred citizens if anyone in a certain village wears
a red shirt on Tuesday. The village takes the threat seriously, and
everyone is informed. If some adult citizen slips up and wears his
favorite red shirt on Tuesday, he will be responsible and culpable, but
the terrorist who set up the situation will be much more culpable.

Once again, my further conclusion is not that God would (like the
parent and the terrorist) be culpable if He were to insert humans into a
situation in which their eternal destiny depended on their exercise of
impaired agency, for I deny that God has any obligations to creatures
(see section 2.2.1). Rather, God (like the parent or the terrorist) would
bear primary responsibility for any tragic outcomes,[29] and God would
be cruel to create human beings in a world with combinations of
obstacles and opportunities such as are found in the actual world and
govern us under a scheme according to which whether or not we go to
the traditional hell depends on how we exercise our impaired adult
agency in this life – cruel, by virtue of imposing horrendous consequences on our all-too-likely failures.

2.4   The possibility of transworld damnation?

Perhaps it will be objected that my arguments in section 2.3 are unfair
because they abstract from one of Craig's important claims: that God

supplies all the graces needed for success and thereby strengthens us, or at least (as early Augustine thought) offers us the means to strengthen our impaired agency, only to have such aid refused. This claim is, of course, connected with Craig's hypothesis of possible transworld damnation, which I reject twice-over.

2.4.1   *True counterfactuals of freedom?*

First, I deny that any counterfactuals of freedom are true for the metaphysical reason that there is nothing to make them true.[30] It follows from the definition of "incompatibilist freedom" that neither God's will not causal nor logical necessity could account for the truth of propositions about the incompatibilist free choices of merely possible persons (or persons considered insofar as they are merely possible). Nor could the creature's actual character or choices make them true, because these are posterior in the order of explanation to the truth value of the counterfactuals about what the merely possible creatures would do were they to be actualized in certain circumstances.

2.4.2   *Transworld damnation and the logical problem of hell*

Second, Craig's notion of transworld damnation is supposed to mimic Plantinga's conception of transworld depravity: just as it is possible that some or all or the vast majority of created persons would be such that they would go wrong with respect to at least one morally significant action no matter what circumstances God strongly actualized, so – Craig maintains – it is possible that some or all or the vast majority of created persons would be such that they would refuse Christ and be damned no matter what situations God strongly actualized. Likewise, just as it is possible that God might be powerless to weakly actualize a world of sinless incompatabilist free creatures, so – Craig alleges – it is possible that God might be unable to weakly actualize a world in which heaven would be filled without the vast majority of created persons being damned. Moreover, just as God's powerlessness to determine the truth-values of counterfactuals of (created) freedom, together with the laudable desire of creating a world with a favorable balance of moral good over moral evil, rationalizes divine permission of moral evil, so God's powerlessness with respect to such counterfactual truth values is supposed to combine with His admirable desire to fill heaven, to explain His acceptance of damnation for some or all or the vast majority of created persons.

This comparison seems fatally flawed, however. Craig's replacement for (III) is:

(III′)   [a] Some persons do not receive Christ, and [b] are damned.

Note that it splits into two parts, which, given divine sovereignty over the soteriological process, are logically independent of one another. That is, it is logically possible that some or all or the vast majority of created persons might refuse to accept Christ or might commit the sin of final impenitence, and yet God need not condemn them to hell but might maintain them in a world much like this one or annihilate them instead. Put another way, the existence of hell and the conditions for admission are among the things that fall within God's powers of strong-actualization, even if the truth values of counterfactuals of (created) freedom are not within His power. Thus, even if, relative to some possible world, the essence of each and every created person were infected with transworld final impenitence, still none would be transworld damned. Transworld damnation is not, after all, a logical possibility.

Given Plantinga's metaphysics, it is logically possible that

(IV′)   Created persons would not accept Christ in great enough numbers to fill heaven unless some or the vast majority of created persons were finally impenitent and consigned to hell forever.

By the same token the following will be taken as logically possible:

(IV″)   Created persons would not accept Christ in great enough numbers to fill heaven unless (in addition to some or a large number who die finally impenitent) some or a large number of those who responded best to Christ were consigned to hell forever.

and

(IV‴)   Created persons would not accept Christ in great enough numbers to fill heaven unless (in addition to some or a large number who die finally impenitent) some or a large number of children two years old and under, who were never even morally competent agents, were consigned to hell.

Although each of (IV′), (IV″), and (IV‴) combines with Craig's hypothesis that God weakly actualizes a world in which heaven is filled, to entail (III'), this does not suffice to establish the compossibility of (I) with (III) or (III'), for the latter conclusion requires the additional premiss that each is compossible with (I). Once again, God would not violate any of His (non-existent) obligations were He to proceed with His plans to fill heaven with incompatibilist free creatures, even in the face of such counterfactual fates. Nevertheless, I submit that God would be cruel to do so, middle knowing that He was bringing some or the vast majority into being for lives it would have been better for them never to have lived. Therefore, (I) would be compossible with (III) only if "good" in (I) were taken in a sense that does not rule out cruelty. Contrary to Craig's hopes, he will not be able to rely on omnipotent powerlessness over counterfactuals of freedom to reconcile hell with divine goodness; he will have to follow the Stoic in tampering with the notion of "good" to be understood in (I).

The logical possibility (on Plantinga's scheme) of (IV'), (IV''), and (IV''') might even call into question an assumption that Plantinga locates at the heart of free-will approaches to evil: viz., that a "world containing creatures who are sometimes significantly free (and freely perform more good than evil actions) is more valuable, all else being equal, than a world containing no free creatures at all."[31] On reflection, is it not anthropocentric, another manifestation of our idolatry of human agency (cf. section 2.2), to suppose that the latter is so valuable that God would accept unredeemed horror to include it? Since our thoughts are not like God's, how can we be so sure that omniscient creativity could not find equally good or better worlds altogether devoid of incompatibilist free creatures[32] – in which case (I) might not be compossible with (III) or (III'), even where divine goodness were evaluated solely in relation to God's role as producer of global goods.

2.4.3 Transworld damnation as theodicy?

Craig offers his reflections as grist for the mill, not only of defensive apologetics, but also of theodicy. Thus, he invites us to agree (a) that (IV') is not only logically possible but true, and yet (b) that for each actual created person, God has done everything He could to win that person over. I reject both claims.

2.4.3.1 Congruent grace versus transworld final impenitence   If I believed that counterfactuals of freedom could be true, I would replace (a) with Suarez's doctrine of congruent grace: namely, that God is able to provide each created person with such grace that she or he would

freely consent to His will, and that God is able to do this for each, no matter which other created persons He additionally makes and graces. Craig considers this move but finds it impotent against his theodicy, because "we have no good grounds for believing" the Suarezian doctrine, and the burden of proof is on the Suarezian to "demonstrate" its truth.[33] By contrast, I see the onus of proof distributed otherwise: it favors his position no more than mine. The issue may be approached at two levels. First, if (as Plantinga assumes) nothing explains why one counterfactual of freedom should be true of an individual essence rather than another, their truth-values would seem to fall like "fates" independently of both the divine will and created wills. And if – so far as the theory of counterfactuals of freedom is concerned – it remains a mystery to us why or how the truth values should be distributed, we are left with appeals to ignorance or epistemic contingency about their actual distribution. Second, we might suppose with Plantinga that, while nothing makes such counterfactuals of freedom true, still some are more plausible than others. Both ways, the arguments favoring transworld impenitence or transworld redeemability[34] will be driven by other considerations: for Craig, by his belief that (III) and (III′) are true because endorsed by Scripture and required to fire the missionary effort; for me, by confidence in God's ability to convince us that He is the Good that satisfies, in His power and resourcefulness to defeat evil thoroughly within the context of each created person's life.

For that matter, I, too, have a synoptic proof text (Matt. 19:24–26; Mark 10:25–27; Luke 18:25–27): Jesus' claim that all things are possible with God does not respond to worries about the size of stones God is able to make and lift or the possibility of His squaring the circle or making contradictories true but to the question how anyone can be saved, about how human hearts can be changed. I understand the answer to imply that God is so powerful, so witting and resourceful, that he can let created persons do their damnedest and still save them.[35] I prefer the mystery of how God accomplishes this with incompatibilist free creatures to the equally impenetrable mystery of how transworld damnation falls on some individual essences rather than others.

Empirically, given that all adults have impaired freedom – where some impairments are worse than others due to factors beyond the agent's control, some increased by the agent's own choices – the belief that any of us is saved implies that God is able to change the hearts of sinners from good to bad. When I consider the way our neuroses are integrated into the cores of our personality, and the difficulty of ripping out such dysfunctions, I doubt that there is much to choose among them from God's point of view: if God can change any of them, there is insufficient reason to believe He could not change the others, too.

2.4.3.2 "Sufficient" grace universally distributed?   Insofar as Craig intends not merely a defense but a soteriological theodicy, he must confront the concrete problem of hell, and construe (III) and (III′) to be about, not just some possible persons in some possible situations or others, but about possible persons in antemortem situations of the sort in which people find themselves in the actual world (i.e., with like traumas, impairments, disasters, and hardships to work against). I do not find it credible that all such actual antemortem situations contain grace sufficient for faith in and cooperation with God (Christ) were it not for the creature's incompatibilist free refusal. (Consider, e.g., the predicament of gangland youths in South Central Los Angeles, individuals who have been subject to physical and sexual abuse from childhood.) Rather, God seems for the most part to have a policy of distributing the graces bit by bit, so that our way out of our sinful habits and so on is itself a developmental process. Some people die before they get very far, and sometimes this seems to be through no fault of their own.

2.5   Pragmatic implications

In my judgment, Craig's theological picture is not only theoretically mistaken, but also pragmatically pernicious. For according to it, a created person can view God as friendly – i.e., as good to him or her – only by counting himself or herself among the elect. But this breeds Pharisaism thrice-over: (1) To the extent that I do succeed in walking the straight and narrow, I will be contrasting myself with my brothers and sisters who don't, which easily leads to self-congratulation. (2) To the extent that it is difficult for me to toe the line, because of my developmental impairments, it produces the feeling of the one-talent man (Matt. 25:14–30; Luke 19:12–27), that God is harsh and demanding. (3) Insofar as sincere obedience to the first and great commandment needs to be laid on the psychological assurance of divine goodness to oneself, it will be difficult to obey the first while obeying the second.

LEEDS TRINITY UNIVERSITY

3   THE HERMENEUTICS OF CHARITY

When authorities seem to say things that are inconsistent or unreasonable, our first move is, not to cut off, but to twist the wax nose a bit, so that without crediting the troublesome pronouncements taken literally, we can "make something" of them by finding some deeper and more palatable truths which (we may claim) they were attempting to express. In this spirit, some agree that the notion of hell as an eternal torture chamber, as a punitive consequence for not accepting Christ, is not compatible with any tolerable understanding of divine goodness. That is, if 'hell' is understood the traditional way, then they construe 'perfectly good' in such a way as to render true the statement:

(3)   If God existed and were perfectly good, he would want to avoid (III).

Rather than abandon the doctrine of hell altogether, they modify or reinterpret it as some other fate involving permanent exclusion from heaven.

3.1   Hell as leaving people to the natural consequences of their choices

On Craig's politico-legal model, the relation between a person's sinning to the end and his or her suffering eternal punishment is extrinsic and contingent (as is that between speeding and paying a monetary fine). Other philosophers think there is a better chance of construing (III) in such a way as to be compatible with (I) if one discovers an intrinsic connection between the created persons' choices and their postmortem punishments or deprivations. Thus, Richard Swinburne maintains that "heaven is not a reward for good behavior" but "a home for good people."[36] He insists on the high value not only of created free agency but also of the autonomy of created persons to determine their own destinies. Noting psychological commonplaces about how patterns of choice build habits of thinking, wanting, valuing, and doing, and the more entrenched the habit, the harder it is to break, Swinburne reckons such habits may become so entrenched as to be unbreakable. For a person may so thoroughly blind himself or herself to what is really worth going for, that she or he can no longer see or rationally choose it. Since heaven is a society organized around the things that are really worth wanting, being, and doing, people locked into their voices could not enjoy it there.

Swinburne is less interested in (III) than in

(III′)   Some persons that God creates are permanently excluded from heaven.[37]

He is willing to recognize "various possible fates for those who have finally rejected the good": (i) "they might cease to exist after death"; (ii) "they might cease to exist after suffering some limited amount of physical pain as part of the punishment for their wickedness"; or (iii) "they might continue to exist forever pursuing trivial pursuits."[38] In Swinburne's estimation, "the crucial point is that it is compatible with the goodness of God that he should allow a man to put himself beyond possibility of salvation, because it is indeed compatible with the goodness of God that he should allow a man to choose the sort of person he will be,"[39] even where these decisions have eternal consequences.

Likewise, dismissing literal construals of Matthew 25:41–46 and Luke 16:19–26 as "a crude and simplistic account of the doctrine of hell,"[40] Eleonore Stump turns to Dante, who understands the fundamental awfulness of hell in terms of eternal deprivation of union with God. Stump takes Dante's "graphic images" at theological face value and suggests that the latter is fully compatible with a Limbo of beautiful physical surroundings "in which the noblest and wisest of the ancients discuss philosophy."[41] Moreover, in the more punitive regions of hell, external tortures are not suffered the way they would be in this world but serve rather as outward and visible signs of inner psychological states – afflictions which are nevertheless compatible with long and leisurely intellectual discussions. So far as the problem of hell is concerned, Stump maintains, "Everlasting life in hell is the ultimate evil which can befall a person in this world; but the torments of hell are *the natural* conditions of some persons, and God can spare such persons those pains only by depriving them of their nature or their existence. And it is arguable that, of the alternatives open to God, maintaining such persons in existence and as human is the best."[42] In other words, when "hell" in (III) is thus reinterpreted, Stump finds the logical compossibility of (I) with (III) defensible.

Once again, my principal complaint about these approaches centers on their understanding of human nature. Swinburne and Stump/ Dante begin by taking human psychology very seriously: that entrenched habits of character, established tastes, and concomitant states of inner conflict are *naturally* consequent upon sinful patterns of choice is supposed to explain the *intrinsic* connection between the sinner's earthly behavior and his or her exclusion from heaven and/ or consignment to hell. By contrast, their estimates of the *natural* effects of vice over the very (i.e., eternally) long run leave human psychology far behind. For vice is a psychospiritual disorder. Just as running a machine contrary to its design leads, sooner rather than later, to premature breakdown, so also persistent psychological disorders caricature and produce breakdowns even in the medium run of twenty to seventy years. My own view resonates with C. S. Lewis's suggestion in *The Problem of Pain*,[43] that vice in the soul preserved beyond three score and ten brings about a total dismantling of personality, to the torment of which this-worldly schizophrenia and depression are but the faintest approximations. A fortiori excluded is the notion that persons with characters unfit for heaven might continue forever philosophizing, delivering eloquent speeches, or engaging in trivial pursuits.[44] Likewise, either union with God is the natural human telos, in which case we cannot both eternally lack it and yet continue to enjoy this-worldly pleasures forever; or it is not, because we are personal animals and unending life is not a natural but a supernatural endowment. For God to prolong life eternally while denying access to the only good that could keep us eternally interested would likewise eventually produce unbearable misery.[45] In short, I think that the Swinburne/Stump/ Dante suggestion that God might keep created persons in existence forever but abandon them to the consequences of their sinful choices collapses into the more traditional doctrine of hell, when such consequences are calculated from a realistic appraisal of human psychology.

3.2   Annihilation by the creator?

Among others, Swinburne mentions the option of replacing (III) with

(III''')   Some created persons who die with characters unfit for heaven will be annihilated, either at death or after the Judgment.

Nor is this suggestion without ancient precedent: the non-canonical apocalyptic work, I Enoch, predicts that after the Judgment, the wicked will suffer for a while until they wither away. As contrasted with the positions examined in sections 2 and 3.1, this move has the advantage of avoiding the claim that God has subjected created persons to cruel and/or unusual punishment by extending their life span into an eternity of horrendous suffering.

True to my Suarezian bias, I reject it, on the ground that it involves an uncharitable estimate of divine wisdom, goodness, and power. St. Anselm reasons that omnipotent, all-wise goodness would do the hard as well as the easy. For God, it is easy to make good from the good; what is more remarkable, it is no effort for Him to make good out of nothing. For Him, the real challenge would be to make good out of evil; so He must be able to do that.[46] Moreover, St. Anselm argued that it is unfitting to omnipotent wisdom either to change its mind or to fail in what it attempts.[47] I agree both ways. To me, it is a better theological bargain to hold the mystery that God will not give up on the wicked, will eventually somehow be able to turn them to good, than to swallow the tragic idea that created persons, finite and dependent though we are, are able ultimately and finally to defeat our Creator's purpose, the mystery of transworld final impenitence ending in the Creator's destroying His own creation.

3.3   Truths told by the doctrine of hell

Like Craig, I take the Bible seriously; indeed, as an Episcopal priest, I am sworn to the claim that "the Holy Scriptures of the Old and New Testaments" are "the Word of God" and "contain all things necessary to salvation".[48] Like Swinburne, Stump, and Lewis, I feel bound to weigh the tradition behind (III). I, too, pay my respects by identifying some deep truths expressed by the doctrine of hell. (T_1) The first (mentioned in section 2.2.1 above) is that created persons have *no rights* against God, because God has *no obligations* to creatures: in particular, God has no obligation to be good to us; no obligation not to ruin us whether by depriving our lives of positive meaning, by producing or allowing the deterioration or disintegration of our personalities, by destroying our bodies, or by annihilating us. (T_2) Second, the horrendous ruin of a created person represented by eternal torment in hell constitutes a (negative and mirror image) measure – perhaps the most vivid we can understand – of how *bad* it is, how utterly indecent, not to respond to God appropriately; and for all that, because of the radical incommensuration between God and creatures, the measure is inadequate.

Nevertheless, I have insisted in print for more than twenty years that
(T3) the doctrine is false on its traditional construal, because neither the
ontological gap between God and creatures nor the radical impropriety
of our comportment toward God is a good indication of God's intentions and policies toward us. God does not stand on rights and obligations, nor does He treat us according to such "deserts".

As I see it, both the defenders of hell and I are confronted with a
theological balancing act. The *prima facie* logical incompossibility of (I)
and (III) and the accompanying pragmatic difficulties force us into a
position of weighing some items of tradition more than others. Like
many Christians, Craig begins with a high doctrine of the authority of
Scripture, which combines with a certain hermeneutic, to make (III)
obligatory. He then appeals to an equally high doctrine of human
freedom to try to reconcile (I) with (III). For this, he pays the price of
denying that God will be *good to* every person He creates (in the sense
defined in section 1.1) and further of understanding divine goodness to
be compatible with the damnation of the vast majority of actual created
persons. Likewise, Craig's God shares the limitations of human social
planners: (i) He cannot achieve the optimal overall good without sacrificing the welfare of some individual persons; (ii) nor can He redeem all
personal evil: some of the wicked He can only quarantine or destroy.

By contrast, I emphasize a high doctrine of divine resourcefulness
(assigning God the power to let creatures "do their damnedest" and still
win them all over to heavenly bliss) and a low doctrine of human
agency (both ontologically, in terms of the gap between God and
creatures, and psychologically, in terms of developmental limitations
and impairments). Because I do not regard Scripture as infallible on
any interpretation, I do not feel bound to translate into theological
assertion some of the apocalyptic imagery and plot lines of the New
Testament. Nevertheless, I do not regard my universalist theology as
un-Scriptural, because I believe the theme of definitive divine triumph
is central to the Bible, is exemplified in Christ Jesus, and is the very
basis of our Christian hope.

3.4   *The pragmatics of universalism*

Surprisingly many religiously serious people reject the doctrine of
universal salvation, on the pragmatic ground that it leads to moral
and religious laxity. Withdraw the threat, and they doubt whether

others – perhaps even they themselves – would sustain the motivation for moral diligence and religious observance.

My pastoral experience suggests, on the contrary, that the disproportionate threat of hell (see sections 2.2 and 2.3) produces despair that masquerades as skepticism, rebellion, and unbelief. If your father threatens to kill you if you disobey him, you may cower in terrorized submission, but you may also (reasonably) run away from home. My brand of universalism offers all the advantages of Augustine's and Calvin's *sola gratia* approaches (like them, it makes our salvation utterly gratuitous and dependent on God's surprising and loving interest in us) and then some (because it gives everyone reason to hope and to be sincerely thankful for his or her life).[49]

4 THE RELEVANCE OF FEELINGS

Craig and Swinburne do not enter at any length into how bad horrendous sufferings are. For example, Craig hurries by with two scant mentions that damnation of many is "a terrible price" and "an admittedly tragic fate".[50] Both close their essays with a quasi-apology, anticipating that some will be offended by their value judgment that the existence of free creatures autonomously deciding their destinies, enough to fill heaven, is worth the price of the eternal exclusion and misery of many. Both imply that those who are offended will be motivated by understandable feelings, which are nevertheless not relevant to a rational consideration of the subject.[51]

I want to close with a contrary methodological contention (one already implicit in my argument in section 2.2): namely, that feelings are highly relevant to the problem of evil and to the problem of hell, because they are one source of information about how bad something is for a person. To be sure, they are not an infallible source. Certainly they are not always an articulate source. But they are *a* source. Where questions of value are concerned, reason is not an infallible source either. That is why so-called value calculations in abstraction from feelings can strike us as "cold" or "callous". I do not believe we have any infallible faculties at all. But our best shot at valuations will come from the collaboration of feelings and reason, the latter articulating the former, the former giving data to the latter.

Personally, I am appalled at Craig's and Swinburne's valuations, at levels too deep for words (although I have already said many). I invite anyone who agrees with Craig – that the saved can in good conscience let their happiness be unaffected by the plight of the damned because the destruction of the latter is self-willed – to spend a week visiting patients who are dying of emphysema or of the advanced effects of alcoholism, to listen with sympathetic presence, to enter into their point of view on their lives, to face their pain and despair. Then ask whether one could in good conscience dismiss their suffering with, "Oh well, they brought it on themselves!"[52]

I do not think this is sentimental. Other than experiencing such sufferings in our own persons, such sympathetic entering into the position of another is the best way we have to tell what it would be like to be that person and suffer as they do, the best data we can get on how bad it would be to suffer that way. Nor is my thesis especially new. It is but an extension of the old Augustinian-Platonist point, that where values are concerned, what and how well you see depends not simply on how well you think, but on what and how well you love (a point to which Swinburne seems otherwise sympathetic).[53] I borrow a point from Charles Hartshorne[54] when I suggest that sensitivity, sympathetic interaction, is an aspect of such loving, one that rightfully affects our judgment in ways we should not ignore.[55]

NOTES

1   Cf. my article "Problems of Evil: More Advice to Christian Philosophers", *Faith and Philosophy* 5 (1988): 121–43; esp. pp. 135–7; and "Theodicy without Blame", *Philosophical Topics* 16 (1988): 215–45; esp. pp.234–7.

2   The ability thus afforded has actually been cited as a strategic advantage by some Christian philosophers.

3   Duns Scotus, *Opus Oxoniense* in *Opera Omnia* (Paris: Vives, 1891), IV, d. 46, q. 4, n. 6; Wadding-Vives 20, 459.

4   Duns Scotus, *Op. Ox.* IV, d. 46, q. 4, n. 5; Wadding-Vives 20, 457.

5   Cf. my *William Ockham* (Notre Dame: University of Notre Dame Press, 1987), chap. 30, 1257–97; and "The Structure of Ockham's Moral Theory", *Franciscan Studies* 46 (1986): 1–35.

6   Alvin Plantinga takes this line in numerous discussions, in the course of answering J. L. Mackie's objection to the free-will defense, that God could have made sinless free creatures. Plantinga insists that, given incompatibilist freedom in creatures, God cannot strongly actualize any world He wants. It is logically possible that a world with evils in the amounts and of the kinds found in this world is the best that He could do, Plantinga

argues, given His aim of getting some moral goodness in the world. See section 2.2 below.

7   Thomas Aquinas, *Summa theologica* I, q. 23, a. 5, ad 3.

8   Cf. my "Horrendous Evils and the Goodness of God," *Proceedings of the Aristotelian Society*, Supplementary Volume 63 (1989): 297–310; esp. 303.

9   Cf. Diogenes Allen, "Natural Evil and the God of Love," *Religious Studies* 16 (1980): 439–56.

10 William Craig, " 'No Other Name': A Middle Knowledge Perspective on the Exclusivity of Salvation through Christ," *Faith and Philosophy* 6 (1989): 172–88.

11 Ibid., 184.

12 Ibid., 182–3.

13 Ibid., 186.

14 Ibid., 176.

15 Ibid., 183.

16 Ibid., 186.

17 Ibid., 184, 185.

18 Ibid., 176.

19 Ibid., 185.

20 Ibid., 176.

21 Ibid., 186.

22 Cf. my early article "Hell and the God of Justice," *Religious Studies* 11 (1974): 433–47.

23 Cf. my "Theodicy without Blame."

24 Cf. John Hick, *Evil and the God of Love*, rev. ed. (New York: Harper and Row, 1966, 1978), chap. 3, pp. 37–48.

25 Duns Scotus, *God and Creatures: The Quodlibetal Questions*, translated with introduction, notes and glossary by Felix Alluntis, O.F.M., and Allan B. Wolter, O.F.M. (Washington, D.C.: The Catholic University of America Press, 1975), q.16, art. II, 377–9.

26 Augustine, *De libero arbitrio*. Corpus Scriptorum Ecclesiasticorum Latinorum, vol. 74. (Vindobonae: Hoelder-Pichler-Tempsky, 1956), passim.

27 This position is especially clear in Augustine, *De gratia et libero arbitrio* (AD 426), and Augustine, *De correptione et gratia* (AD 426 or 427).

28 Cf. my "Theodicy without Blame," pp. 231–2.

29 Contrary to what Craig maintains, " 'No Other Name' ", pp. 176–7.

30 I agree with the arguments offered by Robert Merrihew Adams in "Middle Knowledge and the Problem of Evil", reprinted in his *The Virtue of Faith and Other Essays* (New York: Oxford University Press, 1987), pp. 77–93. I am indebted to him for many helpful discussions of this material, which have corrected various errors in earlier drafts of this section.

31 Alvin Plantinga, *The Nature of Necessity*, chap. 9 (Clarendon Press, 1974), p. 166.

32 I owe this suggestion to Robert Merrihew Adams.

33 Craig, "'No Other Name'", p. 183.

34 David P. Hunt of Whittier College opposes the notion of 'transworld salvation' to Craig's 'transworld damnation' in his interesting paper "Middle Knowledge and the Soteriological Problem of Evil," *Religious Studies* 27 (1991): 3–26.

35 Note, I use the term 'proof text' lightly. I am not so naive as to assume that my citation of these passages and assertion of my interpretation constitutes a proof that the doctrines of congruent grace or universal salvation are biblical. My own general impression is of a variety of different biblical, indeed New Testament views, each of which deserves separate and careful consideration. Certainly, I do not think the biblical witness is so univocal as Craig alleges ("'No Other Name'", pp. 172–4). But neither am I so confident as Thomas Talbot ("The Doctrine of Everlasting Punishment," *Faith and Philosophy* 7 (1990): 19–42; esp. 23) as to advance the doctrine of universal salvation as the biblical view; apocalyptic theology, whatever is to be made of it, strikes too strong a chord in the New Testament. At any rate, this is the work of many other papers (and volumes), some of them mine. Cf. my "Separation and Reversal in Luke-Acts," *Philosophy and the Christian Faith*, ed. Thomas V. Morris (Notre Dame: University of Notre Dame Press, 1988), pp. 92–117; and "Hell according to Matthew?" presented at the Gordon College Conference on the Future of God, May 1989.

36 In several places, including "A Theodicy of Heaven and Hell," in *The Existence and Nature of God*, ed. Alfred Freddoso (Notre Dame, Indiana: University of Notre Dame Press, 1983), 37–54; the second quotation is from page 43.

37 Swinburne, "A Theodicy of Heaven and Hell," pp. 37, 52.

38 Ibid., p. 52.

39 Ibid.

40 Eleonore Stump, "The Problem of Evil," *Faith and Philosophy* 4 (1985): 392–423; esp. 400.

41 Ibid., p. 400.

42 Ibid., p. 401.

43 C. S. Lewis, *The Problem of Pain* (New York: Macmillan, 1979), chap. 8, pp. 124–6.

44 Years ago, I agreed with Dante that philosophy could keep one entertained for eternity. Extensive conversations with the Reverend A. Orley Swartzentruber persuaded me of what Augustine and Anselm confirm: that philosophy can only seem infinitely fascinating because it involves

insights into the Christ, the Divine Word, clearer knowledge and love of whom is the only thing that can satisfy forever.

45   Cf. Swinburne, "A Theodicy of Heaven and Hell", p. 41.

46   St. Anselm, *Proslogion*, chap. ix; *Sancti Anselmi: Opera Omnia*: 6 vols., ed. F. S. Schmitt (Edinburgh: Thomas Nelson, 1946–61); Schmitt I, 108.

47   St. Anselm, *Cur Deus homo* II, chap. IV; Schmitt II, 99; cf. *Proslogion*, chap. vii; Schmitt I, 105–6.

48   "The Ordination of a Priest", *The Book of Common Prayer* (1979), p. 526.

49   To be sure, Augustine thinks the damned should praise the divine justice that damns them, but to do this sincerely seems psychologically impossible for humans. Cf. my "Theodicy without Blame", pp. 221–34.

50   Craig, " 'No Other Name' ", pp. 183, 185.

51   Ibid., pp. 186–87; and Richard Swinburne, "Knowledge from Experience, and the Problem of Evil," in *The Rationality of Religious Belief: Essays in Honour of Basil Mitchell*, ed. William J. Abraham and Steven W. Holtzer (Oxford: Clarendon Press, 1987) 141–67; esp. p. 167.

52   Years ago, Rogers Albritton persuaded me, at the theoretical level, that some suffering is too bad for the guilty. My introspective and pastoral experience since then tells in the same directions.

53   Swinburne, "A Theodicy of Heaven and Hell", pp. 46–9.

54   Charles Hartshorne, *The Divine Relativity* (New Haven: Yale University Press, 1948, 1964), chap. 3, 116–58.

55   Over the years, my ideas about the doctrine of hell have been shaped by others, some of whom ultimately disagree with my conclusions. Among the medievals, I am especially indebted to Anselm, Aquinas, Duns Scotus, Ockham, and Julian of Norwich; among my contemporaries, Robert Merrihew Adams, John Hick, Jon Hart Olson, A. Orley Swartzentruber, and the members of the Philosophy Department at Calvin College in Grand Rapids, Michigan.

Index

Lightning Source UK Ltd.
Milton Keynes UK
UKOW06f1817240416

272839UK00006B/227/P